Profiles of Personality is the one
and rhetorically compelling personality textbooks
available. Returning to personality as a study of (whole) persons, it
foregrounds integration of theoretical approaches towards an
unfolding understanding of life as lived, in keeping with the most
important tenet of humanistic psychology. Coverage of the theories is
clear and informed, blending the best of old and new ideas. The text's
clear structure and engaging narrative make it highly valuable for
face-to-face discussion and online learning environments alike. It will
help students grasp difficult concepts in personality psychology,
engage critical thinking, and develop lifelong tools for self-
understanding and more insightful interactions with others.

Lisa M. Osbeck, PhD
Professor of Psychology, University of West Georgia
Past-President, APA Division 1 (Society for General Psychology)

In light of new discoveries in neuroscience, the plasticity of the brain
confirms a view of the human personality as fluid and dynamic. Most
theories of personality are stuck in old views of the brain and human
nature, but Eugene DeRobertis gives us a holistic and dynamic
perspective on personality that is congruent with these new
discoveries. In this book, his passion for the wonder and mystery of
the human personality comes through, as does his clearly stated desire
to convey that passion to an emerging generation of psychology
students and practitioners.

Ilene A. Serlin, PhD, founder and director of Union Street
Health Associates and the Arts Medicine Program at
California Pacific Medical Center,
editor of *Whole Person Healthcare* (3 volumes)

Profiles of Personality:
Integration, Paradox, and the Process of Becoming

Second Edition

By
Eugene Mario DeRobertis

Colorado Springs, CO
www.universityprofessorspress.com

First Published in 2021, University Professors Press.

Hardcover ISBN:	978-1-939686-97-8
Paperback ISBN:	978-1-939686-74-9
ebook ISBN:	978-1-939686-75-6

University Professors Press
Colorado Springs, CO
www.universityprofessorspress.com

Cover Design by Laura Ross
Cover Art by Violet Void

Table of Contents

Acknowledgments

Many thanks to my wife for granting me the time to complete this project from its inception in 2013 to the present. I would also like to thank Louis Hoffman and Andrew Bland for their feedback in envisioning the second volume of this text. Finally, thank you to Violet Void of True Poison (https://truepoison.com) for providing the artwork for the front cover.

Preface

The teaching of personality comes with certain challenges. Deciding to adopt a comprehensive textbook offers two choices. One kind of text, the more traditional one, organizes content according to historical affiliation and usually begins with Freud. Thinkers who are in some way connected to the historical lineage of psychoanalysis are systematically presented. From there, the text moves on to other traditions, covering each of them in a similar manner. The other, more recently developed kind of text presents personality as a series of research programs, using the study of discrete aspects of personality as foci for its chapters. In either case, students tend to have a difficult time attaining any kind of synoptic grasp of personality. Of the two book choices, I have found the newer kind of text to be poorer in this regard because the student is hit with a virtual buckshot of personality, so to speak. It gives the experience of being confronted with a disparate barrage of research findings from chapter to chapter.

Still, the former, more traditional text presents its own problems. The student's sense of the evolution of personality (not as an area of study, but *personality itself*) has to stop, rewind, and restart every time an entirely new tradition is introduced. Moreover, the conceptual continuity within each section can be strained. One need only consider the cases of Freud and Adler to understand my rationale. Freud and Adler were historical contemporaries who worked together and who now share a common lineage dubbed "the psychoanalytic tradition." However, they produced radically different approaches to personality. Freud is seen by many as a champion of the disavowed "basement" realms of personality, while Adler offered a very progressive, humanistic form of interpersonal psychology. Thus, it makes more *conceptual* sense to cover Adler nearer to more holistic, personalistic theories than it does to introduce Individual Psychology alongside orthodox Freudian thought.

Over the years, I have found that the best alternative for helping students attain some sense of continuity in the study of personality is to use a traditional comprehensive text, along with supplementary primary source readings, and to structure the class according to some meta-narrative that overrides the order in which thinkers are presented in the textbook. The current text was created to assist in carrying out this strategy. It is a companion text, providing a briefer, more conversational, more user-friendly introduction to each theory that is nonetheless academically rigorous and structured according to a meta-narrative for deriving a more continuous learning experience. Pedagogically speaking, the structure has the characteristics of an unfolding story of personality; strategies such as this have been shown to be optimally effective in teaching science from experiential research and brain science alike (DeRobertis, 2017; Fischer, 2009; Martinez-Conde et al., 2019; Szurmak & Thuna, 2013).

Each theory herein is presented as a contributor to the development of an increasingly expansive, multifaceted, integrative understanding of personality and personal becoming. To employ this meta-narrative as a structural guide involved creative envisioning on my part as the author. The overall design priorities were to order the theories in such a way as to enable the reader to simultaneously and recurrently build upon their understanding of the differential–integrative process that undergirds personality formation and their understandings of growth and health. These design priorities allow an instructor to communicate both more coherently and more meaningfully with students about personality, lessening the likelihood that they will look upon personality as "just another psychological concept" they heard about in college. If successful, students will be able to relate to the study of personality as a way of thinking about the evolving, dynamic process of lifelong *becoming* (i.e., becoming both more human and more oneself by the forward-moving, creative striving to realize potentials and actualize possibilities). This is the pedagogical goal of a human science or *humanistic* psychologist (see Bland & DeRobertis, 2017). Organizing the theories as a kind of progressive developmental unfolding makes it easier for students to relate the material to their own developmental processes in a sustained manner throughout the semester. This is a more effective communication strategy for helping students attain an insightful, synoptic grasp of personality than relying on historical affiliations.

Before proceeding, the reader will note that I have not included biographical material on the theorists presented here. Similarly, there are no extended discussions of method or applications, be they academic or applied. As a companion, this book is not intended to be a substitute for a detailed introductory textbook, for primary source material from the personality theorists themselves, or for critical considerations of historical context, methodology, and contemporary application. Rather, the text was designed to go straight to the conceptual heart of each theory, as it were. The coverage stays focused on how the theories go about making their unique contributions to understanding personality as one moves toward a more differentiated integrative viewpoint and explores still more aspects of optimal becoming. This presentational strategy can help to counteract the tendency to leave the study of personality with the feeling that it is suffering from a dizzying, proliferating fragmentation, which M. Brewster Smith complained of long ago (Smith, 1982). As Smith saw it, the responsibility is on humanistic psychology to overcome this seeming fragmentation, as the great personality theorists of the last century essentially laid the foundation for the humanistic revolution. The study of personality was always humanistic psychology *in statu nascendi*. It is long past time to start making inroads to reclaim our heritage. At the end of the day, the fact that a seminal personality psychologist like Gordon Allport, for example, was highly eclectic is evidence for his nascent humanistic orientation. His complex, open system of thought need not be, as is sometimes argued (Nicholson, 1997), evidence against his inclusion in the humanist camp. History has shown that humanistic psychology is mosaic in its overall approach (Maslow, 1961; van Kaam, 1966).

The reader who is familiar with the previous version of this text will notice certain refinements in achieving its aims. Citations have been included throughout the body of the text, and a reference section has replaced the suggested readings that were provided for each chapter. The material on David Buss has pivoted away from his act-frequency approach in order to clarify the way in which his evolutionary perspective has reinterpreted the Big Five. The discussion of the Five-Factor Theory (beyond the research taxonomy) has also been enhanced, and the entire chapter on factor-analytic trait theorizing has been moved to reflect the robustness of the diverse contributions of that chapter.

In response to feedback in the peer review process concerning certain points of contact between humanistic theories and cognitive-regulatory (social learning) theories, I decided to include George Kelly's personal construct theory to the text. His viewpoint provides theoretical connective tissue between the two traditions. The coverage of the individualism–collectivism continuum has been further augmented to emphasize the diversity that exists within those typological designations. "Taking it Further: Food for Thought" and "Make it Work!" subsections have been included to enhance student engagement and deepen their understanding of the material. Accordingly, what were once "Final Remarks" sections are now "Reflections" on chapter contents, specifically with regard to how they play a role in the book's unfolding. Lists of key concepts have also been included at the end of each chapter. Finally, the book sections have been altered to better reflect the narrative thread of the text.

Chapter 1

Introduction

Like so many topics in psychology (e.g., intelligence, emotion, motivation, health, psychopathology), *personality* lacks a universally agreed upon conceptualization. Instead, what one finds is a diversity of viewpoints on the topic, each with its own manner of interpreting what personality is and how it forms. In fact, few personality theorists have taken the time to formally define personality. A notable exception to this general trend is Gordon Allport, the psychologist who coined the term *humanistic psychology* in 1930 (DeCarvalho, 1990). Allport (1961) defined personality as the dynamic organization within the individual of those psychophysical systems that determine their characteristic behavior and thought. This is perhaps the best definition of personality to date. Stated in simpler terms, when psychologists use the term *personality*, it is meant to refer to the relatively stable pattern of experiencing and acting that makes one unique. The term *psychophysical* is used to emphasize the integrational nature of personality, the fact that experiential dynamics (the *psycho* part of the term) and behavioral dynamics (the *physical* part of the term) are interdependent rather than separate or self-contained. The experiential and behavioral dimensions of the person together form a complex, organized *style of life* (Adler, 1979) or "psychological thumbprint," so to speak.

Personality psychologists attempt to understand exactly how human life patterns are integrated, which is a fact that often goes unnoticed on a day-to-day basis. It is only when a person's behavior appears "erratic" or "conflicted" that we seem to notice what we all take for granted: the relatively ordered, organized nature of human living. Our language is revealing. Consider the fact that when behavior appears conspicuously distressed and confused, we start to talk about the possible presence of a *dis*-order. The default condition is that of integrated organization. Personal organization makes for behavioral consistencies that allow one to confidently describe a human being's personality to others. If human beings acted in radically divergent ways from moment to moment, day to day, it would be impossible to describe your friend Kim as "easy-going," for example. Of course, this does not mean that Kim must always be easy-going. We understand implicitly that personality refers to a typical manner of behaving for which there can be exceptions. This is no less expected, as we sometimes see an inflexible excess of order (e.g., compulsion) as a sign of disorder as well. When it comes to personality, a modicum of plasticity is essential.

Personality also has an individualized quality about it. This belongs to the default condition of human living as well. The subfield of abnormal psychology once again provides an illustrative counterexample. The paradox of psychological "disorders" is that the disorder co-occurs with "symptoms" that make behavior appear more stereotypical and reflective of an anonymous diagnostic category (though never fully; thus, depersonalization and stigma are inherent dangers of the diagnostic process). The broader point here is that if all human beings were to act in the exact same manner, there would be no reason to study or even speak about personality. The study of personality would simply be the study of human behavior, nothing more. If all human beings were easy-going, then your description of your friend Kim as easy-going would be a superfluous statement of the obvious. The concept of personality bears with it the assumption that human beings display a relatively integrated, relatively consistent way of living their lives that is particular to each individual.

Personality *theories* are scientific tools that help us understand the achievement of this relatively integrated and consistent, individualized way of living. They do this in two major ways: by providing a means for psychologists to interpret diverse research findings in the area of personality and by stimulating new research on personality. *Interpretation* relates to the fact that scientific theories organize research findings in a way that makes them more comprehensible. Stated simply, theories empower us to make sense of data. They allow the scientist to see select research findings in the broader light of existing knowledge under the guidance of critical thinking skills. Theories of personality provide a means for organizing and making sense of research findings pertaining to personality in particular. The science of psychology is not purely reliant on data collection and specialized data analysis techniques (i.e., research). Theory is involved every step of the way (Lewin, 1951; Popper, 1959). The results of research observations are sometimes the subject of intense theoretical debate, and the results of studies are often reinterpreted over time as theoretical viewpoints in psychology go through metamorphoses, gain popularity, or fall out of vogue (Morawski, 1988). At one point in history, research "findings" are the result of one kind of learning process, then another. At another point, the very same findings are instead attributable to brain anomalies. Sometimes the new interpretation builds upon previous findings, but at other times it does not. The findings are the same; it is *the interpretation* that has changed, which speaks to the often underappreciated power of theory in psychology.

Theorizing is a means for thinking more deeply and more broadly about the "hard data" before us, and the nature of psychology's theories at any given time in history can impact the future of the discipline. Theories can open doors to scientific understanding or close them. In fact, there is currently a largely unheard cry for theory in psychology to save it from the ravages of a myopic focus on data gathering. Theoretical psychology has emerged as a subfield all its own for just these reasons. As Valsiner (2005) put the matter:

> Psychology as a whole has become empirically hyperproductive and theoretically mute—the ideas that are currently presented as "theories" are local, data-driven and methods based (Gigerenzer, 1993)—rather than pertaining to general questions about the basics of the human psyche. (p. 7)

Psychologists are in search of theoretical guidance that allows for analysis at manifold "levels" of human functioning, from the very simple to the infinitely complex (e.g., Sternberg, Grigorenko, & Kalmar, 2001; von Eckartsberg, 1979). This search for theoretical guidance is widespread and can even be observed in the area of research methodology itself! Research psychologists are demonstrating an increasing need for theoretical frameworks that can capture the subtleties of the data they collect. While qualitative research psychologists have long known about the need for such frameworks, quantitative research is now following suit and is slowly transitioning from a narrower focus on null hypothesis significance testing to a broader, more inclusive *modeling* orientation (Rodgers, 2010). This is a *theoretical* shift from proposing that a hypothesis has merit by rejecting the probability that one's research results were random to constructing models that accurately portray multifaceted human interactions. Thus, even at the level of research methods themselves, psychology cannot avoid theory. Still less can theory be avoided in an area like personality, which is usually taken to be the broadest and most multifaceted of all of psychology's areas of inquiry. As Walter Mischel (2004) once put it:

> The study of personality . . . was intended to ask the deepest questions about human nature, and to become the meta-discipline—the hub—for integrating the basic findings and general principles revealed by work at different levels of analysis within the larger science as they speak to the coherence and organization of the individual. (p. 18)

This brings us to the second major benefit of theories. Scientific theories call out for research. They *generate and guide* new scientific observations. When theoretical viewpoints clash, it leads to investigations designed to explore the contested conceptual curiosity. Theories of personality generate and guide research pertaining to personality in particular. So, just as psychology is not based exclusively on data, it is no less true that it is not a purely theoretical discipline. Theories work hand in hand with both quantitative and qualitative forms of data analysis, which inform them and allow them to evolve. This should not be mistaken for a naive advocacy of "data-driven" *methodologism* (DeRobertis, 2012; Kuhn, 1996; Slife, 2000). That would contradict the aforementioned remarks concerning the critical role of theory in the study of personality. Theory and research are meant to work together. This fact does not change, whether one duly recognizes it or fails to do so. As Strasser (1977) once put it:

> The metaphysic which lies hidden in the various psychological . . . "systems" is for the most part already present in the categories and concepts which are selected for describing the normal or pathological movements of the heart. Thus one who is not trained [theoretically] is unaware that, by taking over certain supposedly technical and descriptive concepts and methods, he [*sic*] has already adopted a determinate path which may lead . . . into a hedonistic, naturalistic, idealistic or mechanistic anthropology. (p. xiv)

"Good" Theories: General Criteria

What has been covered thus far implies that there are certain criteria that can be used to evaluate a theory of personality. A good theory has the power to help psychologists interpret research findings in a plausible, insightful way. It can also generate research on established research topics or open new lines of research. However, in order to do so, the theory has to be amenable to research in the first place. A psychological theory is a set of assumptions that research observations and data analyses can in some way or other support or contest. The more a theory is dominated by assumptions that cannot be supported by any sort of observation, the less likely it is to be looked upon favorably by the scientific community. The theory may still garner attention and make headway if it is perceived as having usable value and/or wisdom, but it will nonetheless be dogged by accusations of pseudoscience. If no observations can be used to make an argument for or against a theory of personality, it probably does not qualify as psychologically scientific in nature. Stated differently, if the so-called theory is totally or primarily faith-based, then it no longer falls squarely within the realm of scientific psychological inquiry. However, this does not mean that theories can be proven or disproven wholesale. Theories are large, broad-based narratives, and no single study or group of studies can validate or invalidate an entire theory. Rather, the viability of parts or aspects of a theory can be examined through research. In this way, a theory is distinguished from say, a hypothesis, which is small enough to be tested.

Good theories also demonstrate a conscious recognition of their most fundamental assumptions. They are transparent about the value structure inherent in their viewpoint as well as its scientific and ethical implications. This includes an awareness of the historical, social, and cultural context of the theorizing activity itself. All theories throughout all of the sciences are created from within a time and place in history. Ideally, personality theorizing would be cognizant of the fact that the context out of which a theory arises can have an effect on the final form of the perspective. Without such awareness, the theory can be accused of being biased in some way (e.g., as being ethnocentric, androcentric, heterocentric, and so forth).

Good theories have other characteristics that all students of personality should know as well. For example, a good theory is philosophically consistent. That is, a theory should not violate the law of non-contradiction. If a theory consists of truth claims that simply contradict one another, then the theory will be judged as weak. This is not to say that there cannot be opposing truth claims within a theory. A theory can make opposing claims as long as the theorist demonstrates an awareness of this opposition and provides explanations for what amounts to a seeming contradiction or paradox. Indeed, human existence is very complex, and a theory that lacks such irregularities altogether might be accused of being too linear and myopic. Sometimes behavior can appear radically different under different circumstances. As we will see, Abraham Maslow's descriptions of self-actualizing people illustrate this point in an exemplary manner (see Winston, 2018).

Yet another aspect of good theorizing is that it avoids the opposing extremes of oversimplification and obfuscation. In the absence of compelling evidence to the contrary, the simplest or most parsimonious account of behavior is the best account of behavior. However, it is also true that the simplest account is not always the best account. It depends on what one is studying. The quest for parsimony should never take precedence over faithfulness to the phenomenon under investigation. Accordingly, one must avoid the temptation to lunge at linear, skeletal, or superficial explanations for phenomena that have depth and subtlety to them. To illustrate, consider the school of thought known as *behaviorism*. Behaviorism holds that human behavior (including what we would call personality) is the result of a kind of learning, which is why it is sometimes referred to as *learning theory*. But this should not be mistaken to mean that behaviorists have been open to any and all learning phenomena. From the behavioral perspective, the study of learning is tightly focused on *conditioning*. Using more everyday terms, you would know it as a kind of "training," and you would relate it to how we teach our pets to behave more than to, say, a kind of job training. In fact, behaviorism is largely responsible for popularizing the image of psychologists working in laboratories with animals. Over the years, their research has featured the likes of dogs, cats, pigeons, rats, and vervet monkeys outside of their native habitats and under the manipulative control of premeditated laboratory conditions. This approach, and its associated mindset about learning, has served to selectively illuminate certain elementary forms of learning. But its narrowness has also tended to blind behaviorism to other aspects of learning, not the least of which are those forms of learning that are characteristically human. As Straus (1963) put it:

> There are two kinds of learning: an expansive, gnostic learning and a constrictive, pathic learning. The former rests on the power of the mind to reflect, to negate creatively and thus make it possible . . . to transcend the limits of . . . simple existence. Man [*sic*] learns insofar as he [*sic*] ceases to react directly. However, the individual animal which learns never ceases to react

> directly. The learning of the animal ... concerns the acquiring of habits . . . . It is useful in cases of exact repetition of circumstances, and harmful in every *unusual* case, where precisely the monotony, narrowness, and thus the inadequacy of the accustomed reaction becomes evident. Each habit is bought at the cost of other potentialities. (pp. 192–193)

Behaviorism's penchant for pushing the envelope when it comes to theoretical parsimony has trickled down to many of its concepts, like *extinction*, for example. Extinction refers to the cessation of a previously acquired behavioral response, so learning is held to have thus "gone extinct." But this notion is a direct reflection of the oversimplicity of the behavioral notion of learning. There is much more to learning than an overt behavioral response. As McCall (1983) explains:

> "Extinction" is not a cessation of learning or an "unlearning" (whatever that may be), but a clear instance of *new learning*. And what is learned? That the previously noted connection between the conditioned stimulus and the unconditioned stimulus . . . cannot anymore be counted on . . . and this recognition of a change in the situation is as much a valid piece of information as was the earlier recognition of its utility as a signal. Viewing "extinction" as non-learning is a manifestation of functional blindness. (pp. 116–117)

Good theories are equally careful not to muddle phenomena with conceptual clutter. Ironically, an excessively narrow approach to personality can also give rise to an obfuscating compensatory tendency. To make up for its inadequacies, the theory is forced to come up with all sorts of explanatory conceptual contrivances that trick one into seeing things that are not really there. This is a criticism often made of Freud's psychosexual psychoanalytic theory. People do not like to feel as if they are being "psychoanalyzed," in part for this reason. It is uncomfortable enough to have one's unrecognized or unseen aspects exposed, but it is even more uncomfortable to feel the sting of judgment when the accusations are full of potentially false accusations framed in highly esoteric terminology. Freud made a pointed effort to cast the whole of personality as forming around unconscious sexual and aggressive drives, with an overwhelming focus on the first six years of life. Unimpressed by other kinds of motives or the achievements of later developmental periods, Freud generated a worldview that then insistently interpreted behavior that would otherwise appear more mature, "normal," or healthy through the phantasmagoric lens of primitive fantasies, past conflicts, and all manner of defense mechanisms. *Suspicion* thus becomes psychosexual theory's default manner of attunement to other people (Ricoeur, 1970). As a result, the concrete dynamics of interpersonal communication that occur in real time often cannot appear in their fullness or with unbiased accuracy (e.g., see Smith, 2004; van den Berg, 1972).

Of course, any theory can be accused of either oversimplification or obfuscating distortion. William Stern has been accused of the former (Vygotsky, 1986), Carl Jung has been accused of the latter (Boss, 1982). But in each case the evidence has to be weighed carefully before arriving at final determinations. Sometimes a theory is temporarily written off only to be vindicated by a new generation of psychologists. Again, Abraham Maslow serves as a case in point, as his famous hierarchy of needs has been characterized as an oversimplification on a woefully inadequate and inaccurate reading of his theory for years (Bland & DeRobertis, 2020). Recently, however, it has begun to appear as if the tide is turning, and Maslow's personality theory may see a resurgence in the light of both revised thinking and contemporary research evidence (e.g., Bland, 2019; Bland & DeRobertis, 2020; Bland & Swords, in press; Kaufman, 2020; Valsala & Menon, 2019; Winston et al. 2017).

To sum up, good personality theorizing helps psychologists navigate between very simple and very complex behavioral and experiential dynamics without confusing one with the other. This is an important point, as the ability to insightfully assess the nature of one's observations empowers psychologists to make reasonable, grounded decisions with regard to therapeutic interventions, pedagogical interventions, and various public and institutional policies. This brings us to the issue of praxis. Good theories are tools that can empower professional psychologists to make insightful, prudent decisions with regard to their interventions, whatever they may be. As has already been noted, good theory is a valuable tool in the world of academic research. But the work of psychology does not stop there. As we learn in our introductory psychology courses, psychology is applied in many aspects of human life, ranging from sports, industry, psychotherapy, the military, parenting, pedagogy, and beyond. Armed with good theory, the practicing psychologist has a widened perceptual lens with which to engage phenomena that would be inexplicable to the layman.

Personality Theorizing: A Humanistic Perspective

The above criteria are the kinds of foci that often structure the "evaluation" or "criticism" sections of standard, comprehensive textbooks. They are largely generic and could apply to most kinds of psychological theorizing. The current text also employs standards for evaluating personality theories in particular, and these standards are derived from the perspective of humanistic psychology. They are used to structure the layout of the chapters to follow.

Humanistic psychology is committed to understanding the whole person on the whole person's terms. It resists attempting to relegate the complex organization that makes an individual who they are to any of their "parts" or myriad part-functions. To state the matter in colloquial terms, humanistic psychology is a systematic, disciplined attempt to not mistake the forest for the trees. This orientation demands a kind of thinking that is dynamical, synoptic, and characteristically poised to evolve. It cannot be linear and reductionistic in the name of scientific convention or the status quo. So, on one level—the more abstract level of its scientific theorizing activity—humanistic psychology evaluates personality theories by their integrative potential. It asks: Can this or that theory interface with other theories in a productive way, yielding increasing insight rather than distortion? Even though humanistic personality theorizing appreciates and values even the most narrowly defined, highly specialized theoretical contributions (see van Kaam, 1966), it insists upon a certain kind of intellectual humility, one that is associated with keeping its approach "open and flexible" (Bühler, 1971, p. 378). Accordingly, it looks more favorably upon specialized theoretical contributions when two conditions are met. First, the theory should recognize the limitations of its vantage point so as not to do violence to the whole. Second, its methods and concepts should be "permeable" enough (to borrow the language of George Kelly, 1963) to allow for cross-fertilization with other specialized perspectives and more synoptic approaches to smoothly assimilate its insights as they work toward a more "whole person," comprehensive viewpoint. The theories of George Kelly (Chapter 6) and Erik Erikson (Chapter 7) are exemplary in this regard.

On another level, the more concrete level of *content*, humanistic psychology evaluates theories of personality by their ability to address the unique person's own capacity for integration. But bear in mind, personality is not static. It develops and evolves over time. Thus, personal integration cannot be understood without further consideration of the relative openness and flexibility of the personality in confronting the ever-present paradoxical relationship between stability and change throughout the lifespan. Optimal degrees of openness and flexibility allow for the forward-moving processes of growth that facilitate health. The perspective of the text is that integration and health, though not perfectly identical, are nonetheless indubitably connected at the hip (e.g., Behrends, 1986; Koydemir et al., 2014). These ideas were alluded to at the outset of the chapter in the discussion of the relatively ordered and integrated, individualized nature of personality. Integration and health are mutually implicative. Relative health implies relative integration. Even though there are periods of moratoria, positive *dis*integration (Dabrowski, 1967), or temporary regression (Bland & DeRobertis, 2020) over the course of the lifespan, the development of the healthy personality cannot occur without the evolving capacity to bring together, consolidate, or synthesize its various attributes, capacities, and potentials in some workable way. In Dillon's (1983) words:

> Integration marks the point of intersection between freedom from and freedom for, that is, the intersection between archeology and teleology. To be freed from the conflict between opposed values located in the world structured by one's past is to be freed for the pursuit of becoming . . . . (p. 37)

But there are various "workable ways" of integrating, and not all forms of personality integration are equal. So, to state the matter in the reverse, relative integration implicates relative health. That is, personality integration can be evaluated on the basis of its robustness, genuineness, nuance, and refinement. Some forms of personality integration are rather tenuous, making for personalities that are overtly fragile or prone to compensatory rigidity. Such personalities are less conducive to creative growth and more vulnerable to the potentially deleterious effects of life's many challenges and stressors. There are also superficial, intellectualized, ego-driven forms of integration that look "well-adapted" on the surface and may grow according to age-expected norms, but they display little of consequence when it comes to indicators of well-being, happiness, thriving, fulfillment, and so forth. What is apparent in all such cases is that integrative shortcomings stand in the way of optimal personal becoming. In contrast, other forms of integration have impressive depth and breadth, evidencing a tensile strength that allows the personality to shift and move in dynamically responsive ways, clearing diverse pathways to fulfillment in life. They facilitate ongoing diversification or "differentiation" and, at the most advanced levels, the confrontation with life's many paradoxes.

Assessing personality systems on these bases, one finds a continuum of viewpoints. Some theories lean in the direction of being more atomistic, mechanistic, reductionistic, impersonal, and impermeable in character. Such views tend to deal with the problem of personality integration in ways that are very conceptually restrictive, searching for an explanatory lowest common denominator, so to speak, and could be called *micro-integrational*. Their understandings of personality are either tied to anonymous statistical aggregates or fashioned from concepts taken from the natural sciences and uncritically generalized to humans. Thus, human psychology and the individuality of persons are seen as more or less derivative. They make no distinction between objectivity in the sense of "being objective" and the all-out objectification of human psychological life. These perspectives tend to revolve around normative behavior and/or pathology. The former is considered functional and adaptive; the latter is considered dysfunctional and maladaptive. Within the confines of this conceptual dyad, the highly developed personality is one that is well adjusted to environmental conditions. Having garnered the lion's share of attention in the field of psychology, they are largely responsible for the trend of psychology departments offering courses in "personality and adjustment." Adjustment—normative adaptation—is the way they envision health (Maslow, 1961). These theories are frontloaded in the chapters that follow.

In contrast, there are theories that lean in the direction of being more holistic/holonic, personal (extending out into the interpersonal and the transpersonal), and permeable. Personality is considered a *Gestalt*, a living whole that is not a mere summation of its parts. These views are more macro-integrational and humanistic. Here, the objectifying consciousness of the scientists is counterbalanced by a perpetually open-ended orientation toward the lived experience of situated persons. Part of being objective means knowing when not to objectify human subjectivity. Hence, these theories will be oriented in varying ways toward the vitality, spontaneity, creativity, and narrative meaning-making powers of the personality. Human psychology and the individuality of persons are not considered wholly derivative. Quite the contrary, understanding their originality is considered a central organizing theme of the approach. These personality theories tend to prioritize working from a conception of optimized *becoming* or human thriving that is mindful of both its triumphant and tragic dimensions. Pathology and normative behavior are seen as deviations from and/or opportunities to work toward progressive growth and fulfillment. This more encompassing vantage point is where the originality of the human species and individual persons comes into maximum relief. As described in the Preface, personality is seen as an evolving, dynamic process of becoming more human and more oneself through the forward-moving, creative striving to realize potentials and actualize possibilities. The chapters on George Kelly and Erik Erikson will serve as conceptual bridges to macro-integrational theorizing in the chapters to follow.

Perhaps no one has more clearly and succinctly provided a conceptual foundation for the distinction between these two trends than Abraham Maslow (1961), when he stated:

> Psychology is in part a branch of biology, in part a branch of sociology. But it is not only that. It has its own unique jurisdiction as well, that portion of the psyche which is not a reflection of the outer world or a molding to it. There could be such a thing as a psychological psychology. (p. 6)

Early in his career, Maslow had noted that psychologists on a large scale were borrowing heavily from biology for their concepts and methods. When biology seemed to fall short, they hastily retreated to "nurture," various forms of social determinism and environmental adjustment (which he summarized with the generic term "sociology"). Either way, the person remained a mere pawn, only approached from contrasting vantage points. But, for Maslow, the effort to reach beyond biology to the environment did not go far enough. The problem, as he saw it, was that psychologists habitually viewed the psychology of the person as the residual side effect of biological determinants, sociological determinants, or some combination of both. He saw this as psychology avoiding its task and true calling. An adequate psychology, and thus an adequate psychology of personality, would place psychology at the center of its study while acknowledging its relational connectivity to biology and sociology. The person and personality would have to be seen in terms of what van Kaam (1966) referred to as a "subjective–objective–situational Gestalt" (p. 195). There would have to be a place for subjectivity in personality, envisioned as irreducible to biosocial conditions, as genuinely participatory in its own life and potential future development. To recognize irreducible subjectivity means that the natural scientific inclination toward objectification must be kept in check. Macro-integrational (humanistic) trends in personality embrace this vision of the personality.

To be clear, humanistic psychology respects both micro-integrational and macro-integrational trends. Accordingly, van Kaam (1961) once noted:

> The [humanistic] psychologist . . . is suspicious when a . . . psychologist claims that man [sic] is only a mechanistic stimulus-response organism. On the other hand, he [sic] is as suspicious when personalistic psychologists claim that man [sic] is only a personal being without an aspect that is measurable and without adjustment to a collectivity. (p. 100)

Humanistic psychology does, however, insist on emphasizing the critical contributions of the latter views, which have traditionally been more often minimized or glossed over in psychology as a whole. Thus, van Kaam (1966) would later note:

> The danger of a distortion of the whole of . . . psychology is the necessary consequence of the fact that modern research is so . . . one-sidedly directed, and therefore so time and energy consuming that it is impossible for the researcher who works in limited areas of personality to relate . . . findings to the explicated fundamental structure of human personality and to all the findings of all the studies of personality. Therefore, there is only one choice for humanity today: either to develop on a global scale specialists of the whole personality who counterbalance the process of individualization of certain aspects of personality, or to resign itself to an otherwise inescapable distortion . . . . The last course will mean our gradual destruction because we will lose contact with our own psychology. There is only one choice today: to integrate or to perish. (p. 181)

The penultimate task of humanistic psychology, far too ambitious to accomplish here, is to show in detail how the more personalistic (macro) theories can actually incorporate the best that other, less personal (micro) theories have to offer in the hope of achieving the best possible integrative understanding of personality in the process. Their aim is not to merely negate "opposing" views but to work creatively toward the achievement of a more refined, profound form of scientific dialogue. As Maslow (1961) once noted, humanistic psychology is a "hierarchical-integrative way of thinking, which implies simply that . . . the higher . . . *includes* the lower" (Maslow, 1961, p. 2, emphasis mine). This is humanistic thinking. It is guided by the ideal of being both critical and inclusive, in contradistinction to the superficial images of self-actualizing romanticism that are repeated ad nauseum in popular discourse, even in many academic circles. This is why Maslow insisted, "We shouldn't have to say 'humanistic psychology.' The adjective should be unnecessary. Don't think of me as being anti-[any other school of thought]. I'm anti-doctrinaire" (Hall, 1968, p. 57).

Regrettably, the theoretical language of the humanistic orientation can sometimes be confusing for students for at least two reasons. First, when studying personality, humanistic psychology describes its own theoretical approach in much the same way that it describes personality itself. On the whole, humanistic psychology aspires to be both differential and integrative (van Kaam, 1966). In any area of psychology (including personality), humanistic theory respects specialized, narrowly defined lines of inquiry, but it is also an open systems theory that seeks an expanding integrative organization to contextualize the findings of these specialized perspectives. Likewise, diverse forms of humanistic psychology (of which there are many) approach personality as follows: Differentiating characteristics, such as new skills and abilities, new ways of experiencing and understanding, new challenges and hardships are all seen as presenting themselves as possibilities in the process of human development. These possibilities are held to emerge from the nexus of the preexisting whole and are then actualized by the way the person reintegrates them into the personality, which then changes and refines its total organization. Ideally, the personality displays the requisite openness (to the world in general, to other people, and to one's own genuine desires) to carry out its integrative work in a creative manner that allows for both growth and health. The viewpoint of the current text is that humanistic psychology's particular synoptic emphasis is uniquely suited to the study of personality because, as Buss (2004) observed, "Personality psychology might be the broadest and most encompassing branch of psychology" (p. 394). Further, personality theorists of all persuasions— even those that are more atomistic, mechanistic, and reductionistic— acknowledge the need for some principle of integration that would allow personalities to come into being, even if their theories are not particularly well equipped deal with it.

The second source of potential confusion comes from the fact that humanistic psychology demands that one think in highly dialectical and dialogal/dialogical ways that contrast with the linear, logical determinism to which we Westerners have become so accustomed. To illustrate, even though humanistic psychology has championed the cause to recognize individuality, it nonetheless maintains that personality is always situational, manifesting within contexts. Correlatively, for a context to actually *be* the context of personality development (i.e., its occasion or live setting), there must be persons experiencing, interpreting, and acting in and through it. Person and context are always mutually implied and interpenetrated, so neither rules over the other with an iron first. As this text unfolds, the student has to transition from linear images of personality integration that is at the mercy of causal forces, to reciprocal causation, to more humanistic forms of thinking that cannot be adequately subsumed under either model. Here, person and world are not approached exclusively from the third-person perspective of causes and effects, even reciprocating ones. Humanistic psychology adopts the view of a more intimate interrelationship between person and world, one that is commensurate with the firsthand experience of the living person. It sees irreducible subjectivity as *irreducibly relational*. Accordingly, it embraces an open-ended approach to human interaction and is willing to explore myriad forms of meaningful mutual involvement, presence, or encounter (Luijpen & Koren, 1969; Robbins, 2015). It dives headfirst into topics like vulnerability, finitude, angst, suffering, devotion, love, wonder, awe.

Irreducible relationality is a major manifestation of a deeper underlying theme in humanistic psychology: the centrality of dynamic, polar tensions and paradox. The first hint of paradox appears early in the text, with Freud's (Chapter 3) observation that human existence is shot through with powerful forces of both creation and destruction. It resurfaces in the chapter on George Kelly (Chapter 6) due to the inherent bipolarity of constructs in his construct theory as well as a growth paradox that will be noted in connection with his viewpoint. Paradox becomes still more explicit toward the culmination of the chapter on Erik Erikson (Chapter 7), and then remains an integral theme until Chapter 11, especially in its interpersonal aspects. Alfred Adler's work serves as a clear illustration in the sense that, for Alder, the person is more human and more *themselves* the more they are capable of caring about cooperating with others in the spirit of community feeling. From Chapter 11 through Chapter 15, the theme of paradox becomes increasingly prominent and is exposed in relation to ever-diversifying relational matrices. The humanistic view maintains that there is an essential incompleteness to personality integration that drives the process of becoming, so no vision of "oneness" can negate the fact that human beings are always "in relation to . . . ." More advanced forms of integration recruit simultaneously deepening and expanding relational dynamisms. Later chapters headings thus feature the word "nested" because they delve into select aspects of irreducible relationality in a systematic fashion. The term *nested* denotes the co-constitution of a medium or media through which the drama of human existence unfolds (it helps to think of the metaphor of making a nest or the gerund form, "nesting").

Taking it Further: Food for Thought

Psychology is typically defined as the study of human behavior and mental processes, with an overall focus on the individual. This is what distinguishes it from sociology. Yet, the study of what makes people individuals has been relegated to a single specialized subfield: personality! Moreover, personality psychology has had to contend with strong criticisms over the years and, at times, has had to struggle just to survive (McAdams & Pals, 2006; Smith, 1982). This is indicative of a kind of contradiction deep in the heart of psychology, having ripple effects across its many areas of concentration. Take the following observation from the area of lifespan development:

> Academic developmental psychologists neglect the subject of development, namely the individual, in whose subjectivity all fragmented processes are amalgamated in a meaningful way. Mainstream developmental psychology excludes an important dimension of development: The Gestalt of development, or a subject's development from a holistic perspective, or development based on the real experiences of the developing subject. In mainstream psychology it is not even considered a legitimate research question to talk about the subject in whose mind and body these basic processes and fragmented parts form a totality. Or worse, this problem is not even discussed as a problem. Not only journals and monographs demonstrate that the Gestalt has been lost. A look at contemporary textbooks of

developmental psychology—which would be most appropriate to do justice to the Gestalt of development because they are not restricted in legitimizing their content by doing original research—demonstrates that parts are proliferating while the totality of development is nowhere to be found. (Teo, 2003, p. 75)

Just as with developmental psychology, perhaps even more so, personality psychology needs brave champions to work toward an integrative understanding of personality and bring their insights into fruitful contact with the rest of psychology to help the discipline achieve its aims and fulfill its scientific mission.

Make it Work!

Personality is not "inside your head"; it permeates your behavior and communicates who you are to other people in many subtle ways. Personality is *in the world*. When you pick out things like clothes and furnishings, they tend to bear the mark of your personality even if only in the smallest of ways. If you had been living somewhere for a time and someone visited while you were not home, what aspects of the environment would provide the most valuable clues (maybe even dead giveaways) that this was the place where *you* lived? More important, what aspects of the environment would be indicative of your general style or way of living (i.e., your personality)? This "profiling" is the kind of thing criminal investigators must do as part of their job.

Key Concepts

Atomistic perspective/reductionism
Becoming
Bias
Characteristics of good personality theories (humanistic perspective)
Characteristics of good theories
Characteristics of human personality
Differentiation
Hierarchical-integrative viewpoint
Irreducible subjectivity
Irreducibly relationality
Macro-integrational orientation
Micro-integrational orientation

Normative adaptation
Obfuscation
Oversimplification
Personality
Personality and praxis
Relationship between theory and research
Relative integration
The law of non-contradiction
Theories
Theories of personality
Usable value of theories of personality
Whole person perspective/holism

Part I

Micro-Integrational Theorizing: From Illusion to Adaptation

Chapter 2

Watson and Skinner: Personality as an Aggregate of Conditioned Responses

In this chapter, we will examine approaches to personality that look to the *environment* for the causes of behavior and, by default, personality formation. Although these approaches acknowledge that something like personality formation occurs within inherited genetic parameters, they focus their attention on the situational behavioral exchanges that occur during the organism's lifetime. Thus, B. F. Skinner (1969) warned that heritable *evolutionary* factors must be approached with caution because they are not directly observable. They are hypothesized and inferred from evolutionary theory, and what is held to be the result of inheritance may in fact be something that is shaped by current experience. Skinner distrusted hypothesis testing (which is derived from theorizing) on large groups of participants and instead tended to work in a more freeform fashion, manipulating environmental conditions on his research subjects case by case (Hall & Lindzey, 1978; Tesch, 1990). Moreover, strict behaviorists reject the use of internal mechanisms, be they physical or mental, as a *primary* means for explaining behavior or personality. Rather, behavior and personality are considered the result of repeated exposure to specific environmental conditions. Hence, these theories are called *conditioning theories*. They come from the school of thought known as *behaviorism*. From this vantage point, if one were to inquire as to the origin of certain patterns of behavior, one should not look "inward." Rather, one ought to look outward for the causes of behavior in the individual's "readily observable" environmental conditions. Thus, conditioning theory similarly does not consider how much things like your mother, your home, or your dog might *mean* to you to be valid environmental data. For a strict behaviorist, the *meaning* of your environmental interactions is far too intrapsychic (meaning inside the mind) to be given focal consideration. Conditioning theories take the very strict position that anything that is to be considered truly scientific must be measurable, and environmental interactions that cannot be measured are thus deemed inherently problematic.

Classical Conditioning Theory

The first behavioral learning theory to appear in the history of psychology was classical conditioning theory. The fundamental principles of what would go on to become known as classical conditioning were first discovered in the United States by Edwin Burket Twitmyer (1902, 1905). But for reasons unknown, Twitmyer's research has been systematically ignored throughout the history of psychology. Instead, the history of classical conditioning is regularly presented as the brainchild of Soviet physiologist Ivan Pavlov (1927). Pavlov was studying the reflexive (i.e., involuntary) responses involved in the digestion of food. In order to study digestion, Pavlov studied dogs. In order to study their digestive processes, Pavlov had to feed his dogs. Over time, Pavlov came to notice that his dogs were salivating *before* he presented them with food. This was strange to Pavlov. As a physiologist, he knew that the involuntary response of salivation was naturally elicited by the sight, smell, or taste of food. What he saw, however, was that the response of salivation could be elicited without seeing, smelling, or tasting any food. This was not natural; therefore, it must have been *learned*.

Pavlov hypothesized that the dogs were salivating before they perceived food because a simple form of learning had taken place called *associative learning*. He ventured that an *association* had occurred, a linking or joining of some stimulus accompanying the food with the food itself. Each stimulus became an indicator of the other. What has now become known as *classical conditioning* is the process by which the systematic pairing of stimuli creates associative links. As a result of such links, any response brought on by one of the stimuli spreads to the other, so to speak, so that the organism in question comes to elicit the same response to the new (previously neutral) stimulus.

To test this, Pavlov surgically implanted tubes into his dogs' salivary glands so that he could measure the amount of saliva that they produced. He was able to compare how much saliva was in a dog's mouth at any given time as opposed to how much saliva would be produced when presented with food. Pavlov then searched for something that would act as a neutral stimulus. That is, he searched for something that would not elicit any more salivation than usual in the dogs' mouths. His choices for neutral stimuli varied, including the sound of a metronome, a buzzer, and tuning fork. For our purposes, let us use the tone of a tuning fork as the example. Pavlov sounded the tuning fork and noticed that the dogs did not salivate any more than usual when they heard it. At this point, Pavlov began systematically pairing the tone of the tuning fork with the presentation of food. Over and over again, the tuning fork would sound before feeding time. Eventually, Pavlov was able to demonstrate that after systematically pairing the tuning fork with the presentation of food, he could get the dogs to salivate to the sound of the tuning fork similar to the way they would salivate to the presentation of food *even in the absence of any food perception*. In other words, the dogs would produce copious amounts of thick saliva when they heard the tuning fork, even though they were not seeing, smelling, or tasting any food. This, for Pavlov, was evidence in favor of his ideas concerning associative learning.

Pavlov gave names to the variables in his study. The food was called the *unconditioned stimulus*. In simpler language, this means that the food was the "not taught" stimulation. One does not have to teach dogs about food. They have a preexisting response to it, which is salivation. Thus, salivation was called the *unconditioned response*. The sound of the tuning fork, in contrast, was dubbed the *conditioned stimulus*. Dogs do not naturally salivate when tuning forks ring out, so the sound of the tuning fork was the *taught* or *learned* (environmentally conditional) stimulation. The dogs learned to salivate to the sounding of the tuning fork. Their salivation to the sounding of the tuning fork was dubbed the *conditioned response*. The conditioned response is the brand-new reaction of the organism. It is the new learned behavior and the evidence that classical conditioning has taken place.

Pavlov won the Nobel Prize in physiology for his work. Recall that his field was not psychology. However, in the United States, the up-and-coming psychologist John Watson (1994) saw in Pavlov's physiology the fulfillment of a new form of psychology that he was developing called *behaviorism*. As he described it:

> Psychology as the behaviorist views it is a purely objective experimental branch of natural science. Its theoretical goal is the prediction and control of behavior. Introspection forms no essential part of its methods . . . . The behaviorist, in his [*sic*] efforts to get a unitary scheme of animal response, recognizes no dividing line between man [*sic*] and brute. (p. 248)

For Watson, the principles of conditioning furnished a way of doing psychology that was precise and unhampered by concepts that he found vague and troublesome—like mind, consciousness, and introspection. He sought the "elimination of states of consciousness as proper objects of investigation in themselves" for psychology (p. 253).

In one of his more controversial studies, Watson and his associate Rosalie Rayner (Watson & Rayner, 1920), secured the "participation" of an eight-month-old baby boy who was given the pseudonym "Little Albert." The aim of their study was to condition Albert to have an emotional reaction of fear. They would thereby demonstrate that the kinds of procedures at play in Pavlov's experiments were also operative in determining the behavior of human beings. Watson and Rayner found that if they struck a suspended steel bar with a hammer, they could frighten Little Albert. They then proceeded to expose Little Albert to a white (laboratory) rat and noted that Albert showed *no* apprehension with regard to this stimulus. That is, he was *not* afraid of the rat. They then systematically paired the presentation of the rat with the loud, sharp sound of the hammer hitting the steel bar. Over and over again, when Little Albert would encounter the rat, he was made afraid by the frightening sound of the hammer hitting the steel bar. Over time, simply presenting the rat alone to Albert caused him alarm. Little Albert did not fear rats at first. But after the successive presentation of the rat with the fear-evoking stimulus of a clanging metal bar, Albert came to fear the laboratory rat. Through this systematic pairing, Little Albert was classically conditioned to elicit an emotional reaction of fear.

The kinds of studies done by Watson and other early behaviorists were believed to have important implications for a theory of human behavior that could be transferred to the study of personality. From this perspective, our relatively consistent behavioral patterns would be seen as an aggregate of conditioned responses, like those in Pavlov's and Watson's studies. Consider the following behavioral discrepancy: one young lady is quite fond of school while her friend is apprehensive about school and dislikes it. To shed light on these personal differences one would consider their histories of associations with school. From this perspective, we might expect to find a process similar to what occurred in the case of Little Albert. Perhaps the first young lady repeatedly had fun in school, had a teacher who liked her, found it easy to get help, and found school to be a generally pleasant place. These pleasurable associations would lead us to predict that she should be fond of school. Perhaps her friend was teased, perhaps she had negative interactions with her teacher, or maybe she had a difficult time with her studies. From these aversive associations, we would predict that she should indeed dislike school. The point is, we would not look to their genes or mental processes to explain this kind of difference in personal style. Instead, we would focus our attention on their environments for clues to the history of their associations with school. It is here that one would find the "objective" evidence or *cause* of their respective dispositions toward school.

At this point, you might be asking yourself if all of human behavior can be explained in such simple terms. After all, there is a lot of diversity in human behavior. This is a valid point, and the behaviorists have not overlooked this fact. Watson himself contributed to the behaviorists' response to this query. When Watson and Rayner conditioned Little Albert to fear a rat, they soon noticed that his conditioned response of fear was not limited to the conditioned stimulus (i.e., the rat). They reported that his fear reaction generalized beyond the rat to all sorts of stimuli that were vaguely similar to the rat, such as a dog, a rabbit, a fur coat, and a white bearded Santa Claus mask. This phenomenon was dubbed *stimulus generalization*, and it is used as a way of explaining how human beings develop so many diverse and strange behavioral patterns. Given the way new learned responses can spread far and wide to all kinds of related stimuli, it thus makes sense that we should see diversity in human behavior.

Consider the development of phobias as an example. There are a great many phobias among the general population, and some of them are bizarre. For example, I was once acquainted with a young lady who was phobic of pasta! Now, being afraid of something like a dog or a snake seems understandable to people. All it would take would be an instance of being bitten, or at least seeing someone bitten. But how can we explain a pasta phobia? She had never been hurt by pasta or even injured in the presence of pasta. It turned out that this young lady associated pasta with maggots, which were associated with rot and death. As she probed into the source of the behavior, she began to unearth a series of associations, which led to maggots. Now, many forms of pasta could be seen as sort of worm-like in appearance (e.g., spaghetti). Thus, a behaviorist could explain her phobia by searching for the initial environmental interactions or learning experiences through which she first became afraid in the presence of maggots and thereby generalized her fear response.

Here you might object, "But not *all* learned responses generalize!" This is also true, and behaviorists have a way to explain that as well. It is called *discrimination learning*. Sometimes organisms come to elicit conditioned responses to a specific stimulus apart from all others. The organism can learn to discriminate among the stimuli by unambiguous properties or traits, like training a dolphin to take hostile action against predatory sharks rather than docile sharks to protect divers. An interesting instance of discriminatory learning is the *Garcia Effect* or *conditioned taste aversion* (Garcia et al., 1955). When an organism experiences nausea or vomits, it is not unusual for that organism to avoid that particular food or drink in the future. Other forms of food or drink are unaffected.

So, classical conditioning theorists assert that all learning and thus personality formation proceeds from the establishment of basic associations to more complicated and varied associations, which facilitates *higher-order conditioning*. This is the process by which an organism forms new associations through exposure to a previously conditioned (i.e., learned) stimulus. So, for example, Pavlov's dogs were conditioned to salivate to the tone of a tuning fork. From here, one could then expose the dogs to the color green each time the tuning fork was struck, and we might eventually see the dogs salivate to the color green.

Before moving on, it must be noted that this kind of learning does not have to be permanent. Behaviorists have noted that if the particular kind of pairing in question (i.e., the particular environmental exposure) is stopped, then over time new learned responses can go extinct. *Extinction* refers to the phenomenon where a learned behavior stops occurring due to the elimination or alteration of the environmental conditions that were responsible for the appearance of that behavior in the first place. However, this is not to say that extinction is necessarily permanent. In fact, sometimes a response that has gone extinct can suddenly reemerge for a brief period. This is called *spontaneous recovery*, though such responses are rarely as powerful as the initial learned response.

Operant Conditioning Theory

Operant conditioning theory is the second major viewpoint to appear in the behavioral tradition, and it expands the basic ideas of classical conditioning theory. In agreement with classical conditioning theorists, operant conditioning theorists consider human personality to be the result of environmental conditions that give rise to associations that come to elicit new learned behaviors. However, operant conditioning theory is less about the generic pairing of stimuli and more about associations tied to *the consequences* of an organism's *actions*, as we will see momentarily.

Operant conditioning was first termed *instrumental learning* by Edward L. Thorndike (1932). Thorndike paved the way for this new development in behaviorism. Thorndike studied the behavior of cats trying to escape from puzzle boxes (think of escape room for cats). At first, it took the cats a long time to escape. Over time, however, incorrect solutions were phased out and successful responses occurred more frequently. This pruning and honing of responses allowed the cats to escape faster with practice. With his *law of effect*, Thorndike theorized that responses that produce satisfying consequences become forged in memory, which makes them occur more frequently over time. In contrast, unsuccessful responses (which produce frustrating consequences), are discarded and thus occur less frequently. In other words, rewarding consequences *strengthen* a behavior and frustrating consequences *weaken a* behavior.

B. F. Skinner (1953) later called this form of learning *operant conditioning* because he felt it was more descriptive. For Skinner, organisms operate on things in the world. An *operant* is thus a method that can be used to modify behavioral interactions over time. These operations have consequences that have a direct impact on future behavior or future "operations," as it were. According to the principles of Skinnerian conditioning, an action can be strengthened or suppressed depending upon whether the organism receives reinforcements (i.e., rewards) or punishments after performing the behavior. If an organism carries out an action and, as a consequence, receives a reinforcement, the behavior that preceded the reinforcement will be more likely to occur again. If an organism carries out an action and, as a consequence, receives a punishment, the behavior that preceded the punishment will be less likely to occur again. In other words, a reinforcer is any event that increases the probability of a behavior reoccurring. A punisher is any event that decreases the probability of a behavior reoccurring.

Skinner noted that there are different forms of reinforcement and punishment. For example, there are positive and negative reinforcement and punishment. The terms *positive* and *negative* are often troublesome for students learning about operant conditioning because the two terms are typically used to make value judgments in everyday life. However, positive does not mean good, and negative does not mean bad. Rather, positive means to *add,* and negative means to *subtract.* Thus, *positive reinforcement* offers a reward by way of adding something pleasurable, such as giving praise or money after a behavior to increase the probability that it will occur again. *Negative reinforcement* means taking something aversive (displeasing) away in order to reward the organism, like removing an unwanted curfew or an unpleasant chore. This is reinforcing because an aversive stimulus has been removed.

In contrast, *positive punishment* refers to the presentation of an aversive stimulus for a behavior. For example, yelling at an organism or hitting it for performing a behavior would likely decrease the probability that the behavior would occur again. *Negative punishment* involves removing something desirable for the purposes of punishing the organism, like taking away a child's allowance or television time.

Skinner also distinguished between *primary* and *secondary* reinforcers and punishers. Consequences classified as primary relate to the basic biological needs of the organism and have a direct bearing on its survival. In other words, primary reinforcements and punishments do not have to be conditioned or learned. One easy way to think about this class of reinforcers and punishers is to consider infants who have not been subject to much by way of learning. If an infant would find it rewarding or punishing, it is likely primary. So, for instance, a delicious drink of milk (as a reward) or the prick of a needle (as a punishment) would both belong to the primary class. However, consider the presentation of a hundred-dollar bill (as a reward) or the loss of a diamond ring (as a punishment). These consequences would be valueless to an infant. They have great potential to influence the behavior of an adult, however, due to the adult's having learned about their potential for reward through associative learning (e.g., the hundred-dollar bill can buy you a lot of delicious milk). Thus, the latter two examples would be called *secondary* reinforcement and punishment, respectively.

Given what has been said of operant conditioning theory thus far, one can begin to see its ramifications for approaching the problem of human personality. The relatively consistent behavioral responses that would be cited as indicative of a "personality" emerge because the individual has been reinforced in those behaviors. Behaviors that have not been rewarded or have been punished would thus be less likely to occur and less likely to become part of the personality in question. Thus, personality types are created or made not only through the repeated pairing of stimuli (as in classical conditioning), but also through the reinforcement and punishment of behavioral responses. If one were to speak of an addictive personality, for example, one would explain its appearance on the basis of the rewarding effects of the drugs that the individual has consumed. With each reinforcement, the behavior that preceded it (i.e., the obtaining and consuming of the drugs) is more likely to occur and become a regular pattern of action. Given enough time, the person will become physically and psychologically adapted to intoxication, such that the absence of the drug will create withdrawal symptoms. At this point, consuming the drug will alleviate withdrawal in addition to creating positive sensations. In effect, the process of creating a so-called addictive personality in an otherwise normal individual is the process of compounding positive reinforcement with negative reinforcement.

With operant conditioning, the gradual process of creating a complex mosaic of behaviors is further comprehensible on the basis of *shaping*. Complex patterns of behavior develop over time with many different instances of reinforcement. Any parent knows this well. In order to get a child to behave in a disciplined, well-structured manner, the parent has to enforce structure through the use of many different reinforcements (and sometimes punishments as well). Shaping refers to the process of reinforcing successive approximations of the desired behavior or behaviors until the organism at last learns the entire behavioral repertoire being taught. So, for instance, a parent can reward a child with praise for picking up their clothes. Then they can be rewarded not merely for picking up their clothes, but also for putting their toys away. Eventually, over time, the child will keep their entire room neat and tidy as long as the parent can maintain patience and persistence.

A favorite operant conditioning technique of parents is to reinforce behavior in accord with *Premack's Principle*. According to this principle, an organism will perform a less desirable activity to obtain a more desirable activity. So, a parent might be able to get a child to clean their room (the less desired activity) if, in doing so, the child is granted the reward of being able to go and play with friends (the more desired activity).

When shaping an organism via the use of reinforcements, it is not always possible to reward each and every response. As an alternative, one may use different *schedules of reinforcement* to operantly condition an organism (Ferster & Skinner, 1957). Reinforcements can be distributed according to amounts of time, in which case they are called *interval schedules*. Alternatively, reinforcements can be distributed according to amounts of work, in which case they are called *ratio schedules*. Interval and ratio schedules can be either fixed or variable. A *fixed interval schedule* means that the organism will be rewarded after a fixed time interval, say, every 30 seconds, as long as it is performing the behavior to be rewarded. This schedule causes high response frequency near the end of the interval, but slower responding immediately after the delivery of the reinforcer. A *variable interval schedule* means that the organism will be rewarded after varying time intervals, as long as it is performing the behavior to be rewarded. This schedule produces a slow, steady rate of response. A *fixed ratio schedule* means that the organism is rewarded after a fixed number of responses or actions. This schedule produces a high, steady rate of responding, with only a brief pause after the delivery of the reinforcer. Finally, a *variable ratio schedule* means that the organism is rewarded for varying amounts of work, like pulling the lever of a slot machine. This schedule creates a high, steady rate of responding.

Reflection

From the behavioral psychology of Watson and Skinner, one finds an approach to personality that is very stripped down and bare-bones basic. The formation of a personality is a very mechanical, mathematical sort of process. Responses that are made to occur more frequently and intensely in an organism tend to persevere over time, and this makes them more likely to be associated with the particular organism in question. "Personality" is a word used to refer to the aggregate of relatively enduring conditioned responses. These responses and the overall pattern that they form are a reflection of the environmental conditions that created them in the first place. If you change the environmental conditions, then you will likely change the so-called personality.

This raises the question of how one would approach the issue of personality integration from a strictly behavioral perspective. To address the question, B. F. Skinner's psychology provides valuable clues. But, be warned, the answer is a bit confusing. In his *Science and Human Behavior* (1953), Skinner includes a section entitled, "The Individual as a Whole," which holds that behavior is more or less organized (i.e., is more or less integrated) on the basis of *objective laws of behavior* (i.e., the principles of conditioning, which are the focus of behavioral theory). The objective laws that produce relative integration are those that control behavior. Thus, as we have seen, behaviorism has long specialized in the manipulation of environmental conditions to learn how to predict and control behavior patterns. The environment has always been the focus of the theory, which is largely how behaviorists defend their scientific objectivity (i.e., the mechanisms for behavioral control are deemed external in origin, thus untainted by human *subjectivity*). In fact, few psychologists have contributed more to the rejection of substantive, irreducible human subjectivity than B. F. Skinner (e.g., one of his most famous books is *Beyond Freedom and Dignity*, Skinner, 1971).

Yet, the first chapter in the "Individual as a Whole" section is entitled, "'Self-Control'" (Skinner, 1953, p. 227). In this section, Skinner somewhat astonishingly asserts, "To a considerable extent an individual does appear to shape his [*sic*] own destiny" (p. 228). From this it would seem that personality integration is suddenly put in the hands of the individual human being rather than the environment. How might this transfer take place? Skinner's answer is that human beings can use the objective laws of behavior uncovered by behaviorism to manipulate their environments in such a way as to effect *self-control*. The human being "controls himself [sic] . . . through the manipulation of variables of which behavior is a function" (p. 228). Thus, were one to identify a core principle of personality integration from the viewpoint of behavioral theory, it would be the adaptational mechanism of self-control. But the devil is in the details. All of Skinner's terminology for discussing self-control—terms like *self-determination*, *choice*, and *self*—appear in quotes to let the reader know that they have more restrictive specialized meanings in the objective science of behavioral psychology. Skinner's concept of *self*, for example, is that of a *hypothetical explanatory fiction* that individuals entertain to control the anxiety associated with the fact that they find themselves reacting to environments in ways that can be unclear, perplexing, or inexplicable (i.e., relatively *dis*integrated; Hunter, 2019). Thus, behavioral theory offers up a mixed dialogue of sorts. It consists of an academic theoretical discourse that is highly mechanistic and depersonalized and a practical, application-based theoretical orientation that speaks in a quasi-humanistic voice about the human potential for shaping one's own destiny. Conscientiously taking both aspects of the theory into account, it seems that personality integration results from self-control conceived as ambiguously lying somewhere between illusion and genuine adaptation.

The behavioral approach minimizes the possibility of unnecessary obfuscation in one's approach to personality through positing all sorts of hypothetical mental constructs to account for behavior. Behaviorists sought to take the mind out of the running when it came to explanations of personality. Mental processes are rejected, not outright, but as a source of explanation for personality. In fact, it is sometimes said that radical behaviorists see the mind as a "black box" about which nothing of substance can be said for developing a truly objective science of human behavior. Anything like a mental event must itself be explained on the basis of prior causes that lie *in environmental conditions*. What goes on "outside" the person has overall priority over what goes on "inside" the person.

The radical, strictly behavioral views covered in this chapter can be said to have a zero-tolerance policy when it comes to the proposal of some private world of intrapsychic processes. It is for this reason that individuals like Watson and Skinner dedicated so much of their careers to creating a more streamlined, parsimonious alternative to Freudian psychology, which they considered too mentalistic. Of course, one could just as easily argue that Watson and Skinner were guilty of the opposing tendency toward oversimplification. In fact, radical behaviorism has lost much of its power of influence in psychology on the basis of this accusation. Behaviorism has largely become *cognitive* behaviorism, wherein mental processes have been used to augment behavioral explanations of human interaction.

Ironically, the focused effort to take on Sigmund Freud is exactly what makes for deep continuities between the opposing viewpoints of radical behaviorism and orthodox Freudianism. As we will see, both approaches are rooted in the desire to make psychology a natural science (though strict behaviorism is far more radical in this regard). Both approaches acknowledge that human beings are born with adaptive physiological processes, emphasizing the selfish, hedonistic tendencies of human beings. Indeed, in spite of all his distancing efforts, Watson was highly influenced by Freud, especially during the period of his Little Albert studies. That entire line of research was inspired by Freudian thought, as Watson attempted to provide alternative interpretations to Freudian psychology concerning the way adult personality can be influenced by childhood experiences. Similarly, B. F. Skinner cited Freud more often than any other author.

Taking it Further: Food for Thought

From a historical point of view, behaviorism is often presented as a school of thought that dominated academic psychology from the early 1900s until the backlash that occurred in the 1960s from movements like cognitive psychology and humanistic psychology. Cognitive and behavioral views have since been wedded in numerous ways, perhaps most widely known by the initialism "CBT" (cognitive–behavioral therapy). What is less known is that there have also been attempts at a rapprochement between behaviorism and humanism (e.g., Dinwiddie, 1975). In fact, there is a deep connectivity between behaviorism as advanced by people like Skinner and the European tradition of phenomenology inherent in humanistic psychology. As Kvale and Grennes (1975) observed, both behavioral and phenomenological orientations reject the bifurcation of psychological life into an intracranial (introspectionist) realm of mentality set against a separate public sphere of worldly interaction. Both viewpoints advanced a highly relational conceptualization of behavior that highlights the critical role of learning in human development (DeRobertis, 2017). Finally, as Skinner maintained throughout his career, radical behaviorism (like phenomenological humanistic science) places a premium on disciplined, systematic description over hypothesis testing in research.

Make it Work!

Drawing on behavioral principles, one's approach to personality relies on environmental contingencies. Stability and change in personality are seen as a direct function of the stability and changes occurring in one's environment. This offers two fascinating lines of inquiry in the new millennium. On the one hand, change has been occurring in virtually every aspect of life at an increasingly fast pace on the heels of industrialization, post-industrialization, and now the information age. Thinking behaviorally, what will be the extended implications of this rapid change as the new normal for the psychology of personality? On the other hand, the information age has brought us social media and algorithms that use data collected from past content interactions to offer up new links. So, to use the language of behaviorism, this "new" reinforces old habits, no? Unprecedented speed of change and unprecedented forces of stability at the same time. How to make sense of it all? Consider the possibilities using behavioral theory.

Key Concepts

Associative learning
Behaviorism
Behaviorism and Freudian psychology

Behaviorism and phenomenological psychology
Black box theory of the mind
Classical conditioning
Conditioned response
Conditioned stimulus
Conditioning theories
Discrimination learning
Extinction
Garcia effect/conditioned taste aversion
Higher-order conditioning
Instrumental learning
Interval schedule
Little Albert study
Negative punishment
Negative reinforcement
Neutral stimulus
Operant
Operant conditioning theory
Positive punishment
Positive reinforcement
Premack's principle
Primary punishment
Primary reinforcement
Punishment
Ratio schedule
Reinforcement
Schedules of reinforcement
Secondary punishment
Secondary reinforcement
Shaping
Skinnerian concept of self
Skinnerian concept of self-control
Spontaneous recovery
Stimulus generalization
Thorndike's law of effect
Unconditioned response
Unconditioned stimulus

Chapter 3

Freudian Orthodoxy and
the Psychosexual Personality

Like Watson and Skinner, Sigmund Freud wished to create a psychology that was patterned after the natural sciences (e.g., physics, biology, chemistry, and so forth). In what is known as his *Project for a Scientific Psychology*, originally released in 1895, Freud (1950) called for an approach to psychology that would be firmly based in neurophysiology. Whereas the behaviorists tended to search for the true or ultimate causes of behavior in environmental conditions, Freud was more impressed by the manifold workings of the human organism's internal world. This difference in orientation is reflected in the somewhat divergent paths taken by the behavioral thinkers and Freud. While the behaviorists specifically prohibited recourse to the mind for explanatory principles of behavior, Freud plunged headlong into the "intrapsychic" world of desire, impulse, memory, fantasy, thought, and emotionally charged conflict. Freud's theory is basically a conflict theory. The distinctive style that one associates with someone's personality is the result of the kind of difficulties, anxieties, and defenses that the person has developed over time. Accordingly, there is no official category or classification for "the healthy personality" in Freud's psychology. When successful, psychoanalytic treatment renews the patient's capability for love and work, but frustration and psychic compromise are what pervade "normal" human interaction, as evidenced by the title of one of Freud's more famous texts, *The Psychopathology of Everyday Life* (1965b).

Behaviorists generally view psychoanalysis as vague and obfuscating. When viewed from the perspective of Freudian psychology, however, behaviorism appears somewhat shallow or incomplete. The Freudian point of view brings a degree of depth and vitality to the study of personality that is lacking in behavioral psychology. Human beings are understood on the basis of their "inner" lives, which are at once neurological and subjective. Again, this is a difference in emphasis only. Freud was not unaware of the power and influence of environmental interactions. Quite the contrary, his theory involves many complex social interactions. However, whereas behaviorists look upon environmental conditions as the primary cause of behavior, Freudian psychology takes a detour through the biologically influenced *interpretations* of the individual in its search for the causes of behavior. The experience of the person is brought to the fore in psychoanalytic psychology in a way that was inadmissible in behaviorism. For Freud, the passions, desires, and motives of the organism are far too complex and important to be relegated to the so-called black box. An adequate theory of personality must contend with the tension-filled inner striving of each individual human being to attain those pleasurable forms of need gratification required for the survival of the individual and the species.

Sigmund Freud's path makes sense considering his beginnings. Freud began his career as a neurologist. In the late 1880s, he became intrigued by certain patients who were treated by two of his colleagues, Jean-Martin Charcot and Joseph Breuer. These patients displayed symptoms like paralysis, muscle cramps, and seizures, which were believed to be psychological in origin. Impressed by these cases, Freud coauthored a book with Joseph Breuer entitled *Studies on Hysteria* (Breuer & Freud, 1955). In essence, Freud and Breuer attempted to explain how the symptoms of this strange psychological presentation (then called hysteria) were the result of having repressed disturbing, traumatic memories. Over the course of his career, Freud attempted to further demonstrate that these memories were actually psychosexual in nature. The terms *sex* and *pleasure* were virtually synonymous in Freud's work. Accordingly, his theory is referred to as a *psychosexual theory*.

When Freud began formulating his psychoanalytic ideas in the late 1800s, his manner of conceptualizing the mind was markedly different from his contemporaries due to the sheer amount of emphasis he placed on the role of unconscious processes in the mental life of human beings. With their emphasis on conditioned responses, the behaviorists shared Freud's belief that behavior is rooted in processes that lie outside of conscious awareness. However, Freud's ideas predate those of the behaviorists, as was noted earlier.

Freud (1949) saw the mind as consisting of three layers: *the conscious mind, the preconscious mind,* and *the unconscious mind.* The conscious mind refers to explicit awareness and consists of those things that have become the object of focal attention. If you can pay focused attention to something, examine it with your senses, and articulate your experience in words, it belongs to the conscious mind. As you can imagine, however, not everything in life receives one's undivided attention. There are many things that lie on the outskirts of focal awareness. Anything that has the potential to be given focal attention but is not currently conscious belongs to the preconscious mind. Right now, you are not paying attention to what you had for breakfast this morning. But, as soon as you consider what you had, that knowledge moves from the preconscious mind to the conscious mind. Once you return to the task of learning about Freud, the knowledge of your breakfast will move back down to the preconscious. For Freud, there is a constant interplay between the conscious and preconscious minds. Such is not the case, however, for the contents of the unconscious mind, which are blocked from conscious awareness. The unconscious contains memories and impulses that are unacceptable, dangerous, or otherwise anxiety provoking, and are therefore too difficult for the person to acknowledge. They are defensively kept at a distance from consciousness.

Freud explained this topographical model of the mind by embedding it with three interactive systems known as the *id*, *ego* and *superego* (Freud, 1949). He considered the id to be a repository of animal drives inside a person. Many authors refer to Freudian theory as a theory of "instincts." However, Freud used the German word *instinkt* somewhat sparingly. He tended to prefer the term *trieb*, meaning urge, impulse, impetus, desire, or drive. Instincts and reflexes were both too rigid to suit Freud's purposes.

The id is the wellspring of libidinal energy or *libido*. Freud compared the functioning of the mind to a hydraulic energy system. The most potent form of energy that pumps through this system is libido, a Latin word that means *wish* or *desire*. For Freud, libido is a person's appetite for pleasure, particularly those forms of pleasure associated with tension reduction. It is aggressive, highly impersonal, and constitutes the majority of the unconscious mind. Later in his career, Freud (1961) framed the id in terms two opposing forces: *eros* (a life instinct) and *thanatos* (a death instinct). The id's libidinal energy gives rise to *primary process thinking* (Freud, 1949). Primary process thinking is a kind of thinking that is rooted in hedonistic and selfish tendencies; it consists of narcissistic fantasy and operates according to the pleasure principle. Freud used the term *pleasure principle* to indicate that human beings are creatures who crave immediate gratification from the time they are born. To sum up, the core system of the human mind (the id) houses a force of energy (libido) that unconsciously drives us to get pleasure for ourselves on demand (the pleasure principle).

As is obvious, if everyone were to only act on the basis of primary process thinking, there would be no civilized society. Therefore, the id must be restrained. As a result, at some point in the development of the personality, the person has to develop another psychic structure to acquire some means for living amid other people. This structure is called the ego. The ego is the source of patience, control, and reason. It is the conflict manager of the personality. The ego refers to the aspect of the mind that realizes that drive satisfaction must be accomplished in ways that are not only effective, but also conducive to having to live with others. This is called *the reality principle*, and it governs the functioning of the ego. The ego's functioning enables the person to delay the initial, infantile impulse to get one's own needs met immediately. As a result of ego formation, a new, more mature-looking manner of seeking self-gratification emerges, which is said to operate according to *secondary process thinking* (Freud, 1949). The ego thus provides the means for the individual to adapt to the social world beyond early infancy. Aspects of the ego reside within all three layers of the mind. That is, there are aspects of adaptive functioning that are conscious, some that are only preconscious, and some that are unconscious as well.

As the developing person confronts the reality of living with other people, it is inevitable that they will discover that people make value judgments. At some point during development, the child perceives that words like "good" and bad" are associated with certain behaviors. More important, they come to find that there are punishments associated with the things that are labeled "bad." As a result, it becomes necessary for the child to learn the rules of civilized society to avoid punishment. This is the birth of the superego, which is the closest thing to a conscience to be found in Freudian psychology. The person will develop an inclination to appear moral and ethical. This tendency will also need to be kept in check, as too strong a superego would prevent the person from satisfying the id. Like the ego, the superego exists within all three levels of the mind.

According to Freud, the process of adapting to a world that does not permit unbridled immediate gratification is not easy. The development of the personality is fraught with frustration and conflict at every step of the way. The id would like to be satisfied immediately, but the demands of reality and the opposing inclinations of the superego stand in the way. The ego is stuck in the middle of all of this conflict and must find solutions to life's problems. One of the ways that the ego learns to deal with difficult, frustrating life predicaments is to look for people who appear to have developed effective coping strategies and use them as models for one's own behavior. This is called *identification* (Freud, 1949). However, when the ego cannot find the means to cope with frustration through identification, excessive anxiety may build up and result in the appearance of *defense mechanisms*. Defense mechanisms are strategies employed by the ego to manage anxiety by distorting reality. They tend to operate outside of conscious awareness. That is, they are preconscious or unconscious in nature. These mechanisms cover over both the source of what is threatening to the person and the fact that a cover-up is taking place (Freud, 1949; Mitchell & Black, 1995). In other words, defense mechanisms are not just lies; they are lies that the person believes on some level. They are not just deceptions; rather they are self-deceptions as well. Some common defense mechanisms are:

- *Displacement*: The shift of libidinal energy from its original object to something less threatening. (Example: Taking out your aggression toward your boss on your children when you come home from work. Your boss can fire you, but your children are easy targets.)
- *Sublimation*: The shift of libidinal energy from its original object to something socially acceptable and productive or creative. (Example: Turning your aggression toward your boss into the creative energy that fuels a series of paintings that symbolize powerful emotions.)
- *Suppression*: A selective avoidance of alarming, anxiety-producing impulses, thoughts, images, or memories. Suppressed information is relegated to the preconscious. (Example: A person sees their cat hit by a car, but then refuses to talk about it or even think about the event.)
- *Repression*: The act of repelling alarming, anxiety-producing impulses, thoughts, images, or memories from the conscious mind. Repressed information is relegated to the unconscious. (Example: A person sees their cat hit by a car, but then cannot recall the shocking event.)
- *Regression*: The act of retreating from an anxiety-evoking step in development to an earlier period of development. Specifically, the person seeks to rely on the coping mechanisms typical of the last period of development that felt safe.

(Example: A young lady who resorts to crying and stomping her feet when her teacher does not allow her to make up an exam.)

- *Projection*: Attributing the source of an anxiety-producing impulse to someone else. (Example: A young man with wandering eyes constantly accuses his girlfriend of looking at other men.)
- *Denial (or Disavowal)*: The refusal to acknowledge the reality of a danger or threat. (Example: An alcoholic insists they do not have a drinking problem despite their many alcohol-related arrests and health problems.)
- *Rationalization*: The interpretation of anxiety-provoking impulses or their morally reprehensible consequences as reasonable, logically consistent, and/or ethically sound. (Example: Cutting down your neighbors' favorite flowers because you did not like them, noting, "It's the end of the season and this will make them grow back better next season anyhow. I actually did them a favor.")
- *Reaction formation*: The adoption of an attitude or characteristic style of presenting oneself that is the exact opposite of one's true desires, inclinations, or impulses. (Example: Becoming an outspoken radical conservative regarding sexuality when you are actually quite lustful and promiscuous.)

One of the more talked about defense mechanisms pertaining to Freud's thoughts on personality development is *fixation* (Freud,1960). Fixation occurs when a developing person refuses to face the challenges brought about by a new stage of life. As a result, they remain at a more primitive state of psychological development. Moving on to a new phase of life can evoke anxiety in a maturing person. Change means that old comforts and previously secured means for libidinal gratification might be threatened. Thus, fixation is usually discussed in terms of its relationship to certain stages of child development that Freud identified. In particular, Freud outlined five stages or phases of psychosexual of development: *oral, anal, phallic, latency*, and *genital*. At each stage of development, the id seeks gratification from a different part of the body called an *erogenous zone*. If the child is under-satisfied or over-stimulated at any stage, they may become fixated on the erogenous zone of the stage in question. Freud's stage theory of development is widely considered critical to his explanation of personality formation. The idea is that the way the child learns to manage physical desires colors or influences the general style of personality that develops. The ways in which we are conflicted, frustrated, and fixated thereby become the defining features of the individual personality. While Freud did mention connections between stages of development and personality types, it was actually a psychologist named Karl Abraham (1965) who really articulated this aspect of Freudian theory, with some degree of approval from Freud.

Psychosexual Stages of Development

The oral stage is the first to appear and is identified with early infancy. The anal stage emerges just before the typical period of potty training for Westerners and spans a time frame of approximately 1 to 3 years of age. The phallic stage is typically identified as a preschool age period, ranging from about 3 to 6 years of age. The latency phase is pre-pubescent, spanning an approximate time range of 6 to 10 years. Finally, the genital stage is associated with puberty and onwards into adulthood. However, Freud believed these stages were only loosely ordered. For Freud, it would be a mistake to suppose that these phases appear in a perfectly clear-cut fashion. One may appear at the same time as another, they may overlap, or they may be equally present alongside one another.

During the oral stage, the child seeks pleasure by using the mouth. The mouth can be used to incorporate food to satisfy hunger. However, Freud noted that the child derives such enjoyment from the mouth that they will continue to seek pleasure from that erogenous zone even when there is no longer a need for food. Thus, the child will suck on their hands or use a pacifier. The child can get oral stimulation "receptively" from sucking, licking, and swallowing, or "sadistically" (i.e., aggressively) by biting, chewing, and so forth. Normally parents understand that the child seeks oral pleasure and will try to accommodate the child accordingly. At a certain point, however, parents attempt to wean the child. They try to get the child to stop sucking their thumb, to stop using a bottle, and to stop using a pacifier. If the child is under-satisfied or over-stimulated during this time, an oral fixation may become a trait of the developing personality. The child might go on to pursue pleasure associated with the mouth far beyond the time of the oral stage. This could be done receptively or aggressively. So, for example, the child might grow to be a person who feels driven to smoke or drink or suck on candy, which are *oral-receptive* traits. Freud even considered a gullible person to be oral-receptive, since such a person would "swallow anything," so to speak. On the other hand, the child might grow to be a person with a nail-biting habit or become verbally abusive to others, which are *oral-aggressive* traits.

During the anal stage, the child seeks pleasure by holding on to and letting go of waste. There is a pleasure that the child experiences from controlling the stimulation of the anal sphincter muscles. The child is given time to enjoy the pleasure of expelling fecal matter at will through the use of diapers. However, parents know that the child is developing control over the anal region, so they eventually attempt to potty train the child. This can be experienced as a threat to the child's immediate gratification of anal pleasure. Fixations stemming from this stage include anal retention and anal expulsion. *Anal-retentive* personalities display stinginess, stubbornness, and an exaggerated tendency toward control, orderliness, and cleanliness. *Anal-expulsive* personalities are just the reverse, displaying excessive tendencies toward impulsivity, disorganization, messiness, dominance, and cruelty.

The phallic stage is the stage where the child discovers the genital zone and the pleasure that can be had by manipulating that area of the body. However, whereas there were outlets for the satisfaction of the oral and anal drives (e.g., pacifiers and diapers), the child is obstructed from manipulating their genitals. Such manipulation is deemed socially unacceptable. This leads the child to conclude (unconsciously, of course) that the key to getting genital satisfaction must lie in relationships with members of the opposite sex. As a result, the little boy seeks to win the affection of his favorite female, and the little girl seeks to win the affection of her favorite male (i.e., mommy or daddy, respectively). Freud called this unconscious desire to sexually possess the parent of the opposite sex the *Oedipus complex* (Freud, 1949, 1960). The Oedipus complex leaves a major mark of tragedy on the developing mind, since it is inevitably confusing for the child, and it must end in failure and some degree of disappointment. After all, it revolves around a cultural incest taboo.

According to Freud, little girls and little boys find female genitalia virtually incomprehensible. Males have penises, and this makes sense to a child. There is a clearly identifiable sex organ. However, female genitalia appear to be missing. There is no clearly identifiable organ. This has far-reaching implications. For the boy, the pursuit of mommy places him in competition with daddy. If the father enforces personal boundaries that let the boy know he cannot be so attached to mommy his whole life, the boy child will come to experience *castration anxiety*.

After all, some people (i.e., girls) are missing their penises! A suspicion that the father might castrate him disposes the boy child to back away from his pursuit of mommy and learn how to attract a woman of his own by identifying with his father. Girls, however, find that they have already been castrated and develop *penis envy*. They enter into competitive relations with their mothers and try to become daddy's girl. In time, daddy has to again enforce personal boundaries so that his daughter will come to identify with her mother and learn how to become a woman to attract a man of her own. In both cases, the parents are supposed to make their children feel special and desirable for a time, but then impose boundaries that allow for a workable resolution of the stage. If this is disrupted, the child may develop an Oedipal fixation, which would become evident in problems revolving around gender, sex, and/or relationships (especially intimate relationships).

For Freud, the first three stages of development were the most important in the formation of the personality (Freud, 1949, 1960). At the fourth stage, there is no erogenous zone that dominates development. The id is restrained, and libidinal energy is sublimated into the socially acceptable activities of youth, such as school, hobbies, sports, etc. This all ends, however, when puberty arrives. With the onset of puberty, the genital stage has begun, and the child rediscovers the genitals, only now in a more mature, adult manner. However, behavior, mental processes, identity, sexual identity, and so forth are all already well underway by the conclusion of the phallic stage.

Reflection

Freudian psychology brings a level of dynamic psychological depth and meaning to personality theorizing that is wanting in traditional behavioral conditioning approaches. From a Freudian point of view, individuals like Watson and Skinner begin with a valid insight into the fact that human beings are naturally attracted to pleasurable activities, some of which satisfy basic biological needs. However, to then relegate one's understandings of this attraction to the sheer mechanics of processes like positive and negative reinforcement stops short of a full grasp of its interactive complexity. The mental or intrapsychic aspects of pleasure seeking (for Freud, the dynamics and folly of the id, ego, and superego) must be taken into account.

According to psychosexual theory, the biological determines the psychological. In this sense, Freud is more sympathetic to the genetic paradigm of inheritance (Ritvo, 1990), which will be taken up again in the next chapter. When it comes to human beings, biological development proceeds faster than mental development and thereby prefigures the final form of the human personality. For instance, the genital region of the body becomes a highly active erogenous zone at the *phallic* stage, long before the child comes to grasp the nature of genital functioning or realize the social import of that functioning. It is not until the genital stage that some degree of insight appears, but by that time, the form of the individual's personal style has already been set in motion. Moreover, this style has been determined by many interactions that will remain unconscious. Each stage of development marks an attempt to manage a physical need, which then gives shape to the overall experiential and behavioral tendencies of the individual.

Freudian psychology introduces a pronounced element of passion and desire into personality theorizing. Freud's view highlights not only the influential power of hedonistic longing, but also the sheer depth and complexity of mental life. What behaviorists would describe as the result of repeated exposure to environmental conditions, psychosexual theory sees as rooted in numerous interchanges between diverse psychic systems on several levels of awareness.

In spite of these differences, however, it is important to bear in mind that there are also deep continuities between the behavioral and orthodox Freudian viewpoints covered thus far. Both traditions make an attempt to turn psychology into another kind of natural science, albeit to different extents. At least in their traditional interpretations, each prioritizes the physical over the psychological. Both look at human beings from a primarily self-serving vantage point. And both traditions see human personality as rooted in and abundantly determined by processes lying outside of conscious awareness and control. Moreover, this inherent connectivity allows the contributions of the two traditions to be combined in various ways. For example, drives can be shaped and even created according to behavioral principles (Dollard & Miller, 1950). For that matter, the functioning of the entire topographical landscape can be analyzed with respect to the principles of conditioning. In turn, one can examine the associations that are the focus of behavioral analysis from the viewpoint of a depth approach, analyzing their significance with respect to the person's developmental conflicts and associated intrapsychic dynamics.

Significantly, the Skinnerian notion of self-control provides a point of theoretical convergence with orthodox Freudian theory regarding the issue of personality integration. Freud's highly subdivided personality approximates organizational footing by way of ego functioning, which is managerial in overall nature and thus control-oriented. The ego must be properly modulated to keep intrapsychic conflict at workable levels to prevent psychic collapse. It cannot over-control the id's needs for pleasure (and aggression) at the risk of neurosis, and it cannot over-control the superego, since the fear of punishment is a necessary civilizing force in the personality. Frustration is ubiquitous and conflict is inevitable, but "just enough" ego control allows one to function normally. Of course, much of what we believe to be under our control is illusory for Freud, just as it is for Skinner. But Freudian psychoanalytic treatment also makes genuine appeals to conscious ego functioning to effect "cures." As Freud (1965a) stated, "Where id was, there ego shall be" (p. 100). Thus, psychosexual theory also (like Skinner) offers an ambiguous, mixed dialogue concerning the integrative self-regulatory propensities of the personality. Freud's "pure" theory is at variance with his theory of praxis. By conscientiously taking both aspects of his theory into account (just as we did with Skinner), personality integration is once again seen as the result of self-control (here, as derived from properly modulated ego functioning) conceived as ambiguously lying somewhere between illusion and genuine adaptation.

Taking it Further: Food for Thought

Freudian psychology has been refined and reinterpreted in many ways since Freud produced his original formulations. History has seen everything from revisions of Freud's theory that hold to his basic assumptions to full-blown reworkings of his ideas. Freud has been taken up by thinkers from diverse traditions, some as seemingly far away from Freudian orthodoxy as neobehaviorism (Dollard & Miller, 1950) and existential psychology (Binswanger, 1967). In a sense, there are many Freuds. Medard Boss (1982), in fact, reminds us that there has always been a minimum of two Freuds: Freud the aspiring natural scientist and Freud the clinical practitioner with an eye (and ear) for the very personal and tragic aspects of human existence.

Probably the most popular offshoot of Freudian thought in the United States comes from the work of his daughter, Anna Freud (1936): ego-psychology. Staying close to Freud's formulation of psychoanalysis, the ego-psychology of Anna Freud focuses on the ego's preconscious and unconscious mechanisms, ranging from the more functional to the more defensive, which are used to keep the id in check. Anna Freud articulated many of the defense mechanisms mentioned in this chapter, showing how they can become building blocks of a person's overall style or total personality structure. In this sense, Anna Freud is more of a personality theorist, properly speaking, than Sigmund Freud. The version of ego psychology that has risen to prominence in the United States, however, comes from Heinz Hartmann (1939). With Hartmann, non-conflictual aspects of ego functioning come into relief. As Mitchell & Black (1995) described it:

> Freud had derived from Darwin the notion . . . that having evolved from other species, humans were not wholly different creatures from other animals. Much of Freud's vision of the instinctual source of human motivation, the primitive forces of infantile sexuality and aggression, could be traced to this Darwinian view. Hartmann put his emphasis on the notion that animals were designed, through the process of survival of the fittest, to be highly adapted to their surroundings . . . . Hartmann envisioned not a dreamily drifting baby who is suddenly forced to get to work, but a baby who arrives with built-in ego potentials . . . . Rather than being forged in conflict and frustration, certain "conflict-free ego capacities" were seen as intrinsic potentials . . . . (pp. 36–37)

This more adaptive aspect of the personality will briefly reemerge toward the end of the next chapter. It will then take center stage when we encounter cognitive-regulatory and ego-psychological theories.

Make it Work!

Freudian psychology remains relevant and interesting in an American context, if for no other reason than it remains controversial. It is often hated by academic psychologists because it is too "clinical" and, in their view, too reliant on case-based observations and thus anecdotal. Clinicians, in contrast, tend not to judge Freud as negatively, and his works remain standard reading for students of psychology. Students tend to love Freud for the depth of his insights into the dark side of humanity or hate his theory, often for what seems to them to be an inordinate focus on sex. At first glance, it seems easy to peg Freud as a pervert. I have had feminist students who hate him for misogyny, gay students who hate him for implying that homosexuality is a perversion, and religious students who hate him for advancing a distasteful pansexualism (and blaming social problems on religion). Then there are those students who simply find him frustratingly obscure and seek to discount him as a "cokehead." And yet, through it all, could his enduring relevance really be denied? For Freud (1961), the id is sexual and aggressive in nature, which he referred to with the terms *eros* (the life instinct) and *thanatos* (a death instinct, which includes both destructive and self-destructive tendencies). With this in mind, what was the "Nipplegate" incident of 2004? On average, how many acts of violence will the American young person witness before the age of 18 on television? How would a Freudian make sense of these striking facts of American culture?

Key Concepts

Anal stage
Anal expulsive
Anal retentive
Castration anxiety
Conscious mind
Defense mechanisms
Denial (or Disavowal)
Displacement
Ego
Ego-psychology
Erogenous zone
Eros
Fixation
Genital stage
Genuine appeals to the ego
Hysteria
Id
Identification
Instincts/drives
Latency stage
Libido
Oedipal fixation
Oedipus complex
Oral stage
Oral aggressive
Oral receptive
Penis envy
Phallic stage

Pleasure principle
Preconscious mind
Primary process thinking
Projection
Psychosexual
Psychosexual theory and Skinnerian theory
Rationalization
Reaction formation
Reality principle
Regression
Repression
Secondary process thinking
Sublimation
Superego
Suppression
Thanatos
Topographical model of the mind
Unconscious mind

Chapter 4

Personality as a Reflection of Inherited (Common) Traits

At present, psychologists on a mass scale are enamored with the biological aspects of human living. There are many factors responsible for bringing about this turn of events, such as the numerous technological advances that have enabled scientists to probe the brain and the human genome. Thus, it should come as no surprise to find that there are psychologists who have suggested that personality can be looked upon as a genetically inherited phenomenon. In fact, this idea underlies the most popular form of thinking on the topic of personality today, which is the *Big Five trait theory* or "FFT" most closely affiliated with two individuals, Robert R. McCrae and Paul T. Costa (2003).

The story of trait theory, however, begins with the aforementioned Gordon Allport (1955, 1968). Allport observed that individuals tend to display a relatively unique collection of behavioral and experiential characteristics that seem relatively consistent over time and across a variety of situations. He called these characteristics *traits* and set out to gather together the various trait descriptors that have been employed by human beings through a study of the English language. Allport (Allport & Odbert, 1936) poured through unabridged dictionaries and accumulated thousands of trait words. He entertained the idea that one could study these descriptive words and develop relevant insights for personality theorizing. Allport observed that in the lives of individuals some traits appear more frequently than others, while some have a stronger motivational influence than others. He also differentiated between widely shared *common traits* and highly individual *personal dispositions*, thus moving dynamically between multiple levels of analysis (Allport, 1961). Overall, his focus returned again and again to the concrete object of personality psychology, which is the organized inimitable whole that is the living, breathing human being.

As it happened, various psychologists to come along after Allport decided that it was not enough to consider the breadth of human trait descriptors and study the diverse ways they cluster in the lives of individuals. These psychologists were inclined to bundle traits into generic parcels that they believed would illuminate individual differences among many individuals. Psychologists like Raymond Cattell (2007), for instance, initiated a psychometric, factor-analytic program of research wherein traits were mathematically analyzed in a way to reduce many traits down to a set of more "basic" summative categories (i.e., broad classifications or general headings). These basic factors were defined by clusters of trait descriptors found to correlate with one another.

By using instruments to make inquiries of research participants (e.g., self-report questionnaires, biographical data, and various tests constructed to study personality), clusters of traits were pulled together and dubbed *factor loadings*. Cattell targeted the attitudes of research participants. These were studied factor analytically to progressively drill down and arrive at the most fundamental or "source" traits intrinsic to the universal undergirding of human personality. Attitudes, of which there are many, were deemed outwardly observable expressions of *ergs* and *sentiments*. An erg is what Cattell considered a constitutional or instinctual source trait with motivational force (i.e., curiosity, sex, gregariousness, protection, self-assertion, security, hunger, anger, disgust, appeal, self-submission), while a sentiment was seen as a source trait that also possesses motivational force but is environmental in origin. The most important of the sentiments is *self-sentiment*, which provides a modicum of stability and organizational structure to the personality. Interestingly, even though self-sentiment would by default fall on the environmental (rather than ergic) side of things, Cattell (2007) presented self-sentiment in a conspicuously Freudian manner, as a kind of orientation toward satisfying one's own needs, with an overall emphasis on survival. Cattell further noted the importance of self-sentiment as "a *necessary instrumentality*" for adaptively "maintaining the self correct by certain standards of conduct, satisfactory to community and super-ego" (p. 272).

Cattell first arrived at a list of thirty-five surface-level traits, which were then further factor analyzed down to a core of sixteen primary or "source" trait categories (i.e., the traits deemed most important for determining personality style). It was at the tally of sixteen that Cattell finally felt comfortable. These sixteen traits included abstractedness, apprehension, dominance, emotional stability, liveliness, openness to change, perfectionism, privateness, reasoning, rule consciousness, self-reliance, sensitivity, social boldness, tension, vigilance, and warmth. Each category comprised traits that would indicate if a person had more or less of the primary factor in question. So, for instance, scoring low on warmth would be described with words like impersonal, distant, cool, reserved, detached, formal, or aloof. However, scoring high on warmth would be described with words like warm, outgoing, attentive to others, kindly, easy-going, participating, or likes people. Moreover, and this is vitally important to the current discussion, Raymond Cattell gave constitutional traits scientific primacy in his theory. The erg level was considered most foundational to the development of personality, followed by sentiments, then attitudes.

This established an important precedent. Soon, another psychologist named Hans Eysenck (Eysenck & Eysenck, 2006) would come along, develop his own factor-analytic depiction of traits, and even more strongly assert that traits rooted in genetics should have top priority in personality research. Eysenck further asserted that the genetic influence on these traits should be readily apparent in the architecture of the brain. Eysenck drew inspiration from the personality theory of Carl Jung (1964) in his research. Jung is one of the people responsible for bringing an evolutionary sort of perspective into psychology via psychoanalysis. Thus, Eysenck's basic or primary trait categories (dubbed *superfactors*) have a strong Jungian ring to them, as well as a strong clinical flavor and an overall focus on biology as the foundation of personality traits. Aiming his focus more tightly around the notion of biological inheritance, Eysenck brought the total number of core personality traits down to two, which he later expanded to three. The initial superfactors were *extraversion/introversion* and *neuroticism/stability*. The third superfactor, added later, was *psychoticism/superego impulse control*. As an example of Eysenck's model, the factor-loading for *psychoticism* includes aggressive, cold, egocentric, impersonal, impulsive, antisocial, unempathic, creative, and tough-minded. Its contrasting tendency toward *superego impulse control* includes altruistic, highly socialized, empathic, caring, cooperative, conforming, and conventional.

Today, the previously noted Big Five theory of Robert McCrae and Paul Costa has risen to veritable superstar status, achieving a higher degree of popularity than any other approach to personality. More and more it seems that Cattell and Eysenck are being considered mere precursors to the establishment of the Big Five model (which neither of them endorsed). The Big Five research model is comprised of *extraversion* and *neuroticism* (already identified in Eysenck's model), *openness to experience, agreeableness*, and *conscientiousness*. Each of these factors has a bipolar nature, such that certain trait descriptors are affiliated with scoring high with regard to the factor in question while opposing descriptors are affiliated with scoring low with regard to the factor in question. So, for instance, high extraversion includes descriptors like affectionate, joiner, talkative, fun loving, active, and passionate. Low extraversion is comprised of descriptors like reserved, loner, quiet, sober, passive, and unfeeling.

The reader should note, however, that what is being described here is the Five-Factor *research model* (also called the Five-Factor model or FFM). It is commonplace in factor-analytic trait theorizing to work first on establishing a "taxonomy" (i.e., a system of categories) of trait names before fully committing to the hard work of theoretical analysis. McCrae and Costa worked diligently to establish that the "correct" number of primary traits is five. They have done an efficient job of promoting the quantity of their research data, asserting that the final tally of five has been "discovered" and that the pieces of the personality puzzle are finally beginning to "fall into place" (in spite of the fact that there is no universal agreement on this point in the field of personality research (McCrae & Costa, 1996, p. 78). In other words, McCrae and Costa crunched the numbers to convincingly establish a statistically derived taxonomy (not a unified theory) of trait categories rather than moving back and forth between critical theoretical analysis and empirical observation, which is not uncommon in the factor-analytic, psychometric tradition. They then designed a Big Five theory of personality (a Five-Factor theory or FFT) retroactively or post hoc, meaning after they established their taxonomy of trait categories. In doing so, they gathered together a cluster of concepts like characteristic adaptations to environments, emotional reactions, life events, dynamic intrapsychic processes, and the development of a self-concept (e.g., self-schemas, personal myths). Cultural norms are held to contribute to individual differences in personality as well, but all of these aspects of personality development have long been present in other major theories of personality. As Block (2000) observed, The FFT is exemplified by 6 broad postulates:

1. There are individual differences in personality.
2. Individuals seek to adapt in any way they can.
3. The perceptions and behavior of individuals are multiply influenced.
4. Individuals have a sense of self.

5. Individuals are influenced in their behavior by their situations in conjunction with their predispositions and, subsequently, these influences affect their behavior.
6. The functioning of a person reflects in part a universal human nature. (p 104)

He then goes on as follows:

> This set of five-factor theory postulates, as illustrated here but also in its entirety, impresses me as inclusive of widespread, certainly not wrong, broad recognitions. There is no serious approach to the study of personality and development that would not subscribe to these backgrounding tenets. However, in this age of psychological science, it should be recognized that these orienting "postulates" do not function as a committed, implicative theory. No specific theoretical consequences are entailed by the five factor postulates; no sense is provided of the specific dynamics of personality. It is not a theory in the sense of "an interpreted deductive system." If these postulates apply everywhere, then they offer no help in directing efforts at understanding. (pp. 104–105)

When it comes down to it, the FFM and FFT make the argument that the fundamental bases of personality are biological (i.e., genetic, neurological, and hormonal) in origin. The Big Five traits, conceived as endogenic and relatively impermeable to sociocultural influences, are considered the most fundamental elements of personality (McCrae & Costa, 1999). It is inherited traits that are held to ultimately account for the deep structure and stability of personality. According to this view, personality integration is a reflection of the way the Big Five are fashioned into characteristic adaptations to environmental conditions. Personality traits (and thus the essence of personality) are passed along through genes, are embedded in the architecture of the brain, and manifest in behavior through adaptive processes:

> The core components of the personality system . . . are designated as *basic tendencies, characteristic adaptations*, and the *self-concept*—which is actually a subcomponent of characteristic adaptations . . . . (McCrae & Costa, 2008, p. 162)

All in all, McCrae and Costa basically adopted a somewhat less biogenetically restrictive version of Eysenck's general approach to personality (Eysenck did not endorse the Five-Factor model). Thus, McCrae and Costa (1996) noted that their theory offers few surprises, adding little to what had already been contributed by the great personality theorists.

Today, the five-factor *research model* (the FFM) is thrown about without much care for the fact that it is not a theory of personality. The distinction between the research model and the personality theory is often overlooked, blurred, or minimized. In accounting for the relatively unique contours of an individual's personality, the idea is that human beings inherit varying amounts of each "Big Five" factor. These inherited quantities accumulate to form the basis of *who* one is. The Big Five have thus become a master recipe of sorts, and they are regularly misapplied and mistaken as explanations for personality (Marsh & Boag, 2013). Advocates of the approach have even gathered data from samples of people from other cultures to argue that the Big Five are universal.

As time has gone on, various branches of biological psychology have been joining forces to help make the biological argument for personality. For instance, neuroscience has been recruited into the Big Five literature. Studies have surfaced claiming to provide evidence that Big Five traits are embedded within the architecture of the brain. For example, in a study done by Colin G. DeYoung and his colleagues (DeYoung et al., 2012), the authors noted that certain Big Five traits can be seen to covary with the volume of neural tissue in various parts of the brain. Extraversion covaries with the volume of medial orbitofrontal cortex, which is a brain region involved in processing reward information. Neuroticism covaries with the volume of brain regions associated with threat, punishment, and negative affect. Agreeableness covaries with the volume of neural tissue in areas that process information about the intentions and mental states of other individuals. Finally, conscientiousness covaries with the volume of brain tissue in the lateral prefrontal cortex, a region involved in planning and the voluntary control of behavior. However, openness to experience was not found to covary with the volume of neural tissue in any significant way (in general, openness is perhaps the most problematic trait to localize neurologically). This research led the authors to hypothesize that there might really be only two essential personality indicators, one being *stability* (comprised of agreeableness, conscientiousness, and neuroticism) and the other being *plasticity* (comprised of extraversion and openness to experience).

A similar line of thinking is being examined from the viewpoint known as the *biopsychological theory of personality*, which Jeffrey Alan Gray (1981) initially developed in response to disagreements with Eysenck. In Eysenck's initial two-factor theory, the trait of impulsivity was under the superfactor of extraversion. When Eysenck expanded to three superfactors, impulsivity was moved to psychoticism. Gray took issue with this, as he associated impulsivity with reward-seeking behavior. In his own system, Gray proposed two brain-based systems as controlling a person's interactions with their environment: *the behavioral inhibition system* (BIS) and the *behavioral activation system* (BAS). BIS relates to sensitivity to punishment and a general motivation toward the avoidance of stimuli. BAS is associated with sensitivity to reward and a general motivation to approach stimuli. Other researchers, like Smits and Boeck (2006), have since found that the Big Five traits of neuroticism and extraversion can be explained well by the BIS/BAS model, while relatively consistent results for agreeableness and conscientiousness can also be established.

In the area of genetics, a variant of what has been termed the *5-HTTLPR gene* (a serotonin-transporter-linked polymorphic region gene) has been linked to the trait of neuroticism. However, the effects of this allele are small and cannot be replicated consistently, much less universally (Pluess et al., 2010). A discrete, unambiguous link between genes, brain structures, and all of the traits discussed here will likely be difficult to come by, and so these studies serve to demonstrate both the enthusiasm and the hesitations that the Big Five approach has evoked among social scientists. To cite a different example, evolutionary psychology has also been used to support the Big Five approach to personality (e.g., Nettle, 2006).

The transition to evolutionary thought has not come without complications. The focus of theories like the Big Five is to identify the core ingredients that contribute to individual differences, while the focus of evolutionary psychology has traditionally been the identification of species-typical mechanisms of adaptation to environmental conditions. As Buss (2004) has noted, individual deviations from the species behavioral norm have long been considered genetic junk or noise that is unrelated to the core of the evolutionary process. The focus of evolutionary thought is species typicality rather than individual difference. Put another way, "most of the genetic variation between human individuals is neutral or functionally superficial" (Nettle, 2006, p. 622). But this has not prevented evolutionary psychologists from advocating for the Big Five. The two traditions share significant theoretical common ground. On the one hand, the factor-analytic approach is similarly founded upon aggregate data. On the other hand, "heritable variation is ubiquitous in all species . . . [so] each of the Big Five dimensions of human personality can be seen as the result of a trade-off between different fitness costs and benefits" (Nettle, 2006, p. 622).

An Evolutionary Reinterpretation: David Buss

The most popular of the evolutionary approaches is that of the aforementioned David Buss (1991, 1995, 2004). Buss (2004) has come out in strong advocacy for the importance of personality psychology, and he has become a kind of advocate of the Big Five by reinterpreting them within his own theory of personality. With his conventional natural science background in evolutionary theory, he has been (unsurprisingly) most attracted to the factor-analytic tradition, with its strong leanings toward quantification and biology. For Buss, the statistical identification of central trait concepts is a vital theoretical task for personality psychology (Buss & Craik, 1981, 1983, 1985). In this, he agrees with factor-analytic trait theories. He is further sympathetic with their appeal to biology in searching for the origins of their core traits, allowing for environmental factors to varying extents depending on the approach in question. But, for Buss, the character of this reliance on biology has been left too vague and indeterminate. As a result, Buss considers factor-analytic trait theorizing to be wanting in terms of explanatory power. He sees it as lacking in regard to its ultimate (biological) principle of causality, insisting that evolutionary naturalism ought to define the parameters for interpreting why certain traits are adapted to certain environments in certain ways over others. In effect, the perception of a certain theoretical impotence of the factor-analytic trait tradition (with a most favorable eye on the FFM and FFT) created a convenient opening for Buss to enter the field of personality (e.g., see Buss, 1991; Buss & Craik, 1985). In establishing his theoretical interface with factor-analytic trait psychology, he has extended his criticism of biological vagary to all personality theories. In his view, personality theories in general have lacked adequate conceptual grounding in the explanatory principles of contemporary evolutionary natural science.

In Buss's approach, trait dispositions like the Big Five do have biological origins, but they are nonetheless *sociocultural emergents* derived from the interaction of "nature" and "nurture." He has thus called for a properly conceived emphasis on both heritable and environmental factors in the formation of personality. As he put it:

> Individual differences can emerge from a variety of heritable and nonheritable sources. Evidence from behavioral genetic studies of personality strongly suggest that both are important. Personality characteristics commonly show evidence of moderate heritability, typically ranging from 30 to 50 percent (Plomin, DeFries, & McClearn, 1990). Simultaneously, these studies provide the strongest evidence of environmental sources of variance, ranging from 50 to 70 percent. (Buss, 2004, pp. 395–396)

In response to these numbers, Buss has espoused a reciprocal–causational approach to the nature and nurture of personality, using evolutionary biology as his conceptual base of operations. What is passed along genetically emerges in the life of an individual only and always as a response to the specific challenges inherent in adapting to a given environmental niche.

For Buss, the most foundational question comes down to how a psychology that has traditionally focused on species typicality (i.e., evolutionary psychology) can address individual differences. Beyond expected random variations, mutations, and genetic defects, Buss (2004) has outlined several avenues of exploration. For example, natural selection favors mechanisms of adaptation that cause some individuals to deviate from the norm in seeking environmental niches where the competition is less intense, thereby allowing for the average payoff to these individuals to be higher. Also, evolution creates decision rules that guide the behavior of each species. When confronted with situations in which the organism has to select a path of behavior from a number of given options, random heritable individual differences provide input to the schematic of decision rules. This produces individual differences in things like aggression and cooperativeness (which are typical foci for evolutionary biology). Buss (2004) noted that Tooby and Cosmides (1990) coined the term "reactive heritability" to describe this phenomenon. This view posits that there are evolved mechanisms designed for appraising one's own inherited characteristics. As a result, individual differences are not directly heritable but indirectly by way of the individual organism's genetic predisposition to assess available heritable information. Another possibility is that although more adaptationally successful heritable variations tend to replace (and eliminate) those that are less successful, there are exceptions to this regularity by way of *frequency-dependent selection*. Here, two or more heritable variants can be sustained in equilibrium simultaneously. The payoff of each strategy will decrease as its frequency of use among a population increases, thus making the other viable strategies rise in frequency in response. Overall, however, none are driven out completely. Another source of individual differences is early environmental experiences, such as father presence or absence, which creates a need for individuals to come up with different strategies to cope with the contingencies of their circumstances. Finally, differences in behavior can arise from different organisms occupying different environments in adulthood as well, which recurrently activate a particular mechanism or set of adaptive mechanisms over others.

These last two options in particular implicate one of the more contemporary tends in genetics: *epigenetics* (a term coined in 1942 but which rose to prominence only in the 21st century; see Deichmann, 2016). The "epigenome" refers to various chemical compounds that tell the human *genome* what to do. The epigenome attaches to DNA and activates or deactivates genetic codes, thus controlling the production of proteins in particular cells. Epigenomic compounds change the way cells are affected by genetic instructions, and these changes can endure throughout the process of cell reproduction. They can even sometimes be passed on to offspring (Radtke et al., 2011). This is relevant to the current discussion because lifestyle and the environmental factors involved in an individual's manner of living generate chemical responses that bring out or suppress genetic potentials. Though such responses can sometimes be detrimental to the organism, epigenomic adjustment to the challenges and pressures of life is part and parcel of normal human functioning.

As you can see from this development in the history of genetics, Buss's evolutionary appropriation of the factor-analytic style of approach is rooted in a view of environmental adaptation. Human behavior and personality are seen as built upon adaptative mechanisms for solving the two fundamental evolutionary problems of survival and/or reproduction (e.g., mate selection, friend selection, kin investment, coalition formation, and hierarchy negotiation). Other than the noise/junk mentioned above, human behavior in general is seen as trickling down from adaptations and those characteristics and behaviors that are byproducts of adaptations, like the kinds of things specific to industrial or post-industrial society, such as operating machinery or computing skills. Such skills are not absolutely essential for human survival (Buss, 1991). For Buss, the Big Five are adaptations: mechanisms that signal to other people the extent to which we are adaptive and up to the tasks of survival and reproduction. He thus tends to refer to extraversion as *surgency* and turns the focus of neuroticism around to *emotional stability*. So, his Big Five are surgency, agreeableness, conscientiousness, emotional stability, and openness. These core traits are seen as playing a role in the dynamics of competition and cooperation among people as they try to vie for resources and find mates for themselves (the overall thrust of the perspective tends to return to the benefits or "payoff" that "can accrue to individuals," Buss, 1995, p. 17).

David Buss's primary aim has been to shore up factor-analytic theory's specifically *biological* underpinnings, providing relevant evolutionary context for characteristic adaptations. The Big Five become so many tools in the hands of the individual struggling to survive and reproduce like any and every other living organism on the planet. As he described his inspiration:

> All personality theories seemed "arbitrary" in the sense that they were not anchored in any fundamental set of principles. There is no reason to think that humans have somehow been exempt from the fundamental causal forces that have fashioned all other species—particularly evolution by natural selection. (Buss, as cited in Hergenhahn & Olson, 2007, p. 361)

In Buss's (2004) view, all of the major personality theories have explicit or implicit views of human nature embedded within them, but he considers them all arbitrary and at best "hypothesized" (p. 394) because they do not begin from the premises of a physicalist, historical-causal explanatory framework (quite an ironic claim considering that evolutionary psychology must rely on its own theoretical reconstruction of human history and prehistory). Moreover, in Buss's view, every other theory of personality sees human nature as completely formless and vague until the external environment stamps the personality with its shape (Buss, 2001). This raises the question as to whether Buss and his sympathizers (e.g., Marsh & Boag, 2013) treat all theories of personality as if their basic principles are the same as what one finds in radical behaviorism (or some fancier version of it).

Further, while most theories of personality do not dwell on evolutionary principles to the same extent, this in no way means that other theories see humans as merely "exempt" from the evolutionary process. To imply this is a straw man argument. As we have seen, the seeds of Darwin can be found in the Freudian lineage, and there are even traces of Darwin in Maslow's thought by way of two of his major influences: William James (whose admiration for Darwin is now famous) and Alfred Alder (e.g., 1979).

Buss's critique of other personality theories hides an excluded middle fallacy: that one must frame one's theoretical foundations strictly in terms of a biologistic interpretation of evolution, or one is engaging in mere speculation (see also, McAdams & Pals, 2006). In his view, no theory of personality ever "properly conceived" of the biological contributions to personality (Buss, 1991, p. 486), assuming that reductionistic naturalism is the only valid way of interpreting the role of evolutionary context. But there are different ways to take up Darwin and the theory of evolution (e.g., Herring, 2018; Jung, 1964; Loye, 2010; Smuts, 1926). For Buss (1995), the evolutionary perspective casts human beings as living fossils, collections of mechanisms for adapting to the demands of days long past recapitulated in the present. In contrast, there is a tradition of process philosophy, as represented by thinkers such as William James, Henri Bergson, and Alfred North Whitehead, which has confronted Darwin in a more forward-looking, productive manner and is more commensurate with the tradition of holistic biology inherent in humanistic psychology (e.g., Goldstein, 1995; von Bertalanffy, 1968; von Uexküll, 2010). As Eisendrath (1971) described it:

> James viewed evolution as the adaptation effected by the introduction of novel ends or purposes. Whitehead's analysis is the same: the adaptation effected by the novel end, or negative prehension, is an aesthetic adjustment by the organism to the novelty of the environment. (p. 145)

Later, he goes on, "The problem, for Whitehead, is to explain not survival, but the creation of a higher order of life, with greater spontaneity and intellectuality" (p. 198).

According to this view, evolution is neither mechanistic nor teleologically laid out in advance for humankind, but a matter of our creative involvement in the process of productively and ethically confronting life's givens. Evolution is "creative evolution" (Bergson,

1998). Contemporary human beings may be genetically and physiologically similar to their ancient ancestors, but they have the potential to reorganize their environments in the service of thought, the improvement of human life, and the ability to assist one another (Eisendrath, 1971). Having been greatly influenced by this tradition of thought, Abraham Maslow (e.g., 1993) and his humanistic colleagues sought to build an adequately human psychology that would not only integrate but also move far beyond the motives of survival and reproduction. From this point of view, many of our current challenges may not stem merely from being so many walking fossils. Instead, they may also relate to the struggle to bring the highest potentials of human nature to bear. The plentitude and creative expansion of post-industrial life have created unprecedented change, which comes with both unforeseen challenges and new opportunities for growth (Shaw, 1961).

Reflection

This chapter considered the idea of looking at personality as founded upon an aggregate of inherited traits. Varying degrees of each trait are used to account for individual differences among humans. There are many trait theories, the most popular of which is the Big Five theory. This theory proposes that individual differences are best understood on the basis of extraversion, neuroticism, openness to experience, agreeableness, and conscientiousness, each of which is held to be genetic in origin. The Big Five theory comes from the psychometric factor-analytic tradition (sometimes called *differential psychology* or "the psychology of individual differences"), which deviates significantly from the vision of the originator of trait theory: Gordon Allport. The factor-analytic strategy involves the mathematical process of reducing thousands of culturally embedded trait descriptors down to the handful (and there have been many tallies) that can most convincingly allow researchers to probabilistically account for variations in behavior on a mass scale. This, in and of itself, does not constitute a personality theory. Regrettably, the conflation of taxonomic research model and theory that has permeated the discipline of psychology on the whole reflects a form of bias in contemporary psychology in favor of viewpoints that are *atomistic* in nature and prone to oversimplification. Atomistic psychology takes complex structure and reduces it down to its minimally workable elements or lowest common denominator. For this reason, it is sometimes referred to as *reductionistic*. In this instance, we are dealing with biological reductionism or biologism and statistical reductionism or *statisticism* (Lamiell, 2013). Allport (1961) saw this coming:

> The statistical units discovered are remote from the individual organism. Scores on many tests from a large population of people are put into a statistical grinder, and the mixing is so thorough that what comes out is a link of factors in which every organic individual has lost his [*sic*] identity. His [*sic*] dispositions are mixed with everyone else's. The factors derived in this way seldom resemble the dispositions discovered by clinical methods when an individual is intensively studied. There is no proof whatsoever that the functional units correspond to "source traits," i.e., to the genetic composition of human nature—as claimed by some enthusiasts. (p. 329).

Here, Allport was addressing the psychological "bottom line," as it were, which is the question of the individuality of the personality. But it is no less important to note that many have taken issue with the reductionism of factor-analytic trait theory from a cross-cultural viewpoint. By moving directly to the business of establishing a taxonomy in search of the most replicable and thus biological traits, theories such as these have been essentially accused of a form of confirmatory bias that marginalizes culture (e.g., see Bijnen & Poortinga, 1988; Laher, 2013). On the basis of cross-cultural data, cultural psychologists are taking the Big Five concept seriously. But many researchers have reservations about this research, particularly as regards the extent of its applicability and its thoroughness. For example, Paunonen and Jackson (2000) have noted that the Big Five theory does not account for a host of traits such as religious, sly, honest, sexy, thrifty, conservative, masculine-feminine, egotistical, humorous, and risk-taking, which may be better able to account for variations in culturally relevant behaviors in places like Canada, England, Germany, and Finland. In fact, cultural critiques have led to the development of a Big Six personality theory (Ashton et al., 2004), which added an honesty–humility dimension to the Big Five, and a Big Seven personality theory (Waller & Zavala, 1993), which added two new dimensions (*positive valence* and *negative valence*), reflecting extremely positive and negative self-evaluations, respectively.

So how do the theories in this chapter deal with the problem of integration? Let's begin with how psychometric trait theories compensate for their lopsided differential focus. Cattell spoke of self-sentiment. For their part, McCrae and Costa offered up the FFT, which expands on this idea of self by including things like self-concept, self-schemas, and personal myths, contributions that illustrate the integrative promise of the Big Five approach. Taken alone, however, the concept of "self" says little. Everything depends on how one theoretically frames, describes, and conceives of selfhood. Cattell defaults to what looks like a psychometric mutation of Freudian psychology, from its emphasis on instinctual source traits to adaptive societal adjustment in the form of "superego." If we look closely at the FFT and inquire about its core dimensions, we find that human beings are born with five stylistic predispositions, representing a common human nature that must be adjusted to the demands of the world by way of characteristic adaptations to environmental conditions. Adaptation thus remains the central organizing principle of personality integration, but without an ambiguous, contradictory theoretical emphasis on the illusory nature of self-control because of one's history of reinforcements (behaviorism) or the power of one's unconscious animal drives (psychosexual theory) (see Costa & McCrae, 2011).

Reinterpreted by David Buss, the Big Five traits are themselves considered adaptive mechanisms for survival and/or reproduction. They are sociocultural emergents, which are the product of natural selection. Thus, there is additional integrative promise inherent in Buss's evolutionary reinterpretation of the Big Five in its ability to work past the antiquated bifurcation of "nature" and "nurture" while maintaining an explicit commitment to the foci of differential psychology. That is, it works at a broad level of discourse revolving around universal human evolutionary factors that can be used to explain why people differ from the group and one another (Buss, 2008). Buss has sought to integrate the entire field of personality, but the essential theoretical thrust of the evolutionary approach remains entirely commensurate with the conceptually "conservative," relatively narrow or restrictive (micro-integrational) foci of previous theories: the need for an integrative principle in the form of adaptational strategies for meeting the basic biological needs of the individual, conceived differentially as situation-specific variations on a species-wide genomic design. Buss's theory is relatively new as personality theories go. Only time will tell how it evolves (no pun intended). From the viewpoint of the current text, his aspirations are too ambitious to be handled within the scope of his limited (micro-integrational) theoretical lens. It is critical that the limitations of this viewpoint be recognized; otherwise his theory is left open to charges of unchecked adaptationism (Panksepp & Panksepp, 2000). Hergenhahn & Olson (2007) rightly note that relatively few human behaviors qualify as evolutionary adaptations, a generally recognized fact among evolutionary psychologists. Still, this does not alter their more basic claim, which is that the personality's complex organization can be reduced to the biosocial process of natural selection. The adaptations that it gives rise to are what ultimately determine personality integration; everything else is incidental in comparison. Adaptation in any form, however, remains but a micro-integrational structural support of the Gestalt that is the total personality.

Taking it Further: Food for Thought

At the end of the day, one has to reckon with the fact that the "personality traits" of factor-analytic trait theory are indicators of *temperament*. Temperament-based factor-analytic trait theory is an extension of a line of thought as old as Ancient Greece, when Hippocrates suggested that personality could be described on the basis of four bodily fluids or "humors" (yellow bile, phlegm, blood, and black bile). The Roman physician Galen took up this line of thinking and identified four personality types that correspond to a predominance of each fluid: choleric (yellow bile - quick tempered and fiery), phlegmatic (phlegm - sluggish and unemotional), sanguine (blood - sunny, cheerful, and optimistic), and melancholic (black bile - sad and prone to depression). Ideally, a person would display a blend of these tendencies, which would allow them to live well. Fifteen of Cattell's sixteen traits are temperament traits; the sixteenth—reasoning (in its crystallized and fluid forms)—is an ability trait. Eysenck's (1991) superfactors are temperamentally focused, and the Big Five have similarly been deemed temperament characteristics as well (Piekkola, 2011). And what we know from research on temperament in the area of lifespan development is that it is influenced by environmental variables (Saudino & Micalizzi, 2015) and can change over time, especially in the earlier years of life when a person is most impressionable. What is more important in the overall scheme of things is the *goodness of fit* of a temperamental disposition and its environmental setting (Thomas & Chess, 1977). As McAdams and Pals (2006), have observed, "Developmental and life span psychologists study meaningful and orderly change over time. The Big Five trait taxonomy provides one valuable take on personality development, but the emphasis is mainly on the stability of dispositional traits over time" (p. 214).

Make it Work!

Think about the most significant interpersonal relationship in your life (or pick one that is very important). Now consider the particular dynamics of that relationship. What are its traits? How would you describe its primary characteristics, the major dynamics that make it the kind of relationship that it is? Now consider the five bipolar trait categories of surgency, agreeableness, conscientiousness, emotional stability, and openness. Do you think that relating these trait categories to you and the other person adequately accounts for the kind of relationship that you have described? If not, what is missing?

Key Concepts

Agreeableness
Attitudes
Basic tendencies
Behavioral activation system (BAS)
Behavioral inhibition system (BIS)
Big Five trait theory
Biologism
Biopsychological theory of personality
Characteristic adaptations
Conscientiousness
Creative evolution
Emotional stability
Epigenome
Ergs
Evolutionary adaptations
Extraversion
Factor loadings
Factor-analysis
Five-Factor model (FFM)
Five-Factor theory (FFT)
Frequency-dependent selection
Goodness of fit
Honesty–humility
Introversion

Mutations
Neuroticism
Openness to experience
Plasticity
Positive valence–negative valence
Psychoticism
Reactive heritability
Self-concept
Self-sentiment
Sentiments
Sociocultural emergent
Source traits
Statisticism
Superego impulse control
Superfactors
Surgency
Taxonomy
Temperament
The evolutionary approach
Traits

Chapter 5

Rotter, Bandura, and Mischel:
The Cognitive-Regulatory Personality

In this chapter, we begin to see with a lot more clarity the (micro) integrative power of the adaptive tendency that has been repeatedly referenced in previous chapters. The chapter revolves around insights into personality that have been developed by Julian Rotter, Albert Bandura, and Walter Mischel. The term *social learning theory* is sometimes used to refer to the kinds of views covered in this chapter (e.g., Bandura, 1977; Rotter, 1982). The logic behind the term is that the views presented here emerged from the behavioral tradition in psychology (e.g., Watson, Skinner, etc.), which has sometimes been referred to as *learning theory*. However, it is equally true that social learning theory moved beyond the strictures of traditional behaviorism by securing a place for the efforts of the socially interactive organism amid the determining forces of the environment. The details of what goes on in the mind of the individual are considered vital to understanding personality structure, and that sentiment deviates from the traditional behavioral distain for mental processes.

Social learning perspectives seek to avoid the opposing extremes of strict behaviorism, which grants overriding priority to the environment, as well as factor-analytic trait theorizing, which grants overriding priority to relatively discrete characteristics of the person irrespective of environmental context. There is perhaps more overlap with the evolutionary perspective due to their shared emphasis on reciprocal determinism. The particular importance granted to the individual's mental processes in the current chapter is a point of convergence with psychoanalysis, but not so much with the psychosexual variety. For Freud, as we have seen, the most important aspects of the mind are its unconscious processes, drives, and conflicts. The perspectives discussed below have more in common with ego psychology due to their more conscious, rational, and managerial foci.

Since the early days of his work, Bandura's psychology has been increasingly referred to as *social-cognitive theory* to better match the language of the day (Bandura, 1989). By the mid-1980s, Bandura's increasing emphasis on mental or cognitive processes seemed to call for a new, more modern sounding label. Similarly, Rotter and Mischel are sometimes referred to as cognitive-social theorists or even cognitive social learning theorists (e.g., see Mischel, 1973). The prioritization of the term *cognitive* suggests a somewhat tighter focus on the mental or cognitive processes involved in determining the form of personality than that found in Bandura's works, but one should not make too much of these differences in popular terminology. In fact, some texts will cover these thinkers in the same chapter and refer to all three of them as social learning theorists. The more important issue is that they each see the personality as deeply rooted in environmental contingencies as part and parçel of their behavioral lineage, but they depart from traditional behaviorism on the basis of their attention to the cognitive processes used to interpret and frame the context of their behavior. For these three thinkers, behavior and environment alone cannot override all other considerations when attempting to understand human personality. The cognitively informed regulatory powers of the individual organism are seen as vital co-determinants of personality integration and formation.

Julian Rotter

Like B. F. Skinner, Julian Rotter believes that a human being evaluates new experiences on the basis of previous reinforcement. Personality is learned. In this way, Rotter is grounded in behavioral theory. However, unlike Skinner, Rotter has held that a person's reaction to a reinforcement depends on its subjective meaning and importance rather than on the objective characteristics of the reinforcement only (Rotter, 1982). This insight likely germinated through his contact with George Kelly (1963), the architect of *personal construct theory*. For Rotter, the motivation to continue or abandon a course of behavior depends, in part, on one's goals. Human motivation, human behavior, and human personality are goal directed, which is an insight he took from the individual psychology of Alfred Adler (1935). According to Rotter, reinforcement is most effective when the reward in question promises to bring the person closer to their personal goals.

In the context of Rotter's theory, prediction is indicative of understanding. This is far from certain, of course. It is possible to discover certain methods of prediction without having achieved a deep grasp of an issue. Nonetheless, the notion that prediction indicates understanding has a certain pragmatic appeal because it bears with it the possibility of control. Pragmatism is a deeply rooted value in both American culture at large and those forms of psychology that are patterned after the natural sciences. As an American, natural science-oriented psychologist, Rotter places high value on prediction. Thus, his theory has a tendency to sound formulaic. At the same time, Rotter has legitimately attempted to provide a cogent account of the dynamics of personality formation as they play out in the context of environmental conditions.

Julian Rotter has offered two schemas or frameworks for the prediction of behavior. One framework allows us to size up the probability of an individual engaging in a particular behavior in a specific situation. The other framework is designed to help us get a reliable sense of the behavioral tendencies of an individual in general (which comes closest to the business of understanding the relatively consistent patterns of behavior called *personality*).

Rotter (1982) uses the term *behavior potential* (BP) to refer to the probability that a particular response will occur at a specific time and place. According to Rotter, behavior potential is a direct function of both *expectancy* (E) and *reinforcement value* (RV), giving rise to the heuristic formula $BP = f(E + RV)$. Expectancy refers to a person's expectation that reinforcement(s) will occur in a given situation as a result of the behavior in question. This insight is essentially Skinnerian. However, unlike B. F. Skinner, Rotter does not believe that one's expectation of reinforcement is based solely on one's history of reinforcement. Skinner's worldview is too passive for Rotter, who sees more interactive involvement in the reinforcement process among human beings. Rotter allows for the possibility that an individual's cognitive appraisal or interpretation (whether rational or irrational) of the potential for reinforcement will ultimately determine their expectancy. This opens the door to the possibility that a person could have been reinforced for a past behavior but commit a form of cognitive bias (e.g., focus on the negative) that dissuades them from performing that behavior once again. Or, in contrast, a person may never have been reinforced for a behavior but remain convinced that they will eventually be rewarded for it.

Reinforcement value is the preference a person attaches to a specific reinforcement. It is what gives the reinforcement its particularly rewarding character. As stated earlier, if the particular reward in question is highly valued by the individual, ostensibly because it is congruous with their life's goals, then the reinforcement will be notably rewarding. When the probabilities for the occurrence of a number of different reinforcements are all equal, it is the reinforcement value that best allows us to predict the direction of behavior. Thus, in contrast to Skinnerian theory, the very nature of any given reinforcement is a matter of interpretation and active personal perception. Skinner only discussed the more or less objective aspects of reinforcement, which is referred to as *external reinforcement*. However, when a reinforcement is preferred because it is interpreted as meeting the individual's personal goal structure, this is referred to as *internal reinforcement*. Taking his analysis a step further, Rotter notes that there are factors that tend to determine a person's goal structure as it relates to the potential to engage in a particular action at a particular time. For example, Rotter observes that one must understand the individual's personal needs at the time and place in question (e.g., Are they hungry and in need of food? Are they insecure and in need of some kind of reassurance?). Moreover, one must ask about the total psychological situation that this person is in, since goal structures are not determined by personal traits alone but also by the person's interaction with specific environments, which could lean them in the direction of wanting certain things over others (e.g., Are they fighting with her boyfriend via text message? Have they happened upon a mob scene? Are they going to a nightclub? Are they preparing for prayer services?).

To understand the behavioral tendencies of an individual in general (rather than specific tendencies in a very particular situation), Rotter says that one must appreciate the general needs that all people seek to fulfill (Rotter & Hochreich, 1975). For example, human beings need to gain recognition or achieve some level of social status. Humans need to feel dominant and believe that they have a certain degree of control over others. Human beings seek to achieve a sense of independence, protection, love, affection, and physical comfort. Each need can be satisfied with a whole host of behaviors. General needs such as these are the keys to understanding people's goals, since they tell us about the kinds of motives that can potentiate action. In order to refer to the potential that a group of functionally related behaviors will be brought together and coordinated to satisfy some need, Rotter used the term *need potential* (NP). It is perhaps easiest to think of this as *need satisfaction potential* or *need potentiation*. As for what determines whether or not a person will act on one or another need depends on two factors, each of which is analogous to an element of Rotter's formula for predicting specific behaviors.

For Rotter, need potential is a function of *freedom of movement* (FM) and *need value* (NV), giving rise to the heuristic formula, $NP = f(FM + NV)$. Freedom of movement refers to one's overall expectation of being reinforced for one's actions, meaning that it is analogous to what was previously referred to as expectancy. Need value refers to the degree to which the person prefers one set of reinforcements (associated with certain needs) over others. Need value is thus analogous to what was previously referred to as reinforcement value. Together, need potential, freedom of movement, and need value are components of the individual personality's overall *need complex*, which accounts for the way in which individuals prioritize their personal needs and resultant life goals.

Before moving on, it ought to be noted that Rotter's personality theory also relies on the notion of *locus of control* in assessing both specific and general behavioral tendencies. In fact, locus of control is perhaps the most famous concept of his entire approach to personality. According to Rotter (1966), people come to develop a sense of where the control over their circumstances lies. They form an impression of whether or not the control over punishments and reinforcements lies within them (i.e., an *internal locus of control*) or outside of them (i.e., an *external locus of control*). Locus of control is thus the degree to which people perceive a causal relationship between their own efforts and environmental consequences. Accordingly, a person's locus of control has a direct impact on expectancy and freedom of movement, depending on the level of analysis in question. In Rotter's (1966) words:

> People in American culture have developed generalized expectancies in learning situations in regard to whether or not reinforcement, reward, or success in these situations is dependent upon their own behavior or is controlled by external forces, particularly luck, chance, or experimenter control, which are fairly consistent from individual to individual. If subjects perceive a situation as one in which luck or chance or experimenter control determines the reinforcements, then they are less likely to raise expectancies for future reinforcement. (p. 25)

Albert Bandura

Albert Bandura's departure from traditional or "strict" behaviorism can be illustrated by considering the behavior of smoking cigarettes. Typically, when an individual takes a drag from a cigarette and inhales the smoke into their lungs for the first time, they experience things like burning, nausea, light-headedness, and a foul taste. If we were to use the language of operant conditioning theory, one would say that the act of taking a drag from a cigarette is immediately followed by a set of consequences best understood in terms of punishment. According to traditional behaviorism, punishments suppress behavior. Yet, it is quite common for a person to take yet another drag, then another, finish the cigarette, and then try it again.

This is puzzling. At this point, one would have to do some clever maneuvering in order to explain this behavior using the traditional behavioral concepts of reinforcement and punishment. For example, one might wonder if there are really a number of powerful unconscious or non-conscious reinforcements affecting the person's nervous system that go undetected. In this case, it would only appear on the surface that the drag from the cigarette had a primarily aversive effect. Such an explanation would lead us to a viewpoint that moves closer to Freudianism or neurological psychology. Or perhaps one could explain the behavior on the basis of the possibility that there are people in the individual's environment reinforcing them with praise or some other form of rewarding attention. This is quite possible.

While Bandura was aware of these possibilities, he developed another line of thinking. Bandura (1977) proposed the idea that there are reinforcements, overlooked by traditional behaviorism, that nonetheless exert a powerful influence on people and provide a fuller explanation of something like smoking again after being punished. According to Bandura, it is important to note that an individual's patterns of action are influenced not only by the reinforcements and punishments that they have received directly. A person is also influenced by the rewards and punishments that they have witnessed other people receive for their actions. Thus, Bandura's work is sometimes referred to as a *theory of observational learning*.

Modifications in behavior that occur as a result of having witnessed *someone else* get reinforced are called *vicarious reinforcements*. Social learning thus begins with the observation of a model of behavior or role model, as it is more commonly known. This model of behavior can be internalized by the observer, mentally represented, and remembered.

At this point, the observer may develop a *cognitive expectancy* of being rewarded for performing that same behavior. If the behavior appears within reach (i.e., is doable), the observer will thus imitate the role model in order to be directly reinforced by a process known as *the modeling effect*.

According to Bandura, human beings tend to model their actions after those who appear skilled, competent, or otherwise powerful in some way. In other words, we use others who appear to be the most capable of obtaining reinforcement in a given setting as our template for future courses of behavior. People who lack competence or who are otherwise lacking social status in a given setting are the most likely to look to others for a model of behavior. Moreover, modeling is more likely to occur in situations where individuals have no frame of reference for differentiating between appropriate and inappropriate behavior. Such situations are inherently disempowering and evoke a general sense of uneasiness, which results in the search for a competent model of behavior. This explains why it is that children are so "impressionable," as is often said. Because of their age, children are inherently less experienced than adults and often have no frame of reference for how to behave in various circumstances. They are thereby disposed to see adults as more competent and look to them as role models (whether they really are or not).

As is obvious, Bandura's theory relies on numerous factors that are cognitive in nature (e.g., attention, perception, mental representation, memory, and cognitive expectancy). His thinking became even more cognitive in orientation when he observed that modeling is more likely to occur when the observer perceives the witnessed behavior and its consequences to be valuable in a given circumstance. The question of values strongly implicates the beliefs and views of the individual. As a consequence, Bandura helped to transform a highly anonymous, depersonalized tradition of behaviorism into an approach to personality that begins to scratch the surface of what is "personal" in personality. Older forms of behaviorism were sometimes referred to as S–R theory, meaning that a stimulus gives rise to a response. Bandura's theory belongs to the tradition of S-O-R theory (Woodworth & Schlosberg, 1954), where the "O" refers to the involvement of the individual organism.

These days, the word *person* is often used in lieu of the word *organism* when referring to Bandura's viewpoint (Bandura, 1989, 2008). Bandura explains personality functioning in terms of *triadic reciprocal causation*, which implicates three factors in the final determination of personality. He saw personality as originating within the context of an interactive system of environment, person, and behavior (E-P-B), which supersedes S-O-R (stimulus-organism-response). By integrating the concept of "person" into his thinking, Bandura wished to emphasize that humans have some capacity to select or restructure their environment so that certain things are picked out, paid attention to, valued, and remembered for future reference.

Bandura (1989, 2008) identified a number of "personal" factors that govern the process of observational learning. As alluded to earlier, in order for the modeling effect to occur, a person has to pay attention to a potential role model. The person also needs to mentally represent the model of behavior and remember this model's actions in some way. In addition, the observer must develop some kind of expectancy or anticipation of being rewarded for the behavior that has been witnessed. Moreover, this reward must appear valuable to the observer in order to mobilize their motivation to emulate the role model.

Should the reward be deemed valuable, the observer will approach or withdraw from the possibility of action on the basis of four additional factors. To begin with, their social status will be implicated. All things being equal, a person with less social status would be more likely to emulate a model of behavior by a person with more social status. However, this assumes that the individual with less status feels that they would be able to perform the behavior without negative consequences. They would thus need to have the requisite *self-efficacy* to attempt the proposed behavior. Self-efficacy is a term that Bandura introduced into his theory to refer to the belief in one's ability to succeed in carrying out specific tasks. It is essentially skill-specific self-confidence (rather than a global judgment). A person can have high-efficacy in one situation, but low-efficacy in another. In addition, there is the issue of *behavioral production*. This means that the person has to find workable answers to the question, "How can I accomplish this?" Finally, the person has to engage in the requisite planning in order to carry out the behavior in question.

All of these factors are indicative of the *agency* aspect of the personality in question. Bandura's theory has an agentic dimension in the sense that things like attention, mental representation, value judgments, planning and so forth implicate the involvement of the person in codetermining their circumstances. In particular, Bandura noted that the agency of the person is grounded in four major factors. First, people do things deliberately, with intention. This is called *intentionality*. Second, people set goals for themselves based on desired outcomes and select behaviors that they believe will produce these outcomes. This is called *forethought*. Third, people monitor their progress as they attempt to fulfill these goals. This is called *self-reactiveness*. Finally, people think about and evaluate their motives, their values, and the meaning of their goals. This is called *self-reflectiveness*.

Having endorsed this capacity for self-regulation, Bandura held that, in addition to observational learning, human beings are capable of *enactive learning*. This is learning that occurs as a result of having thought about and evaluated the consequences of one's own behavior. At this point, it might be tempting to assume that Albert Bandura is an advocate of the notion of personal freedom in decision making. However, it is interesting to note that Bandura (2008) has explicitly rejected any and all notions of free will. This is strange considering his apparent advocacy of an active, agentic organism in his model of triadic reciprocal causation. Bandura considers people to be self-adjusting, proactive, and self-reflective, and this would otherwise be an implicit advocacy of some measure of personal freedom. The fact is that his explicit denial of the notion of freedom comes as a result of his desire to maintain his reputation as a descendent of natural science. Thus, Bandura has referred to freedom of the will as an antiquated relic of medieval philosophy. He considers the notion of free will to be superficial, Pollyanna-like, and undisciplined since people obviously act from within a nexus of environmental exchanges and influences. However, those personality theorists who advocate for some degree of free will agree with Bandura on this last point, and in the end, Bandura has made what philosophers call a straw man argument against free will. That is, he has painted a mere caricature of free will that is easy to discredit in order to maintain a certain kind of reputation as a scientist (i.e., as a natural science-inspired psychologist who sees the world in terms of cause and effect). In the process, he has unnecessarily limited his theory's power to tap into the agentic dimension of personality:

> [Bandura] maintains, at least implicitly, that people who are pawns to reward contingencies or to other controlling events are agentic so long as they feel able to carry out the activities they feel coerced or seduced into doing. It is here that inconsistencies in the apparent metatheory of self-efficacy become apparent, because without acknowledging intrinsic activity and an inherent growth tendency, self-efficacy theory is

not equipped to deal with a more complex and meaningful conceptualization of agency. (Deci & Ryan, 2000, p. 257)

Despite this problematic metatheoretical issue, Bandura (1977) has provided some highly practical insights concerning the ways that personal efficacy can be acquired or enhanced. According to Bandura, the most influential source of self-efficacy is successful performance, which he called *mastery experience.* In other words, when hard work leads to success, the result is increased self-efficacy. Various states of arousal and emotionality can affect performance and thereby have an impact on self-efficacy as well. So, in order to build self-efficacy through mastery experiences, it is helpful to know the kinds of physical and emotional states that are optimal for the task in question. One's performance will also have to be judged as successful if one is to experience increases in self-efficacy. Thus, one's personal standards ought to be realistically gauged to the difficulty of the proposed task. Further, one ought to be able to regulate one's self-reaction or emotional response to one's own performance.

Self-efficacy can also be enhanced through social means. For example, social modeling and social persuasion can increase self-efficacy. In the case of social modeling, Bandura observed that a person's belief in their abilities can be strengthened by observing other people who are similar in overall competence and social status perform a task successfully. Social persuasion refers to the idea that self-efficacy can be increased through verbal support from other people. Bandura also believed that self-efficacy can be modified via *proxy agency*, wherein an individual enlists the help of others. This aspect of his theory is illuminated by the old adage that there is strength in numbers. Personal efficacy can be enhanced through group membership, assuming that the group in question possesses a superior degree of collective efficacy. However, this is not a guarantee. Bandura has noted that various social forces have been posing obstacles to the development of both social and personal efficacy. These include the changing nature of an increasingly diverse society, our reliance on rapidly changing technologies, complex and slow social machinery (i.e., "red tape"), and mounting social problems.

Walter Mischel

Like Rotter and Bandura, Walter Mischel believed that human beings interact with the environment in a meaningfully coherent way, such that there is "internal" structure to the personality (Mischel, 1971). Traditional behaviorism envisioned personality as a set of reactions that occur at the mercy of environmental contingencies. Mischel, however, felt that behaviorism created a conceptual framework that allowed behavior to shift too freely in the hands of the surrounding situation. As a result, older versions of learning theory would be inadequate for understanding the stabilizing structure inherent in personality.

At the same time, Mischel stood opposed to those attempts to account for this stabilizing structure in the manner of a factor-analytic trait theory. As we saw last chapter, such theories move in the opposite direction of traditional behaviorism. They attempt to identify the basic ingredients (i.e., traits) that form the basis of all personalities irrespective of situational variables. Mischel considered personality structure to be too context dependent to be understood on a recipe-styled trait basis. In agreement with Allport (1961), Mischel (2004) rejected the notion that common, context-independent traits can account for personality.

For Mischel (Mischel & Shoda, 1995), the relative stability of the personality could only be found in *psychologically meaningful personality signatures,* which are always only expressed relative to environmental contexts. Borrowing from George Kelly (1963), Mischel held that these signatures have an "if-then" character about them in the sense that if the environment presents in one way, then one behavior might occur, but if the environment is different (or is perceived as different), then a different behavior will be elicited. This conceptualization, therefore, allows one to grasp situation-based differences in behavior but still allows for the possibility of an underlying structure that provides unity to the personality.

As an interactionist, Mischel (1971) did not want to simply abandon the idea of stable personality characteristics. Rather, he believed that researchers should pay attention to both situational and personal characteristics that influence behavior (i.e., attention, goals, values, expectancies, feelings, etc.). Personal traits are meaningful and motivating, but only given the right set of circumstances. Personality signatures are too context sensitive to be isolated and quantified the way a factor-analytic trait theorist would have it. Personality is dynamic. It is the result of an interactive system of *cognitive–affective units* resulting in an interactive *cognitive–affective personality system*. This systems view allows that a person's behavior might change (sometimes drastically) from situation to situation, but in an always-meaningful way that is comprehendible if one were to study the individual's stable life patterns of reacting to the world.

What are life patterns made of or built from? Mischel identified five cognitive–affective units (i.e., emotionally toned knowledge structures) that he believed to be the building blocks of personality formation and personality functioning. He referred to these as "cognitive social learning person variables" and describes them as follows:

> Cognitive social learning person variables deal first with the individual's *competencies* to construct (generate) desired behaviors under appropriate conditions. Next, one must consider the individual's *encoding* and *categorization* of events. Furthermore, a comprehensive analysis of the behaviors a person performs in particular situations requires attention to his *expectancies* about outcomes, the *subjective values* of such outcomes, and his *self-regulatory systems and plans.* (p. 265)

To review, the first cognitive-affective unit is comprised of *competencies*, which refers to the degree to which the person can cognitively and behaviorally generate adaptive behaviors that will bring them what they perceive to be beneficial consequences (Mischel, 1973). It is important to note that it is not just the person's actual performance that counts, but also their beliefs concerning their particular skills, plans, and strategies for carrying out life goals. Since this cognitive-affective unit includes an individual's expectations of success as well, it would be related to concepts like locus of control and self-efficacy. The second cognitive-affective unit is comprised of *encoding and categorizing strategies* and refers to how a person selectively pays attention and conceptualizes the world. Borrowing again from George Kelly (1963), *encoding and categorizing strategies* include the person's constructs concerning self, others, and reality at large. So, a person's self-concept and general ways of classifying things in the world (situations, events, interactions, and so forth) would all be included here. The third cognitive-affective unit is comprised of *expectancies* and beliefs, including a person's expectations regarding the consequences of specific behaviors, whether or not they will result in reinforcement or punishment. The fourth cognitive-affective unit consists of a person's goals and subjective values and is the motivational aspect of the person. The final cognitive-affective unit, *self-regulatory systems and plans*, consists of a person's self-reaction (e.g., self-criticism or self-satisfaction), and the overall self-evaluative tone that permeates the systems noted here. It includes affective responses (the way a person feels about the consequences of their actions) and is based on "self-imposed criteria" for evaluating one's own behavior (Mischel, 1973, p. 274).

Of all Mischel's cognitive-affective units, the one that has likely been given the most attention is that of self-regulatory systems. The issue of self-regulation played a central role in Mischel's thinking, especially in the form of *delay of gratification*, which he has argued correlates strongly with life successes in numerous domains of personal functioning (e.g., psychological, behavioral, health, and economic) spanning early childhood to mid-life. These findings are the result of his now-famous "marshmallow test":

> Resisting temptation in favor of long-term goals is an essential component of social and cognitive development and of societal and economic gain. In the late 1960s, Mischel and colleagues sought to identify and demystify the processes that underlie "willpower" or self-control in the face of temptation in preschoolers. With that goal, Mischel developed the delay-of-gratification paradigm (popularized in the media as the "marshmallow test"). This now-classic laboratory situation measures how long a child can resist settling for a small, immediately available reward (e.g. one mini-marshmallow) in order to get a larger reward later (e.g., two mini-marshmallows . . .). (Mischel et al., 2011, p. 252)

The role that this "willpower" or self-control plays in the functioning of the personality is explained as follows:

> Willpower requires skill in overcoming tempting immediate rewards, distractions and frustrations in favor of greater but delayed rewards. This skill, in turn, requires that individuals encode only information from the environment that is relevant, keeping wanted information active in working memory and suppressing unwanted information and selecting desired responses while withholding responses that are not optimal. (p. 256)

From this narrative, one gets a sense of the overall picture of personality that derives from Mischel's thinking. Life patterns or personality signatures are formed by way of the reciprocal determining interactions of cognitive-affective units and specific life circumstances, with the former acting in the capacity of a mediator of environmental information, the functioning of which is optimized by the power of self-control.

Reflection

Rotter, Bandura, and Mischel see people as subject to the forces of conditioning, but not in an exclusively reactive way. What they add to personality theorizing is an appreciation of the sheer degree to which human beings actively adjust to and interact with the environment. The cognitive social learning perspective sees human beings as goal-directed, cogitating animals whose active interpretations of events are at least as important if not more important than the objective features of the events themselves. With these theories, reciprocal causation has come to the foreground with considerable force, and their articulation of the mechanisms that make reciprocal causation possible add a great deal of detail to our understanding of the integrative, organizational propensities of the personality. Their contributions make these propensities far more tangible when compared to previous theories. Rotter, Bandura, and Mischel have provided a wealth of information concerning the cognitive structures that undergird the overt behaviors that have been the focus of traditional behaviorism. They have allowed us to develop a deeper understanding of the pragmatic goals and aims that guide personality formation where there had previously been (in behaviorism) only an accumulation of conditioned responses and an ambiguous, perhaps altogether illusory, measure of self-control. The personality is now seen as capable of emotionally colored information processing and self-regulatory processes that surpass anything we have seen in previous chapters. In fact, it would not be inaccurate to say that Rotter, Bandura, and Mischel collectively bring personality theorizing to the threshold of genuine agency and self-determination; but, ultimately, they do not cross over that threshold.

For all their interest in subjective perceptions, beliefs, constructs, standards, values, goals, "person" variables, motivations such as the need for love and affection, and (at least in Mischel's case) the unique pattern of personality signatures, cognitive social learning theory nonetheless relegates the agency of the personality to the confines of biosocial adjustment. Human subjectivity is thus approached on a decidedly restrictive basis. The cognitive social learning approach revolves around functionalistic, adaptational foci as represented by the following:

- Needs for recognition, social status, dominance, control over others, independence, and protection
- Encoding and representation
- Intentional forethought and planning
- Cognitive expectancies concerning behavioral outcomes
- Self-reflectiveness
- Self-regulatory strategies
- Self-reactiveness
- Delay of gratification, self-control, or "willpower"
- Self-efficacy within a reciprocal causation network
- Locus of control

To sum up, the theories that comprise this entire section of the text collectively operate at the most primitive levels of analysis when it comes to the development of the personality. Their approaches are a reflection of their underlying meta-psychologies, all of which ultimately seek to "explain away" the psychological (albeit to vastly different extents) on the basis of things believed to be more fundamental. All of the theories that have been discussed thus far employ strategies for attempting to explain the whole of personality integration on the basis of certain of its more elementary component part-functions. They have systematically framed the personality in terms of its potentials for adapting to prevailing biosocial conditions.

If we return to van Kaam's (1966) insight that personality is a subjective-objective-situational Gestalt, we would say that these theories disproportionately emphasize the objective-situational aspects of personality. They all recognize subjectivity in their own ways, as we have seen. But they all stop short of directly confronting *irreducible* subjectivity and thus the relational intricacy and sophistication of the personality's integrative structural organization in the process. This as-yet micro-integrational emphasis restricts personality to primarily self-serving aims and spans a range of forms from self-deluded illusion to genuinely self-regulated reciprocal determinism. But, as you may have surmised, the story of personality does not end here. Recall Maslow's (1961) aforementioned observation concerning the complex nature of psychology as a discipline:

> Psychology is in part a branch of biology, in part a branch of sociology. But it is not only that. It has its own unique jurisdiction as well, that portion of the psyche which is not a reflection of the outer world or a molding to it. There could be such a thing as a psychological psychology. (p. 6)

The theories covered thus far lean in the opposite direction, subjugating what would be psychology's unique jurisdiction to the biological and/or sociological in one way or another. Accordingly, they are not designed to handle the integrative dimension of the personality in its full humanity or intrinsic relative uniqueness. But there are theories that take the adaptational baton and run so far with it that they cross over into the realm of a genuinely psychological psychology of personality. George Kelly and Erik Erikson have fashioned two such theories, and they are the focus of the next section.

Taking it Further: Food for Thought

With Rotter, Bandura, and Mischel, the insights of behaviorism have been made more intrinsically harmonious with Alfred Adler's individual psychology, the developmental works of Jean Piaget, and the ideas of clinicians like Aaron Beck and Albert Ellis among others. Perhaps no other theory comes closest to the perspectives discussed in this chapter than George Kelly's personal construct theory. For Kelly, the processes intrinsic to personality functioning are "psychologically channelized" or set on a relatively consistent course via the typical ways that the person conceptualizes and anticipates events (Kelly, 1963). A human being develops a total, relatively organized *construction system* that mutates as they successively reconstrue and reconceptualize events that yield varying results. The person chooses for themselves those constructs that appear to have the greatest potentials for the development, extension, and progressive redefinition of the construction system and, by default, the personality. With regard to issues of individual choice, however, Kelly is likely closer to Alfred Adler than to Rotter, Bandura, or Mischel. It is to Kelly's more agentic, more synoptic theory that we now turn.

Make it Work!

My wife loves to cook and bake. Unlike days past, she can jump on YouTube and see how certain challenging meals are prepared. I enjoy playing guitar. I can now watch video tutorials to see how certain difficult songs are played. Due to the COVID-19 pandemic, my daughter is more socially isolated than she has been since we brought her home from the hospital. On a daily basis, she watches other children play (sometimes called onlooker play) on our family computer. Based on the number of views reported beneath these videos, we are not unusual. The perspectives in this chapter would tell us that the information age has brought with it an unprecedented potential for increased self-efficacy (i.e., skill-specific self-confidence). Has the internet made people more confident, and genuinely so? If that is the case, in what important ways? If not, why not? Try to apply cognitive social learning concepts to analyze the issues.

Key Concepts

Agency
Anticipation
Attention
Behavior potential
Behavioral production
$BP = f(E + RV)$
Cognitive expectancy
Cognitive social learning theory
Cognitive-affective personality system
Cognitive-affective units
Competencies
Delay of gratification
Enactive learning
Encoding and categorization
Expectancies
External locus of control
External reinforcement
Forethought
Freedom of movement
If-then structure
Intentionality
Internal locus of control

Internal reinforcement
Life-patterns
Locus of control
Marshmallow test
Mastery experience
Memory
Mental representation
Motivation
Need complex
Need potential
Need value
NP = f(FM + NV)
Observational learning
Perception
Personal standards
Planning
Proxy agency
Psychologically meaningful personality signatures
Reinforcement value
Role model
Rotter's theory of needs
S-O-R theory
Self-control/willpower
Self-efficacy
Self-reaction
Self-reactiveness
Self-reflectiveness
Self-regulatory systems and plans
Social modeling
Social persuasion
The modeling effect
Triadic reciprocal causation
Values
Vicarious reinforcement

Part II

Incipient Macro-Integrational Theorizing

Chapter 6

George Kelly: Personality as a Personal Construction System

Having noted the influence of George Kelly on both Rotter and Mischel, it is now time to confront Kelly's viewpoint head-on. Kelly is often classified as a cognitive theorist, and there is clearly a cognitive bent to his approach. He is to be counted among those advocating for a cognitive revolution, but in more humanistic terms (see DeRobertis, 2021), especially with respect to his time in history (cognitive psychology has seen many transformations and permutations over the years). Kelly refused to align himself with the cognitive psychology of his day, which he considered logico-analytic to a fault and thus too artificial in its manner of conceptualizing the mind. Instead, he had a more cordial relationship with the founders of the humanistic revolution, as evidenced by his participation in the groundbreaking Old Saybrook Conference of 1964 alongside Gordon Allport, Henry Murray, Gardner Murphy, Abraham Maslow, Carl Rogers, Rollo May, James Bugental, and Charlotte Bühler (Kelly, 1965; Taylor, 2000).

Kelly's approach to personality highlights the way people construe and conceptualize reality, generating evolving construction systems. At the same time, it is mindful of the finite, real-life dynamics inherent in any system of constructs dealing with the overflowing complexity of a person's concrete interactions with themselves, other people, and the world at large. For Kelly (1963), the development of a system of constructs, can be quite an ambiguous affair depending on the individual and their situation, and construct systems cannot be understood on the basis of "classical logic" (p. 61). Reality has a sometimes-messy character about it that is too often obscured by black-and-white thinking resulting from either the impulse to hastily grasp at easy answers and/or unbridled analytical logic. In Kelly's view, people generate constructs by forming opposing dialectical pairs, like *raw* and *cooked*. Each aspect takes on its meaning when juxtaposed with the other. For Kelly, construct formation allows a person to identify things that are similar (i.e., these are raw) and things that are different (i.e., these are not raw; they are cooked). This set of notions will then trickle down into other related notions, like edible and inedible, healthy and unhealthy, and so forth. But the establishment of this portion of the total construction system in question is not always logical. Consider the diversity that exists in the world concerning what is too raw or too cooked, edible or inedible, healthy or unhealthy. It does not abide by a singular, uniform logic. Selfhood provides another example. For Kelly, "self" is really only understandable by its relation to "other," whether this is clearly stated or left unarticulated. The standalone notion of self that bears little to no relation to the other sometimes found in highly analytic, individualistic-leaning thinking is an example of an unarticulated (and thus confused) construct for Kelly. Moreover, the dialectical relationship between self and other is culturally diverse, taking on varied configurations around the globe.

This dialectical style colors the whole of Kelly's approach to personality. He works with pairs like uniqueness and commonality with regard to people's conceptual construction systems, freedom and determinism as two sides of a coin, and the relative permeability and impermeability of constructs and construction systems. This approach gives his work the character of a cognitive-existential-humanistic hybrid. Similar things could be said of Erik Erikson, covered in the next chapter, whose interdisciplinary holism and emphases on identity and the developmental emergence of interlocking psychological strengths make his work a kind of ego-psychological-existential-humanistic hybrid (see Erikson, 1961; Knowles, 1986).

On the whole, George Kelly saw his work as an alternative to mechanistic behavioral and intellectualistic cognitive theories. The cognitive flavor of Kelly's thought has its origins in his notion that human beings are like incipient scientists. A similar analogy can be found in the much more famous work of Jean Piaget, though Piaget takes this analogy a bit more literally than Kelly (see DeRobertis, 2020). Kelly (1963) emphasized the language-based, culturally embedded capacity of the person to create conceptual models of the world and their relationship to it, rather than just reacting to the world (as in behavioral theory) or responding to it in a more logico-analytic manner (as in traditional cognitive theory). According to Taber (2020), Kelly's theory is a unique contribution to personality theorizing that can be seen as residing somewhere between those of Piaget and Lev Vygotsky. This insight notwithstanding, Kelly's keen sense of tragedy and his tragic optimism make him more humanistic than both Piaget and Vygotsky.

In agreement with a certain trend within classical cognitive theory, Kelly maintained that each person seeks to predict and have some sense of control over the course of the life events unfolding before them (as should be obvious, this aspect of his theory left a deep impression on Julian Rotter and Walter Mischel). At the same time, Kelly was less influenced by the model of the detached scientist and more influenced by Hans Vaihinger's (1924) philosophy of "as if." According to this philosophy, human beings always have a limited, perspectival understanding of the world, which can prove to be uncomfortable or even frightening at times. In response, people construct systems of thought (i.e., construction systems composed of implicit and explicit concepts, classifications, taxonomies, narratives, etc.), and then proceed "as if" the world is accurately portrayed by the models of reality that they have constructed. As Kelly (1963) described it, people look at the world through transparent patterns or templates that they create and then attempt to fit them to the realities before them. *Constructs* are the names of the patterns that are tentatively "tried on for size" (p. 9).

Once adopted, constructs (and, by default, construction systems) can be revised, updated, or replaced by newer ones. Kelly (1963) observed that human beings would be hopelessly bogged down by the limitations and biases of their preexisting constructs were it not for the fact that they can assess the outcomes of their predictions at a different, more inclusive level of construction from that at which they originally made them. As Maslow (1961) described it, speaking in reference to Piaget:

> We may remind ourselves here . . . of Piaget's children who could not conceive of being simultaneously Genevan and Swiss until they matured to the point of being able to include one within the other and both simultaneously in a hierarchically-integrated way. (p. 3)

This similarity aside, it is important to recognize that Kelly's theory of construct revision is more radical than Piaget's, whose work is dogged by an assimilation bias (see DeRobertis, 2021). In Kelly's (1963) view, any "alert" person (note the subtle value judgment concerning the relative normalcy or health of the individual here), like a good scientist, tries to bring their constructs up for testing (p. 13). All preexisting interpretations of everything in the universe are subject to potential revision or replacement, and this is what Kelly means by the term *constructive alternativism*, which is what he calls his perspective. As Epting and Paris (2006) noted of Kelly's theory, no one need be the victim of their own biography. Be aware, however, that bias-free construct testing is by no means universal, and revision and replacement are only human possibilities, not guarantees, as we will see.

For Kelly, what constitutes the "person" of personality is the ability to learn, which enables and empowers the evolution of one's system of constructs. In his words:

> The burden of our assumption is that learning is not a special class of psychological processes; it is synonymous with any and all psychological processes. It is not something that happens to a person on occasion; it is what makes him a person in the first place. (Kelly, 1963, p. 75)

The person is, moreover, always *in process* (i.e., in a process of learning and creating constructs), so the study of human personality involves the study of processes more than static traits or attributes. Again, for Kelly, people are perpetually seeking to accurately anticipate the future, operating with varying degrees of efficacy and success. This emphasis on prediction and control gives Kelly's theory a certain cognitive–regulatory/ego–psychological character in the sense that prediction and control are functionalistic/adaptational behavior patterns. But this is just a general emphasis, and he, like Erik Erikson, has a tendency to move in directions that extend beyond this focus, as will be further shown below.

Like the theories covered in the previous chapter, Kelly's theory has a strong psychosocial dimension. His view of the person and personality are inevitably and inherently interpersonal as a matter of philosophical anthropology. Different people's construction systems will inevitably bear certain similarities to greater or lesser extents, making for the possibility of a deep connectivity between diverse individuals. At the same time, however, once one moves to the level of concrete psychological functioning, depth of connectivity is not at all certain. It remains but an inherent possibility of human growth and development that must be actualized and brought to fruition. To the extent that someone takes the time to *construe* the construction processes of another human being, they may become able to "play a role" in the social world and interpersonal processes of the other (Kelly, 1963, p. 95). But this alone is not a guarantee either. There must be a psychological disposition for the person to enter the world of the other and, beyond this, a more or less accurate construal. So, two people can actually have very similar construction systems and still not demonstrate any degree of mutual understanding or compassion! The actualization of the social dimension of the personality comes from the twofold movement of construing the construction system of the other *and* achieving relatively accurate results. In fact, Kelly (1980) outlines an entire construal cycle involving initial anticipations, investment, encounter, confirmation/disconfirmation, and construct revision. A disruption in any one of these moments in the construal process can stand in the way of successful interpersonal connectivity and mutual social development.

Beyond these general features of construction, Kelly left the more specific question concerning what constitutes the "person" in personality largely (though not totally) open and unspecified. This was done deliberately in order to design a theory that operates at a high level of abstraction. Why use such a strategy? In Kelly's view, the benefit of a "high-level" theory would be that it could prove amenable to working in consort with other theories whose focus was any one of the more concrete domains of human behavior (e.g., physical, emotional, moral, etc.). This is part of why it is so easy for Kelly to be claimed by diverse schools of thought. Compounding the situation, Kelly (1963) claimed allegiance to numerous (sometimes contrasting) philosophical traditions in order to remain at this high level of abstraction, including empiricism, pragmatism, rationalism, realism, and what he called "neophenomenology" (p. 40)—a distinctly American current of phenomenology concerned with understanding the formation and structure of the self (see Snygg, 1959).

Kelly's interest in neophenomenology is connected to the need for a theory of freedom that is compatible with determinism, one that is dialectically related to deterministic thought rather than strictly opposed to it. For Kelly, the issue of freedom and determinism is a relative, dialectical one. Freedom and determinism are both a function of the relative degree of openness or constriction of one's construction system. Against strict determinism, Kelly maintains, "Natural events themselves do not subordinate our constructions of them; we can look at them any way we like" (Kelly, 1963, p. 20). Of note, this approach is clearly cognitive, but it is not dominated by the algebraic, logic-centric models that one tends to find among more traditional cognitive psychologists (e.g., Piaget and Garcia, 1989). For Kelly, it is the socially embedded individual as such (not some mechanical or computational subsystem of the personality) that determines the nature of constructs. Here we can begin to see Kelly's characteristically cognitive way of approaching the patently humanistic dialectic of relative freedom and limitation, and it is on such a basis that Kelly (1963) can hold that it is ultimately the person as a self-determining agent that sets the measure of their own freedom (or bondage). Indeed, this chapter is a turning point in this book because Kelly's is the first theory to unequivocally embrace the transcendent dimension of human personality that has always been a time-honored hallmark of humanistic psychology's holistic, integrative perspective (Frankl, 1967; Maslow, 1961; May, 1958). As Giorgi (1992) described it:

> Every human situation has a certain gap or leakage which prevents the situation from being closed deterministically, and the gap is human subjectivity which has the power to transform situations through meaning bestowal or interpretation . . . . [Transcendence is] the ability of a person, on his or her own initiative, to overturn any given received structure . . . the capacity of going beyond created structures in order to create others . . . . Humans are not trapped within the context of a specific fixity. One could say that it is the relationship to possibilities that matter, and the power to bring possibilities into being. (pp. 434–435)

As a relevant contrast to the social learning perspectives of the previous chapter, Maslow (1961) observed that *transcendence* bears with it the implication that a person has the ability to transcend not only their preexisting interpretations of the world, but also those interpretations that orient personality primarily toward adjustment to prevailing biosocial conditions (see also, Ryan & Deci, 2004). Kelly's theory crosses over into this way of thinking, as illustrated by the following observation made by Epting and Paris (2006):

> What is so striking in Kelly . . . is his vision of life as being, as he would say, an audacious adventure, as opposed to a series of adaptations or the ultimate outcome of a . . . compromise. Kelly's emphasis is always on hope, on the future, and on what opportunities we might have for improving our lot in life. (p. 35)

Returning to Kelly, he maintained that a person chooses for themselves and creates the alternative constructs through which they see the world and respond to it. However, it must be noted that Kelly was adamant that this ability to make choices is not absolute for at least four reasons. The first reason has to do with the developmentally unfolding nature of knowledge. According to Kelly, constructs are built from construals (which, by the way, makes him a forerunner of not only cognitive psychology but also of cultural psychology; e.g., see Markus & Kitayama, 1991). But construing is not to be confounded with what is currently verbalizable. Construals are typically formed on an implicit, pre-thematic basis. At some point they may be articulated, but this is not always the case, and not always necessary. As a process, construing has a wide range of application, which is by no means limited to those experiences that people can talk about or those that they can think about privately. Kelly (1963) referred to *preverbal governing constructs*, and even acknowledged construal patterns that give rise to constructs that are rarely communicated in symbolic speech, which he called *nonverbal governing constructs*. For example, aspects of a person's anatomy and physiology, like body type or glandular functioning, could influence the way someone sees the world, but the person may not have a language and associated constructions at the ready to think through or discuss their role in their construction system. Developmentally, a person's construction system undergoes a progressive evolution and gives rise to many subtle levels of awareness, with conscious construing representing a high level of awareness. At the lowest levels, one finds nonverbal and preverbal construing at work. What this all means is that sometimes a person's experience and behavior could lie outside of the realm of what would normally be considered self-determination because it is as yet unarticulated and perhaps poorly understood. Kelly (1963) advanced a vision of cognitive functioning that is quite complex, foreshadowing dynamic systems thinking, and its depth and complexity rival what one finds in psychoanalysis:

> A person may successively employ a variety of construction subsystems which are inferentially incompatible with each other. A construction system is continually in a state of flux. Yet, even though it is fluctuating within a superordinate system, his [sic] successive formulations may not be derivable from each other. The relationship is . . . a collateral one . . . rather than a

> lineal one. The old and the new constructs may, in themselves, be inferentially incompatible with each other. (p. 83)

A second way in which freedom is relative concerns the fact that the person only ever has a finite number of constructs in the first place. Further, their various constructs for dealing with reality are only designed to be effective within a certain range of convenience. Recall the earlier example of something being raw or cooked. These ideas simply do not apply to tables and chairs, for example, since we do not eat them. So, there is a double limitation at play with regard to the construction system. Accordingly, thinking is never completely fluid, and so neither is behavior. Cognition is channelized by the design of one's limited constructs, which were made to deal with certain specific aspects of reality. A construct is convenient for the anticipation of a finite range of events. Thus, constructs may or may not carry over and prove effective when encountering issues outside the range of convenience for which they were initially designed. One may think here in terms of Piaget's (Piaget & Inhelder, 1969) *assimilation* and *accommodation*. Some life issues may prove legitimately workable by certain constructs (thus proving amenable to the assimilatory tendency), but others may not. Stymied, the person would then need to update their construction system by "recombining old channels" to create new ones (Kelly, 1963, p. 61).

One can broaden and extend one's construction system by making it more comprehensive, increasing its range of convenience, making more and more of life's experiences meaningful. A construct is said to be *permeable* if it will admit to its range of convenience the addition of new elements not yet construed within its framework. A totally concretized construct would not be permeable at all, would have very limited use value, and would place strong restraints on personal freedom. Recall that for Kelly, it is best to think of freedom and determinism as bipolar, residing on a continuum that can be understood in terms of the relative permeability intrinsic to the construction system the person is building. Those construction systems that are composed of sufficiently open, plastic, and flexible (i.e., permeable) constructs allow the person access to ever more diverse, complex dimensions of reality. Rarely will the person be painted into a corner and forced to succumb to forces that compel a specified action or reaction. However, myopic, rigid, relatively impermeable construction systems will regularly tend to bottleneck experience and behavior within narrow parameters, forcing the person to operate according to a more highly constricted range of possibilities. Personal freedom is a function of the level at which the person chooses to establish their convictions, ranging from a broader, more encompassing construction of reality to a more narrow-minded construct system that is more restrictive in scope. In sum, the relative freedom of the person depends in part on the relative range of convenience and permeability of their constructs.

A third major aspect of the always-relative nature of human freedom pertains to the frailty and fallibility of constructs and construction systems. Construction systems are never completely "logic-tight"; nor do they evidence total internally consistency (Kelly, 1963, p. 85). Logically flawed, inconsistent construction systems can in and of themselves create stumbling blocks that stand in the way of self-transparency, general understanding, and the free exercise of the will. Cognitive therapists have taken these insights seriously and have been using them to carry out the work of psychotherapy for years (e.g., Beck, 1979; Ellis, 2006).

Fourth and finally, freedom is relative to a certain frailty and fallibility lying at the core of human nature itself. The inherent fragility of constructs and construction systems is something that human beings do not relish. In fact, it is something that has to be managed. As Kelly describes it, the tenuous, sometimes fragmentary nature of construction systems is something that a person has to come to tolerate. If they cannot, it may lead the person "to anticipate reality in very bizarre ways" (Kelly, 1963, p. 89). There are people who, for whatever set of reasons (and here we could turn to theories of personality that engage "lower" levels of concretion), have generated construction systems that afford them very few options when it comes to spanning the world of experience and the horizons of potential action. Human beings by and large prefer to feel as if they understand things (e.g., cognitive dissonance tends to create stress). Discrepancies in the viability of a construct can have destabilizing effects on one's entire construction system. For Kelly, the question for each individual human being then becomes how to manage this inescapable and potentially discomforting fact of existence. As Taber (2020) described it:

> Kelly used the metaphor of a person building their own 'maze', or 'labyrinth'—an ongoing building project where the structure was subject to perpetual revision, but where "the complex interdependent relationships between constructs in the system often makes it precarious for the person to revise one construct

without taking into account the disruptive effect upon major segments of the system." (p. 380)

Here, Kelly sees a human need for constancy and stability in construction systems, which is connected to the larger issue of how human beings deal with the radical contingency of life, including the ever-present threat of non-being or death. For him, all human beings differ in the ways they integrate and organize their constructions of events, and each human being must find a way to manage conflicts that appear in the struggle to live in the face of harsh realities. Striving brings the threat of failure, loving brings the threat of rejection, living brings the threat of dying. While one person may seek to resolve conflicts among their life's anticipations by means of ethical behavior, another person may solve their inner conflicts in terms of desperate attempts at self-preservation. Everything depends on how the person "backs off to get perspective," says Kelly (1963, p. 56).

For Kelly, while there are always alternative constructions available to any given person (as a broad generalization), there are situations wherein some people find it more difficult than others to access efficient, effective constructs that allow them the freedom to learn and grow. Sometimes people prefer to stick with constricted (illusory) certainty rather than opening themselves to broadened understandings that upset the order of their current construction system. As Kelly noted, some constructs are "definitely poor implements" (1963, p. 15). Poor implements (i.e., impoverished constructs or construction systems) generate self-made prisons wherein the person repeatedly misconstrues situations and responds inappropriately. Thus, Kelly held that human beings can enslave themselves with their own ideas. Forever the optimist, Kelly nonetheless maintained that the person can then again win back their freedom by reconstruing their life. If a person contradicts what is true within their field of vision, they have the power to reorient themselves on the basis of clearer definitions for their system of constructs. If the person is willing to tolerate some day-to-day uncertainties, they may broaden their field of vision and thereby extend the predictive range of their construct system.

Reflection

Personality integration is made significantly more comprehensible when it is seen as deriving organizational structure from the formation of a personal construct system. George Kelly's metaphor of the person living their life as an incipient scientist provides a global conceptual housing for the myriad contributions of cognitive social learning theory. His construal cycle with its anticipations and confirmatory/ disconfirmatory processes bears striking similarities to that approach, which he influenced, though it would not be accurate to call him a cognitive psychologist (at least not in the traditional sense). This aspect of his theory similarly highlights the need for human beings to adjust to their surroundings and to feel some degree of regulatory power within them. He was explicitly dedicated to advancing what he considered a "high-level" (relatively abstract) form of theorizing. So, for instance, Kelly's theory looks upon emotions as responses that accompany transitions in one's construal system, meaning that they are basically indicators of a change in one's mode of *information processing* (Tully, 1976). Moreover, while Kelly (1963) understands constructs to be mutually cognitive, affective/emotional, and conative (i.e., volitional or agentic), his discussions of emotion typically focused on threat-related topics like fear, anxiety, aggression, hostility, and guilt (Walker & Winter, 2007).

At the same time, it must be recognized that Kelly's theory provides a definite counterpoint to the decidedly adjustive, adaptive trend that we have been discussing thus far by way of Kelly's notion of construal as a creative process that operates outside the confines of logic-centric cognitivism. The reciprocal determinism of cognitive social learning theory, though superior to simpler models of causality, remains too linear and too detached to capture the subtleties of Kelly's contributions to personality theory. As Epting and Paris (2006) observed:

> Kelly's theory does not depend on establishing cause and effect relationships as a basis for gaining psychological understanding of the person. Instead, it is a matter of investigating what people are up to, what they are trying to accomplish, what circumstances they find themselves in and how they go about making meaning out of all of this. (p. 25)

Kelly's constructive alternativism, his emphasis on the creative nature of construction systems, his theory of the permeability of constructs, and his bipolar approach to freedom and determinism introduced the transcendent dimension of the personality, advancements that distance him from strictly adjustment-based theorizing. Kelly also demonstrated a deep and wide-ranging appreciation for the bodily, cultural, linguistic, and existential (tragically optimistic) dimensions of personality, and these collective advancements bring us further into the realm of a robust, macro-integrative psychology of personality. More contemporary work in the area of ego development and well-being confirms this view. Having analyzed data from three studies derived from measures of ego development, well-being, and growth narratives, Bauer, Schwab, & McAdams (2011) concluded that ego development only seems to lead to well-being when a person achieves comfort in their constructs. Specifically, one's construction system must be experienced as capable of facilitating the integration of seemingly incompatible aspects of life:

> People at higher stages of ED [ego development] are in the position of having to accept as satisfying a vision of psychosocial life that appreciates and even identifies with human suffering and inequities. How do these people do this? Perhaps these resolutions come from becoming emotionally comfortable with the conceptual understanding that the conflicts themselves are predicated on mental constructs (Cook-Greuter, 2000) . . . . At the Integrated stage, individuals have had experience with and understand what it means at a lived level that constructs like self-identity, life circumstances, outcomes, and growth are all projections of mental, linguistically bound constructs (Cook-Greuter, 2000). Personal comfort with constructivism seems to accompany an interpretation of everyday life in terms of longer-term process, as well as a greater flexibility in one's interpretations of one's life. At this point, one transcends (at a felt—not merely conceptual—level) a paradox of growth: That to grow one must accept things as they are while simultaneously taking steps to change things for the perceived better. (Bauer, Schwab, & McAdams, 2011, pp. 131–132)

Regrettably, not a word of credit is given to Kelly throughout this article, but one cannot be too hard on the authors. I myself (DeRobertis, 2017) have arrived at conclusions that are in fundamental agreement with Kelly on the centrality of learning and creativity in human development and likewise made no mention of his work. At the time, I was simply too unfamiliar with his corpus, and it seems likely that I am far from alone. Rarely does one stumble across references to Kelly, even in humanistic journals. Alongside William Stern and Alfred Alder,

George Kelly is among the most under-recognized, under-cited psychologists in this text.

Taking it Further: Food for Thought

George Kelly (1963) lamented that the psychology of individual differences (i.e., psychometrics, including factor-analytic trait theory) turned out to be the psychology of group differences and was unsatisfied with the strict reliance on aggregate data for understanding personality. For him, the fundamental unit of analysis is the person, not a part or summation of part-processes and not the group as such, which are all necessary, of course, although he considered them secondary to the aims of psychology and personality in particular. Since academic psychology appeared to reserve no respectable place for the systematized study of individual cases, he (like Gordon Allport and others more or less affiliated with the humanistic tradition) struggled to find a way to navigate between idiographic (case-based) and traditional (quantitatively biased) nomothetic data collection that used many participants. He felt that his notion of construction systems provided a foothold to begin: Individual construction systems display thematic regularities that can be seen across individuals. This was not enough, however. He wanted to have an integrated methodological system that could dialogue the experiential focus of (neo)phenomenology with conventional nomothetic methods that use large sample sizes (see Kelly, 1963, pp. 42–43). Had he lived longer (he died in 1967), Kelly would have been happy to see that Amedeo Giorgi (2009), who joined the psychology department at Duquesne University around the time of Kelly's death, began a lifelong project of creating a phenomenological method that begins with idiographic data, but then goes on to generate nomothetic results.

Make it Work!

Kelly's metaphor of the mind as a kind of labyrinth of our own (situated) life's construction is an intriguing one. It has the depth-like feel of psychoanalytic/psychodynamic psychology but also allows some breathing room for the willing participation of the person at critical junctures of the building process. The image of a labyrinth is meaningful because it implies that we set ourselves up to consistently turn in a predetermined direction when we travel down certain of life's paths. For Kelly, of course, we have the potential (to varying extents) to start a construction project and redesign the labyrinth so that we might turn in new and different directions. Can you identify certain life paths, relationships, or interactions with yourself or others where you seem to always turn in the same unfulfilling direction? Can you begin to envision a personal construction project that would allow you to make a move in a new, more satisfying direction? Which of Kelly's concepts would help in allowing you to conceive of how to begin? Are there dark corners of the labyrinth that seem impenetrable? Considering Kelly's view on the limits of personal freedom, what could be standing in the way?

Key Concepts

Comfort in constructs
Construal
Construal cycle
Constructive alternativism
Constructs
Determinism
Fallibility of construction systems
Freedom
Neophenomenology
Nonverbal governing constructs
Permeability
Personal construction systems
Philosophy of "as if"
Preverbal governing constructs
Range of convenience
Reconstrual
Self
The need for stability in construction systems
Transcendence

Chapter 7

Erik Erikson: The Ego and the Psychosocial Personality

Whereas Rotter, Bandura, and Mischel bring a more multifaceted style of analysis to traditional behavioral theory, Erik Erikson can be said to have done the same to Freudian psychoanalysis. He is not the only thinker to have done so, of course, but his adaptation of Freudian psychology is an exemplary analogue to the way that the cognitive social learning tradition integrated traditional behaviorism into a broadened conceptual framework. Rotter, Bandura, and Mischel moved behavioral thought away from its narrow focus on external reinforcement toward a heightened appreciation for the ways in which human beings make interpretations, form perceptions, derive beliefs, maintain values, forge plans, pursue goals, and so forth. Through their efforts, human personality is better understood in its active, adaptational aspects rather than only its passive, hedonistic aspects. The same can be said of Erikson's reinterpretation of Freudian theory.

Erik Erikson grounded his approach in the psychosexual theory of development put forth by Sigmund Freud. For Freud, human development was to be interpreted on the basis of animal drives. The needs of the id held primacy. Personality was essentially a function of its biological substrate. Far from recognizing the *centrality* of the social aspects of human development, Freud's interpretation of human beings focused on individuals' drives to attain pleasure. Erikson sought to go beyond Freud by integrating a more profound respect for the role of the ego and its attempts to come to grips with the demands of its social milieu into psychoanalytic theory. Thus, Erikson's approach is called both an ego-psychology and a psychosocial theory.

Like the cognitive social learning theorists, Erikson (1963) was explicit that his work was a particular attempt to account for the relationship between the agency of the individual person and their social surroundings. Coming from the psychoanalytic tradition, however, Erikson spoke of this relationship in terms of ego processes.

Erikson identified ego processes as those functions that serve to bring organizational unity (i.e., integration) to the biological and social systems inherent in the personality. So, for example, biologically speaking, a human being develops a need for sexual gratification. However, this need announces itself among a community of other people with a similar need for which a whole host of social norms, mores, beliefs, laws, aesthetics, and so forth (i.e., a culture) has been created. The personality is ever-socialized, and personality development is predetermined to grow in the direction of a widening circle of social relations. Throughout life, then, the individual's sex drive will have to be managed and made commensurate with the social world in which they live. This is the job of the ego. As Freud had asserted, the ego is the managerial aspect of the personality and is associated with rationality and the confrontation with reality.

Psychosocial Stages of Development

Erik Erikson (1963) revisited Freud's stage theory and placed more emphasis at each stage on the needs of the ego and its repertoire of interpersonal relations throughout the development of personality. As a result, he modified the approximated time ranges of the stages somewhat. At each stage of development, Erikson saw the child as needing to resolve a particular "ego crisis." He used the term *crisis* to refer to a critical developmental issue or significant turning point in development, and he considered each ego crisis to be part of the universal evolutionary design of the human organism (Erikson, 1963). According to Erikson, all of the issues in all stages are present in some form at the outset of development, but they nonetheless get their own special time period to take center stage, which he dubbed *the epigenetic principle*. As Erikson articulated it, anything that grows does so according to a predetermined plan. This does not mean that the details of development are already worked out in advance, of course. His theory is in no way a biological determinism. The "plan" is more of a general schematic within which the work of personality integration occurs over the course of the lifespan. Out of this plan, each part arises and has its own special time of ascendancy until all the parts have become unified within a multifaceted, functioning whole. In Erikson's theory, a successful resolution of any ego crisis means that the child will begin to develop new ego qualities and psychological strengths that will allow them to advance to a new, more multifaceted stage of development. Should a failure to resolve an ego crisis occur at any stage, the child will become fixated at that stage or regress to issues of the previous stage, as was the case in Freud's theory as well.

For Freud, the child's id seeks libidinal satisfaction via the mouth during infancy (i.e., licking, sucking, biting, chewing, and swallowing). As is the case at each psychosexual stage, the child requires gratification, but not to excess. Moreover, the child cannot be traumatized, abused, neglected, or in any other way denied adequate satisfaction. If the child is overindulged or undersatisfied, then the child is liable to develop a fixation. At this stage, fixations come in the oral-aggressive and oral-receptive varieties. Whereas Freud emphasized the child's oral pleasure seeking during this stage, Erikson chose to highlight the extreme dependency that the child experiences during this time. Due to this extreme sense of vulnerability, the child's ego seeks out consistent, predictable nurturance from caregivers. Starting with Freud's emphasis on the role of feeding, Erikson noted that while the id needs oral pleasure, the child's ego is in need of a sense of the primary caregiver's dedication to feeding (as well as to the child's needs in general beyond oral gratification). Should the child find their caregivers to be responsive and committed, they will develop an adequate sense of trust in themselves, others, and the world. In addition, they will develop the strength of hope, which acts as the foundation for all future development and socialization. Thus, Erikson saw the first stage of development as a time where the child must resolve the ego crisis of *basic trust versus basic mistrust*, which extends to about the first 18 months of life. However, should some form of emotional neglect prevent the child from developing a basic sense of safety in the world, they will come to rely heavily on attempts to withdraw from shared reality in order to attain a sense of security. For Erikson, an example of the kind of pathology that results from a fixation at this stage is infantile schizophrenia.

In the event that the child successfully resolves the first ego crisis, they will move on to stage two. Erikson called the ego crisis of this stage *autonomy versus shame and doubt*, which spans approximately ages 1 to 3. During this stage, Freud emphasized the child's attempts to obtain an adequate sense of pleasure via the anal sphincter muscles amid parental attempts to enforce potty training. Fixations due to inadequate parenting at this stage included anal-retentive and anal-expulsive character types. What Erikson chose to focus his attention on during this stage of development was the fact that potty training revolves around the issue of control (an ego quality). With bodily maturation, the anus becomes one of the first major things in the child's life that they can control. However, as soon as parents see this potentiality becoming actualized, they seek to use their authority to teach the child the socially acceptable way to regulate bowel movements. If the child comes to feel that the parents are not trying to dominate them but are ultimately attempting to help them develop self-control, the child will develop a sense of autonomy. In addition, the child will develop the strength of will, which is the foundation of notions like freewill and goodwill that always seem to be the subject of intense theoretical debate. However, if parents are emotionally insensitive in their child-rearing tactics, the child will not develop a sense of personal authority. Rather, feelings of shame and doubt will erode the child's sense of agency. For Erikson, the kinds of pathology that result from a fixation at this stage include impulse control disorders and obsessive-compulsive neurosis. Alternatively, if the emotional neglect that the child endures during this stage proves to be overwhelming enough, the child may regress to problems of the previous stage. Such is the case with every new stage.

Erikson saw the ego crisis of the phallic stage as one of *initiative versus guilt*, spanning approximately age 3 to age 5. During this developmental period, the genital region of the body comes into focus. Freud showed us that the Oedipal dream emerges. The child needs to feel like the beloved mommy's boy or daddy's girl for a time and then have this dream manageably come to an end by identifying with the parent of the same sex. If this fails to occur, the child may develop a host of difficulties revolving around relationships, gender, and sexuality. Failures from the previous stages will become more pronounced in the personality. At the same time, however, the child is developing a new sense of mobility. The child is developing new mental and physical skills that give them the ability to envision and undertake projects of their own planning and creativity. According to Erikson, if the child is allowed to enjoy these new abilities under the caring direction and guidance of their parents, then they will develop a sense of initiative. Moreover, the child will develop the strength of imaginative purpose. However, should parents rely on excessive punishment and guilt rather than involvement in their child rearing, initiative will not develop. Rather than being motivated to become involved in projects and relationships, the child will be burdened by a looming sense of guilt over acts contemplated and undertaken. For Erikson, an example of the kind of pathology that results from a fixation at this stage is hysterical neurosis.

During the latency period, the ego crisis that arises for the child is *industry versus inferiority*, ranging from approximately age 5 to11. For

Freud, the latency period was a time when the instinctual urges of the id were sublimated. The child is learning how to be like mom or dad, practicing the skills needed to become a young man or woman. Erikson believed that during this time the ego is attempting to attain a sense of mastery in using the mind and body as tools for building an identity via work and play activities. According to Erikson, the child requires encouragement and sometimes sensitive instruction or coaching to accomplish this task. If the child finds that they can successfully identify with their physical and mental abilities and feel at home in their body, then they will develop a sense of industriousness. In addition, they will develop the strength of competent skillfulness. However, if the child encounters some difficulty during this period, industry will not develop. Rather than becoming enterprising and diligently involved with tasks, the child will develop a pervasive sense of inferiority.

Erikson (1968) characterized the stage five ego crisis as one of *identity versus role confusion*, which begins with puberty at around 11 or 12 years of age and extends to about 18. Freud saw this stage as the time when the genital region is rediscovered, only now in a more adult fashion. Adult sexuality comes into focus and genital maturation brings about a radical change in priorities and lifestyle. Dating and group affiliation become more important and soon others (the adults) will be looking to the young person to make decisions concerning things like college and career. In order to tackle these challenges, Erikson saw the child as needing a strong commitment to the establishment of a sense of identity. Lifestyle choices like who to date, who to befriend, whether to have a family, and what job to pursue all require that the young person figure out who they are. However, Erikson noted that the task of achieving a constant sense of identity is dependent upon both dedication and the success of past stages. In puberty and adolescence all the resolutions of previous stages are more or less questioned again. Adolescents have to refight many of the battles of earlier years. So, for example, the basic trust of others that was won in infancy has to undergo new testing as the adolescent is forced to put their emotions on the line and trust a potential significant other when dating for the first time. Thus, failures throughout development would increase the probability of social difficulties and prolonged role confusion in adolescence. If, however, there is a successful resolution of the ego crisis of identity versus role confusion, the strength of fidelity will arise. The young person will experience the kind of resoluteness and perseverance necessary to figure out who they are supposed to become in their adult years.

As a young adult, the person moves into the stage of *intimacy versus isolation*, which spans ages from approximately 18 to 40. It is common that the search for that special someone to settle down with begins in young adulthood. However, as Erikson saw it, a sense of identity is a prerequisite for a stable, functional relationship with another person. Emotional intimacy with another human being involves sharing who one is as well as knowing what one desires from a relationship. However, these things are out of reach for a person who has yet to establish an identity and commit to a lifestyle. The person who can find the courage to use the newfound strength of fidelity to make genuine commitments to others will eventually discover who they are meant to be with and experience real intimacy. This would mean a successful resolution of the ego crisis of intimacy versus isolation and the strength of love would arise. However, the person who cannot commit to others will eventually come to experience a sense of loneliness and isolation.

In middle adulthood, from about 40 to 65, the person begins the stage of *generativity versus stagnation*. The period of middle adulthood is often the time when a person makes their mark on humanity and becomes most productive in their career and personal life. If fidelity is used during this time period as a commitment and devotion to actualizing one's creative, constructive potential, there will be a successful resolution of the ego crisis of generativity versus stagnation. As a result, the strength of care will emerge. If, on the other hand, the person is lacking a stable identity, is lazy, is disappointed in their choices, or is settling for lesser goals in life, they will experience a global feeling of stagnation.

Toward the close of the lifespan, the person enters the stage of *integrity versus despair*, which extends from 65 onward. According to Erikson, the person is now confronted with the task of developing a sense of meaningful perspective on their life. They need to be able to proudly accept the life they have lived with the people they have lived it with. Perhaps with the help of sensitive others, they can experience a feeling of comradeship with all of humanity and a deep faith in the meaning of their life. This is what is meant by integrity. It amounts to a meaningful old age and a dignified exodus from this world. If there is successful management of the ego crisis of integrity versus despair, the strength of wisdom will be apparent. Since death now waits in the wings, the only other alternative would be disappointment over a life that has been wasted and despair over its untimely end.

Reflection

Erik Erikson's psychosocial ego theory contributes significant experiential breadth toward an understanding of the adaptational efforts that support personality formation. The emotional dynamics brought to light by his theoretical contribution compliment and compensate for the somewhat more intellectual focus of previous theories. Erikson's approach alerts us that successful personal and social adjustment requires qualities like basic trust, autonomy, initiative, industriousness, identity, intimacy, generativity, and integrity to emerge from within a field of growth-conducive social relations, beginning with the mother–child dyad (for most of psychology's existence, "mother" was the default term for the child's primary caregiver). Erikson noted that personality development is in fact rooted in a kind of maternal conviction—a mother's belief that her parenting is a deeply meaningful activity. This conviction will be communicated to her child by permeating her actions throughout the child's development. This then acts as a template for adaptive social relatedness in ever-widening circles over the course of the lifespan. In contrast, psychological dysfunction is rooted in disruptive, maladaptive social conditions that give rise to an unmanageable excess of basic mistrust, shame and self-doubt, guilt, inferiority, role confusion, isolation, stagnation, and despair.

It is most important for the reader to understand that despite these two divergent developmental pathways, Erikson's theory should not, as a whole, be read in an either/or fashion. Overall, his theory offers a consistently dynamical, bipolar, paradox-disposed vision of the lifespan wherein successful resolution of a stage never altogether excludes the so-called "negative" side of each ego crisis. Just consider for a moment what it would be like for a person to develop without the capacity for shame or guilt. We tend to refer to such individuals as sociopaths! Alternatively, ask any parent what it feels like to think of their child going out into the world with absolutely no mistrust of other people. Erikson was quite explicit about the importance of both sides of each crisis and their enduring relevance to each new stage. Traits like basic trust and autonomy are not mere achievements in the sense of being secured once and for all. Erikson said it best when he noted the following in his book *Childhood and Society* (1963):

> Some writers are so intent on making an *achievement scale* out of these stages that they blithely omit all the "negative" senses

(basic mistrust, etc.) which are and remain the dynamic counterpart of the "positive" ones throughout life. The assumption that on each stage a goodness is achieved which is impervious to new inner conflicts and to changing conditions is, I believe, a projection on child development of that success ideology which can so dangerously pervade our private and public daydreams and can make us inept in a heightened struggle for a meaningful existence in a new, industrial era of history. The personality is engaged with the hazards of existence continuously . . . . The stripping of the stages of everything but their "achievements" has its counterpart in attempts to describe or test them as "traits" or "aspirations" without first building a systematic bridge between the conception advanced throughout this book and the favorite concepts of other investigators. (p. 274)

To reiterate, Erikson's overriding focus was the adaptive efforts of the personality as exemplified by the integration of biological and social functioning. Most of the time, Erikson does not dwell on the very core of human personality and focus on what is most personal in the personality. As the existential developmental psychologist Richard T. Knowles (1986) once noted, Erikson never pursued the full significance of the strengths that he mentioned in connection with a successful resolution of each ego crisis. Commenting on Erikson in the light of Heideggerian existential thought, Knowles observed:

Erikson, sensing the narrowness of focus of traditional psychoanalytic thinking, moves toward the inclusion of the person's ego in his framework. It is a definitive move to include the controlling, manipulative aspects of the person. For each stage of development, Erikson points to the specific ego function, using words such as self-control, direction, and technique. Traditional American psychology, with its pragmatic, action-oriented emphasis, unlike psychoanalysis, has always highlighted this aspect of the person. Cognitive approaches and decision-making approaches are particularly representative of this emphasis. Heidegger uses a curious term to express the ego aspect of the person; namely, Being-fallen or fallenness. By this term he means the typical way in which we are occupied by the daily events of life, our everyday tasks, and the way in which this involvement enables us to avoid confronting some other basic issues, such as the issue of death. Rather than seeing the rational, technical person as the ideal . . . Heidegger calls this mode inauthentic, meaning that it is precisely in this aspect that we are *not* ourselves. On the other hand, he does not take a moralistic view here since . . . ego-functioning is an essential aspect of being human and has its place in the total picture. (pp. 10–11)

Yet, it is with the identification of developmental strengths or virtues that Eriksonian theory actually leaves the typical foci of cognitive and ego-psychological theorizing and begins to recruit aspects of the truly human into personality theory (DeRobertis, 2008). It is with, will, purpose, skill, fidelity, love, care, and wisdom that Erikson (1961) decisively crosses over and opens the possibility of appreciating the macro-integrative complexity of personality. For example, Erikson's notion of an interpersonally mediated freewill that comes to the fore during the second stage of development presents personality theorizing with the challenge of understanding the intricacies of socially embedded self-determination. Hope, will, purpose, skill, fidelity, love, care, and wisdom cannot be understood from within the confines of a theory that is adjustment based or limited to a causality orientation. Each strength exhibits a paradoxical world-relating structure or *world-openness* that oscillates as needed between the poles of active control and passive surrender (which will be discussed further below). Alongside Kelly's creative, dialectical, permeable construction systems, Erikson's basic strengths point the way to a form of personality theorizing that is simultaneously more personalized, individualized (self-psychological), and radically relational. This is complemented in no small degree by Kelly's and Erikson's mutual appreciation of the continuously hazardous, "negative," and tragic aspects of human becoming. To revisit the language of the first chapter, Kelly and Erikson have provided decisive theoretical footholds for engaging the irreducible subjectivity and relationality inherent in human personality. Together, they clear a path toward increasingly open, multifaceted, macro-integrative understandings of human personality. This new terrain comes into focus in the chapters to follow.

Taking it Further: Food for Thought

Eriksonian thought has continued to develop since the time of Erik Erikson's death. Toward the end of his life, Erikson collaborated with his wife, Joan. They returned to his work on the eight stages of personality development, considering how to augment them, express them better, and refine them. One of the major outcomes of this work was the identification of a ninth stage of development called *gerotranscendence* (Erikson & Erikson, 1997; Tornstam, 1996, 2005). This stage deals with the fact that older adults reengage the struggles of the previous stages in a new way, as a person in the process of having their bodies (and brains) become less and less capable of meeting the demands of living. Accordingly, it is not unusual for older adults to find themselves becoming increasingly distrusting, to feel guilty about not having been the kind of person they wanted to be in the past or being a burden in the present, or they may struggle with feelings of isolation and stagnation as they become less mobile. Those who successfully overcome these challenges move toward the state of gerotranscendence, wherein one experiences a higher awareness of one's life as a kind of connection to all of creation (past, present, and future), resulting in an increased sense of perspective about life itself. All in all, the description sounds similar to what Maslow (1993) referred to when he discussed the *plateau experience*.

A lesser-known development was instantiated by the aforementioned Richard Knowles (1986). Knowles reinterpreted Erikson's theory in the light of Martin Heidegger's existential–phenomenological philosophy. Knowles used Erikson's virtues as his integrative foci, finding them to be the most "existential," meaning the most human aspects of Erikson's theory and development in general. Altering their names slightly, Knowles called the strengths hope, will, imagination, competence, fidelity, love, care, and wisdom. Overall, Knowles gave greater emphasis to the sense of self that evolves from the progressive integration of these strengths, each bearing a certain paradoxical structure that cannot be appreciated from within the confines of a more functionalistic, adaptational (ego–psychological) viewpoint. To illustrate, Erikson (1963) introduced the second stage issue of autonomy in terms of self-control and tended to speak of willing in terms of "willpower" (p. 274). This is not unusual in psychology. Autonomy is thought of as adaptive self-regulation and (as we have seen in the chapter on cognitive social learning theory) is spoken of in terms like self-regulatory strategies, self-control, locus of control, willpower, and efficacious reciprocal causation. Psychological discourse on control is typically binary, meaning that one is seen as either in control or controlled by something or someone else. Even if one speaks of relative amounts or degrees of control, the conceptual framework remains binary. The psychological structure of willing, however, is essentially and necessarily non-binary. Instead, it is paradoxical, dialectical, and integrative. In an act of willing, one is neither completely controlling one's circumstances; nor is one at the mercy of these circumstances. Both being controlled and exerting oneself to be "in control" result in a stultifying loss of freedom. Willing is discriminatingly responsive, assuming more control as needed while simultaneously partaking of the receptive openness of hope (the strength of the first stage) to know when to let go, and this acts as prophylaxis against overcontrol.

Knowles's approach emphasizes the dynamic (rather than linear) process of growth. The strengths that emerge at each new stage allow for the successful transformation and integration of the issues of each previous stage. More important, Knowles used phenomenological data to show how ego qualities act as legitimate supports for the unfolding process of personality integration, but are by no means indicators of macro-integration or optimal manifestations of becoming (e.g., thriving or well-being, see Bauer, Schwab, & McAdams, 2011). At best, they may be indicators of "normalcy," meaning the person is not dysfunctional or maladaptive in any clinically significant way. Generally speaking, a personality that functions primarily on the basis of adaptive functioning can hardly be characterized as well integrated or healthy. Indeed, the renowned pediatrician D.W. Winnicott (1960) has convincingly shown that a psychic structure dominated by habitual adaptation from the time of infancy is frail and disposed to what he called *False Self Disorder*. Thus, Pfaffenberger (2005) observed that higher levels of ego development, with their accompanying emphasis on intrapsychic differentiation and cognitive complexity, do not necessarily indicate that a person's development can be characterized as "optimal" (p. 288). In contrast, Knowles (1986) systematically describes how optimal development is a process of coming to terms with the fact that one is neither completely determined by biological or psychosocial forces, nor has complete control over them. The relationship is dialectical, involving mutual sensitivity to those aspects of self and world that fall both within and outside the purview of active regulation. From within the matrix of this self-world dialogue, the person is responsible for not becoming "lost in the 'they,' forgetting [one's] own views and conforming to [society's] views" (p. 16) and/or distracting oneself from "basic issues, such as . . . death" via mechanical "involvement . . . [in] everyday tasks" and "the ego aspects of prediction and control" (p. 11).

This existential–phenomenological retooling of Erikson's model of biopsychosocial integration, which shifts his virtues to the center of the model, is the appropriate stepping-off point for the next section of the text. The retooling means, in Knowles's (1986) words, that our study of personality is no longer in danger of committing "a case of mistaken identity with regard to the human being" (p. 5).

Make it Work!

Recall that, for Erikson, the ability to successfully meet the challenges of achieving intimacy with others and figuring out one's future livelihood depends on how one has managed the challenges of the first five stages. Can you see ways in which your relative successes or struggles at these earlier stages have contributed to your successes or struggles with intimacy and/or occupation?

Key Concepts

Autonomy versus shame and doubt
Basic trust versus basic mistrust
Care
Commitment
Competence
Consistent, predictable nurturance
Direction and guidance
Ego crisis
Ego-psychology
False self disorder
Fidelity
Generativity versus stagnation
Gerotranscendence
Hope
Identity versus role confusion
Imagination
Industry versus inferiority
Initiative versus guilt
Integrity versus despair

Intimacy versus isolation
Love
Mastery
Psychosocial theory
Purpose
Self-control
Skillfulness
The epigenetic principle
Will
Wisdom

Part III

Macro-Integrational Theorizing:
The Paradoxical Process of Becoming

Chapter 8

William Stern and Gordon Allport:
The Personal Personality System

This chapter begins a full-fledged, unadulterated journey into the realm of the personal in personality. Unsurprisingly, the kind of personality theorizing represented here comes from what is called the *personalistic* tradition in psychology. Contrary to the way it sounds, the tradition of personalism is not individualistic in character. Instead, it places rather heavy emphasis on self–world–other *relationships.* The term *personalistic psychology* is most closely affiliated with the work of William Stern and his one-time student, Gordon Allport, who will be the subjects of this chapter. William James, Mary Whiton Calkins, and Alfred Adler are the other seminal figures responsible for the emergence of this tradition of thought (Allport, 1937; Hall & Lindzey, 1978).

With the theories of Rotter, Bandura, and Mischel, we were introduced to a reciprocal causational goal orientation to personality formation, supported by a cognitive–social notion of value structuring. For Rotter, Bandura, and Mischel, the goals that guide personality formation can be said to be oriented toward the attainment of various kinds of reinforcements and adaptive life skills. George Kelly and Erik Erikson also generated theories that emphasized the more restrictive, micro-integrational themes of adaptation: the need to adjust to one's surroundings, including things like predictive accuracy, control of one's circumstances, self-control, efficacious regulatory power, the need for constancy, and so forth. At the same time, both Kelly's notion of the situated personal construct system and Erikson's stratified theory, which envelops the psychosexual aspects of personality within the psychosocial (spilling over into the existential) provided superior integrative housing for the more restrictive views of the first section of the text. Kelly and Erikson characterized the integrative, organizational impetus of the personality in terms that put us in touch with certain of its lived, spontaneous, creative, and truly owned aspects. Their theories cleared the way for another manner of approaching personality, which is taken up in the current chapter and remains central for the duration of the text. In Maslow's (1961) terms, we are now assuming an approach that does not prioritize a vision of personality as a mere reflection of biosocial conditions or a molding to them. Rather, we are now facing the challenge of developing a genuinely psychological psychology of personality, a macro-integrative approach that includes the biological and social within it.

Stern and Allport each begin with a holistic, integrative foundation for their respective approaches to personality. Both Stern and Allport viewed personality as *psychophysically neutral*, meaning that personality is not a certain ill-defined psychic "something" mysteriously residing inside of a person's cranium. Psychophysical neutrality is a concept used to indicate that personality is first and foremost understood on the basis of the myriad world-relating activities of the whole person. This viewpoint contrasts with the excessive intrapsychic tendency of Freudian theory and the excessive (yet, opposing) physicalist tendencies of behavioral and factor-analytic trait theories. Person and world are said to converge via the synthetic medium of one's characteristically unique projects and relationships. From this vantage point, the personality cannot be contained within or understood by a theory that habitually privileges or grants overriding priority to discrete forces, conditions, and/or "laws" deemed more basic and objective than the living whole that is the world-relating person. Once the characteristic uniqueness of the personality displaces adjustment to objective conditions as the organizational centerpiece of one's theory, adaptive micro-integration is outmoded by the world-spanning openness of personal, macro-integration.

William Stern

Despite having been a brilliant philosopher and psychologist, William Stern remains an underappreciated figure in the history of both philosophy and psychology. This is especially the case in American psychology, where Stern's name and legacy tend to be narrowly associated with the concept of IQ. This not only diminishes Stern's contributions to psychology on the whole, but also gives the erroneous impression that his approach to psychology was basically psychometric.

William Stern's (2010) approach to personality stems from his general philosophical and psychological viewpoint known as *critical personalism*. Critical personalism refers to the philosophically rigorous and scientifically disciplined study of the person envisioned as a *unitas multiplex* or multifaceted whole. Stern proposed critical personalism as an alternative to the philosophical and scientific tradition of *atomism*, which habitually overlooks the dynamic world-relatedness of the person as such in order to dissect human beings into discrete parts and anonymous part-functions. Stern referred to atomism as an *impersonalism* because it reduces the personality to a collection of mechanisms. Stern repeatedly warned psychologists against too hastily leaving the domain of direct experience in order to posit abstract, artificial "law-like" principles to explain personality functioning. An individual's personality cannot be understood solely as an instance of abstract laws such as those one might attribute to the rest of the natural world. Predominantly hedonistic and adaptational forms of functioning would be inadequate for the purpose of understanding persons and personality because of their inherently impersonal character. The person, in contrast, is always a unique and intrinsically valuable unity and needs to be studied as such. The person is simultaneously a genuine meaning-generating agent and the interpretive receiver of the passive givens of experience. Thus, an individual's first-person viewpoint has to be taken seriously, rather than subjugated to a continuous stream of scientific abstractions.

At the same time, critical personalism offers an alternative to homunculus spiritualism (sometimes referred to as *intellectualism*, *rationalism*, or *dualism*), where the "person" is relegated to the status of a mere ghost residing inside of or alongside a mass of physiological systems. For Stern, this alternative amounts to a *naïve personalism*. Stern rejected any strict bifurcation or dichotomy of self and world. There is no homunculus or "little man" nestled inside of the person orchestrating behavior like a puppeteer. He believed that the study of personality ought to be approached interpretively as it actually operates in the world, forming a unique "field of projection" (Stern, 2010, p. 114). That is, the personality is always manifesting as a distinctive participatory engagement of a situation. As Allport (1937) observed of Stern's perspective:

> Mental phenomena and bodily processes are properties of the person, but the person ... is not a passive theater for the play of psychophysical events; he [*sic*] is their true generator and carrier, and regulator. There are no specific mental or physical elements that are isolable and stable enough to form *between*

themselves a direct relationship independently of the person. (pp. 234–235)

So, for Stern, a person is an experiencing-acting, psychophysically neutral being. A person is not a body and a mind "stuck together," but a living whole that cannot be reduced to the mere sum of its myriad physical and mental characteristics. A person is both "one" and a "one of a kind," being composed of many different "parts," but nonetheless forming a unique and intrinsically valuable unity. Even though a person displays numerous part-functions in the form of things like physiological, intellectual, emotional, and social processes, they are able to achieve a unifying goal-striving self-activation. Goal-striving self-activation refers to the fact that a person is a being capable of taking up and pursuing goals of their own accord (i.e., not as a reaction to impinging stimuli or a mere adjustment to conditions, no matter how proactive that adjustment is conceived). Their psychological and physiological capabilities are mobilized and brought together in the service of pursuing specific intentions and ends that give rise to a novel living form (i.e., the unique personality). Stated differently, the person, with their particular value orientation and myriad interlocking goals, is the primary principle of organized becoming throughout the process of personality formation. Personhood is a kind of sustained achievement that makes it possible for personality integration and formation to unfold. Thus, Stern (2010) defined personality as a living whole that, through its own efforts, strives to realize enduring aims, goals, and purposes.

William Stern (1924) introduced the concept of *convergence* into psychology as part and parcel of this holistic viewpoint. For Stern, the forces of heredity and environment taken alone or combined in a simple additive fashion were equally untenable. The notion of convergence was employed to emphasize the fact that the historical distinction between these two forces had been based upon their prior, dynamic interrelatedness in the life of the acting, living person. Attributes that have been customarily referred to as belonging to nature and nurture simply cannot exist as unadulterated elements of an otherwise random or purely mechanical structure, even an epigenetic one. Nature and nurture are animated and emerge in and through the concrete participatory activities of the experiencing, acting, striving individual. Stern's position was thus that the psychologist must first determine the intentions and goals of the total organism as the requisite frame of reference within which to interpret the relative manifestations of so-called nature and nurture, which are merely abstractions unto themselves. The developing person is the fundamental unity or Gestalt that founds analyses pertaining to inheritance and learning.

According to Stern (2010), the integrative process of becoming that characterizes personality development is a stratified system consisting of phenomena (i.e., experiences), acts, dispositions, and the "I" (i.e., the subject or self). Stern considered the relationship between these constituents to be a "layering" of sorts, a dynamic and interpenetrated hierarchical organization. Each dimension of the person's development is inherently related to the others, but none are reducible to any other. Perceptions and other experiential phenomena occur against the backdrop of actions. That is, the experience of the person is always framed out by their unique *synthetic* (i.e., integrational, organizational) *activity*. In Stern's view, any and all phenomena of experience are synthesized by acting subjects who interpret environmental givens from a particular world-involved vantage point. Actions do not occur randomly (at least not under normal or healthy circumstances) but in accord with dispositions and goals, irrespective of whether these dispositions and goals are clearly articulated or unreflective. Particular goals are themselves organized and contextualized via an overarching goal system (the self-system) that maintains the order and overall integrity of the personality in accord with the person's values.

To reiterate, Stern believed that the unique and intrinsically valuable unity of the person could only be accurately portrayed when their myriad interlocking goals are taken into account. Critically, he spoke of the multiplicity of psychological dispositions as a kind of overabundance to be ordered by the "I" or self in the direction of growth and maturity. Stern (2010) classified the various goal-oriented strivings that characterize personality formation, the major two being strivings toward *autotelie* and *heterotelie*. Autotelic strivings consist of goals that promote individual development (i.e., self-maintenance and self-development). Heterotelic goals, however, extend beyond the self and consist of progressive tendencies belonging to different subclasses depending on their nature. In particular, Stern identified *hypertelie*, *syntelie*, and *ideotelie*. Hypertelic goals are those that join the individual with the unity building goals of family, folk, humanity, or Deity. Syntelic goals are those that join the individual with the unity building goals of their peers. Finally, ideotelic goals pertain to the realization of abstract ideals (e.g., truth, justice, etc.). In and through heterotelie, the individual is prevented from being a closed system of self-concern. At the same time, there is no ultimate incompatibility between *autotelie* and *heterotelie* here. The person's acquiescence to supra-personal goals does not necessitate any form of depersonalization. There is paradox at the core of personality (a theme that will repeatedly reappear in chapters to come). As personality formation proceeds, behavior becomes increasingly multifaceted, diversified, and meaningfully interpenetrated with what lies beyond itself. Personality development is a dynamic, flexible process of moving from simpler to more complicated forms of organized world-relatedness.

Stern's belief in the diverse goal-oriented nature of personality is reflective of a more fundamental underlying belief in the spontaneous, creative nature of personality. He insisted on the possibility of freely willed, personally meaningful engagement with one's surrounding world. The relative freedom of the will in Stern's work is not merely a freedom from conditions, however, but a freedom for the realization of possibilities. Personality integration is thus dynamic and motivational, so freedom does not mean that people act willy-nilly. Drawing on the Aristotelian notion of *entelechie* (which implies the continuous, forward-moving process of actualizing one's potentials), Stern held that actions ultimately serve the actualization of potentials for achieving a relatively ordered, organized form of maturing and personal becoming (as opposed to conflict, disorder, or stagnation). As the psycho-neural organization of the personality complexifies, it comes to operate more and more in the interest of selective perception and self-governed action (though not in any individualistic sense).

Through the integrational momentum of goal-striving, the person brings various potentials together, which result in growth and maturity in the process. *Individualizing form* is thus an achievement that results from successful goal-striving activity in the person's engagement with themselves, others, and the world at large. Relative integration and the sense of personal wholeness are not guaranteed, of course. They are ideals that the person actively pursues, typically without any explicit or reflective awareness of it. Growing, developing, actualizing potentials, and the like are usually not deliberate, conscious aims (though they can become consciously pursued, if one chooses). Stern held that human awareness (including self-awareness) is inevitably *graded*. This means that one's knowledge of anything can range from very diffuse and distributed (or embedded) to very vivid and sharp (or salient) (Allport, 1968). A person may interpret events, objects, others, and so forth in a manner of embedding within or withdrawing from one's own situatedness in the world (Strasser, 1977). Embedding keeps things highly relative to given concrete conditions, while withdrawing abstracts things from their contexts to make them stand out as particulars.

Stern's notions of embeddedness and salience are indicative of a perspective that views the awareness of self and world as many-layered and dynamically oscillating. Stern was explicit that there are "subconscious" aspects to the mind, broadly construed. There are latent dimensions of experience and "supra-conscious" aspects of being in the world that are as yet out of reach. Stern thus displayed a certain sympathy toward psychoanalytic thinking about the mind without resorting to the contradictory sounding notion of an unconscious mind. This style of thinking is repeatedly illustrated in Stern's attempts to explicate the teleological (goal-directed) nature of personality formation. He saw personality as inherently goal oriented, but insisted that dispositions, goals, and their teleological ends may have nothing to do with direct consciousness. Persons can simply pursue goals without being reflectively aware of what they are up to. Moreover, goal consciousness does not have to accurately represent the person's actual goals. It is, in other words, susceptible to distortion and self-deception.

Gordon Allport

Gordon Allport (1961) defined personality as the dynamic (i.e., complex, plastic, and changing) organization of those psychophysical systems within the individual that determine their characteristic (i.e., unique) behavior and thought. The term psychophysical is used deliberately to call attention to the idea of psychophysical neutrality that was introduced by William Stern. For Allport (1955, 1968), like Stern before him, personality is a relative unity comprised of many hierarchically organized, intertwined facets. In Allport's work, these facets include things like reflexes, drives, intentions, habits and attitudes, traits, and selfhood.

Reflexes are the more or less automatic actions of the body, including conditioned responses as defined by the behaviorists. Drives are highly flexible, species-wide innate behavioral tendencies, each of which has adaptive value for the organism, as Freud had shown. Allport readily acknowledged the many pertinent insights into personality submitted by both the behavioral and psychoanalytic traditions. Intentions include the hopes, desires, wishes, ambitions, aspirations, and plans of the person (all of which are themes that emerged in the chapters on cognitive social learning theory, George Kelly, and Erik Erikson). Habits were given a novel place in Allport's thinking via the influence of John Dewey, whom he admired very much. Habits are not the ingrained result of mere repetition as the behaviorists would have it, though they can begin that way. Rather, habits are *selective* regularities in behavior. Habit implicates learning, which includes more than the simple repetitive associations that behaviorists characterized. Habits are specific to particular kinds of life situations, like the habit of taking one's vitamins or of performing an exercise regimen. Attitudes also create regularities in behavior, similar to habits, but attitudes are predispositions to judge or evaluate specific things, people, events, situations, and so forth.

Traits are similar to both habits and attitudes by the fact that they are unique or defining behavioral predispositions. However, traits are more general in nature. When multiple habits are joined together, traits are the result. Similarly, when an attitude is increasingly generalized to more and more things, it takes on the characteristic generality of a trait. Allport was intrigued by traits because he felt that in their generality, they were highly revelatory of the relative consistency inherent in personality as a whole and, more accurately, as an inimitable whole.

Allport (1961) divided traits into two main categories, *common traits* and *personal dispositions*. Contemporary currents of so-called trait theory (i.e., the factor-analytic trait theories covered in Chapter 4) focus on common traits. For Allport, what is most glaringly absent from the factor-analytic tradition are the most important structural aspects of the personality: personal dispositions. The study of personal dispositions requires idiographic (i.e., case-based) research methods to capture the subtleties of their individuality and glean generalizable structural insights. He believed that every person has hundreds of unique dispositions, but also held that about five to ten of these dispositions are the most central to each individual personality. Thus, he distinguished between *cardinal, central,* and *secondary dispositions.* A cardinal disposition refers to an eminent characteristic or ruling passion so outstanding that it dominates one's life. These are rare. A central disposition refers to the five to ten most outstanding aspects of a person's lifestyle. Secondary dispositions refer to those less conspicuous, but nonetheless important, traits that people display under varying conditions, of which there can be hundreds.

On the whole, some traits are motivational and lead to the initiation of action, whereas others tend to be more stylistic in guiding the course of action. Whether motivational or stylistic, however, some traits are experienced as more incidental to one's being, while others are felt to be closer to the core of who one is as an individual (i.e., the ones we most closely identify with). This latter group of traits are thus said to be affiliated with the self or *proprium* of the personality. Allport (1955) called the proprium *the individual quality of organismic complexity displayed by a person*. It refers to that which has experiential warmth and sense of importance in the differential–integrative process of personality formation. Propriate traits are highly individual as a matter of course, but these diverse traits nonetheless admit of scientific classification. Each class represents a dimension of the personality that is largely responsible for its living unity, sense of wholeness, structural integration, orderliness, and hierarchical organization.

Allport (1955) identified eight dimensions of the proprium. The first is a unified *bodily sense*. Another word for this dimension is *coenesthesis*, which refers to overall or general sensibility (rather than a localized sensation in a part of the body). The second dimension is *self-identity* or continuity in time and space. The third dimension is *ego-enhancement*, which is a term often used to refer to unabashed self-seeking or egoism. The fourth dimension is *ego-extension*, which refers to becoming identified with things and others in the world. The fifth dimension is *rational agency*, meaning a reason-informed potential to manage needs emanating from both within and outside the person. The sixth aspect of the proprium is *self-image*, which Allport considered to be the most imaginative aspect of the proprium. Self-image includes the way one sees oneself as well as one's self-ideal or future vision of oneself. The seventh dimension is *propriate striving*, which is the motivational component of the proprium. For Allport, human motivation involves tension creation as well as tension reduction. Thus, personality cannot be fully understood on the basis of drive mechanisms and homeostasis. Human beings strive to create healthy tensions or optimal states of arousal. The final aspect of the proprium is *the knower*, which refers to the reflective, intellectual appropriation and ownership of one's propriate functioning.

Because of the warm, personal, owned nature of the proprium, Allport noted that certain kinds of activity are intrinsically non-propriate. These include reflex behaviors, basic physiological needs and drives, blind conformity to tribal customs and conditioned habits, inherited psychological characteristics, and compulsive symptoms of illness. The disqualification of symptomology is revelatory of the health-oriented focus of propriate activity and of Allport's theorizing in general. According to Allport, it is a natural tendency (which nonetheless can be frustrated) for humans to develop an ever-increasing, differentiated stockpile of traits that will then require unification to allow for ordered functioning and self-expression. This is a dialectic of dividing and uniting that ultimately amounts to an inherent growth orientation at the heart of personality formation:

> We maintain therefore that personality is governed not only by the impact of stimuli upon a slender endowment of drives common to the species. Its process of becoming is governed, as well, by a disposition to realize its possibilities, i.e., to become characteristically human at all stages of development. And one of the capacities most urgent is . . . the formation of an individual style of life . . . . (Allport, 1955, pp. 27–28).

This notion of an *individual style of life* will be revisited and further discussed in the next chapter, when we examine Alfred Alder's personality theory.

Gordon Allport (1955, 1961, 1968) identified a number of characteristics intrinsic to the growth-oriented, healthy personality. Allport noted that a healthy personality tends to emerge from a trauma-free childhood. This provides for the possibility of developing emotional security and self-acceptance. These characteristics give the person the confidence to fully (i.e., unselfishly) participate in events outside themselves. For example, the person would be capable of realistic perception of the environment and demonstrate a capacity to love others in an intimate and compassionate manner. Paradoxically, the person is more fully human and more fully themselves the more they can transcend themselves (Allport, 1961). The person would also have insight into their own behavior, a non-hostile sense of humor, and come to live according to a unifying philosophy of life. All of these characteristics will be revisited in the next three chapters.

Allport further asserted that a healthy personality is motivated by conscious processes in day-to-day living, though he did not flatly deny the existence of an unconscious mind. In Allport's view, personality theorizing should not be bifurcated along the lines of an overall emphasis on conscious versus unconscious motivation. Rather, the healthier the personality, the more likely it will be that the individual is capable of conscious acts of self-determination. Healthy individuals engage in proactive behavior rather than merely reacting or responding to stimuli. The more disturbed the personality, the higher the likelihood that actions will be unconscious and feel automatic or "compulsive" in the generic sense.

Finally, Allport insisted that a healthy personality is not exclusively motivated by past events but also by present interests and future aims. A personality is not a sum total of past experiences playing out in the present. The past acts as a foundation for personality, but the person continues to actively build beyond this foundation. So, for instance, hunger can motivate a person to learn how to grow fruits and vegetables. However, this behavior could eventually give rise to an interest in the pastime of gardening above and beyond the original motivation to eat. Allport (1961) referred to this tendency for activities to transcend their original motives as *functional autonomy*.

Reflection

From Stern and Allport comes an approach to personality that places a clear and strong emphasis on the notion that individual personalities are unique and intrinsically valuable unities embedded within specific world-relating contexts. Personality is in each case an integrative network or system that is comprised of numerous world-responsive potentials such as reflexes, drives, experiences, intentions, acts, habits and attitudes, common traits, personal dispositions, and the proprium (i.e., the self) (consisting of a unified bodily sense, self-identity, ego-enhancement, ego-extension, rational agency, self-image, propriate striving, and a knower).

Of all these world-relating potentials, the proprium/self deserves special mention. The notion of selfhood highlights the interactive, integrative dynamics that stand at the heart of personality formation. "Self" is a word used to designate the core interactive system of the personality whereby hierarchical organization and dynamic stability are derived. William Stern and Gordon Allport both provided clear indications that this system is imaginative, synthetic, meaningful, owned, inimitable, and differentially (diversely) goal oriented (i.e., autotelie, hypertelie, syntelie, and ideotelie). The open, expansive, and very personal nature of this complex goal structure exemplifies the macro-integrational outlook. As we will soon see, this outlook is shared by Alfred Adler (1935), who created an interpersonal framework within which the goal-striving activity of the creative self can be seen as emerging and operating. Adler and the theorists to follow explicate and unpack much of what has been laid out here in their own ways, with diverse emphases, further explicating the growth and health potentials of the developing personality.

Taking it Further: Food for Thought

Literature on the self or selfhood has steadily increased since the middle of the 20th century. What many people do not realize is how controversial this concept has been over the course of its history. Drawing on William Stern, Gordon Allport was at once at the forefront of the psychology of the self and a vehement critic of those who would seek to introduce the concept into psychology as a scientific cop-out or excuse for sidestepping disciplined psychological research (recall Stern's rejection of naïve personalism). Allport (1955) asserted:

> I greatly fear that the lazy tendency to employ self or ego as a factotum to repair the ravages of positivism may do more harm than good. The problem then becomes how to approach the phenomena that have led to a revival of the self-concept in a manner that will advance rather than retard scientific progress. (pp. 38–39)

What Allport feared was the use of "the self" as what is commonly called a homunculus or "little man" that is held to reside within the person orchestrating their functions like an autonomous puppeteer. The cop-out, when a psychologist cannot understand something, thus becomes "the self does it." Similar criticisms have been levelled at the unconscious in psychoanalysis (sometimes called the "blank check" theory of the unconscious). This problem has roots that extend all the way back to Ancient Greece, where philosophers struggled to understand the relationship between the body and the soul (Hoffman et al., 2009; Ricoeur, 1992). Aristotle advanced a hylomorphic viewpoint that envisioned the body and soul as inherently interpenetrated, while Plato saw the soul in the body like a pilot in a ship (the ship being the body). Plato's vision was carried forward by Christianity for centuries until the Aristotelian viewpoint was revived by St. Thomas Aquinas in the Middle Ages. Since the Middle Ages, philosophers and scientists of all kinds have been weighing in on the same basic issue, with the soul being called various things such as spirit, subjectivity, consciousness, and self. Those views of self that are sympathetic to the Platonic tradition tend to slip into homunculus theorizing.

Allport and the thinkers that follow have all sought to think outside the strictures of the Platonic worldview. Among these thinkers, Alfred Adler was especially important to Allport. This is because Allport felt that Adlerian thinking allowed one to envision the self not as a homunculus, but as coextensive with the whole of the personality as its organizational stylizing tendency. Allport (1961) held that Adler's conceptualizing of the personality in terms of lifestyle provided a sound basis for thinking through the problem of selfhood. Adler's thinking allowed viable (non-homunculus) access to selfhood by beginning with the whole rather than parts (i.e., by proceeding holistically rather than atomistically; Allport, 1955). Allport (1961) further considered Adler's viewpoint to be synoptic (macro-integrative) enough to accommodate the findings of diverse schools of thought:

> The individual, says Adler, adopts certain ways of attuning . . . to life. In childhood there is merely a "style of departure," comprised of native equipment and temperament together with societies' requirements for the child. Using these diverse ingredients, the child embarks on a process of self-stylizing and restyling [to] meet, as successfully as possible, the great problems of life, including the problematic nature of life itself. To view personality as a process of stylization has the merit of allowing for limitless individuality (although, for purposes of comparison we may group similar styles into types). It allows for positivist principles so far as they are relevant, as well as for the basic formations of existentialism. Thus as a synoptic concept it has value. (pp. 565–566)

It is to Adler's theory that we now turn.

Make it Work!

The perspective offered in this chapter envisions the personality as a complex/dynamical, relatively organized system (a *unitas multiplex*) comprised of dimensions that vary with regard to their degree of meaning, intimacy/warmth, and ownership. This idea implicates the person's diverse network of goal-striving activity. As inherently goal-oriented, human beings are sometimes more and sometimes less conscious of what they are working to achieve in life at any given time. Using the goal concepts advanced by Stern (i.e., *autotelic, hypertelic, syntelic,* and *ideotelic* goals), can you hierarchically order your goal-striving? Put those with which you feel most intimately identified, owning of, and aware of toward the top of the hierarchy and those that appear to be farther from the proprium toward the bottom. What new insights emerge from this activity regarding who you have been (or have not been) and who you are becoming (or are not becoming)?

Key Concepts

Attitudes
Autotelie
Cardinal dispositions
Central dispositions
Common traits
Convergence
Critical personalism
Drives
Ego-enhancement
Ego-extension
Embeddedness
Entelechie
Field of projection
Functional autonomy
Gestalt
Goal-striving self-activation
Habits
Heterotelie
Homunculus
Hylomorphic viewpoint
Hypertelie
Ideotelie
Impersonalism
Intentions
Motivational dispositions
Naïve personalism
Person
Personal dispositions
Personalistic psychology
Phenomena
Proactive behavior
Propriate striving
Psychophysically neutrality
Rational agency
Reflexes
Salience

Secondary dispositions
Self-identity
Self-image
Self/proprium
Stylistic dispositions
Syntelie
The knower
Traits
Unified bodily sense/coenesthesis
Unitas multiplex

Chapter 9

Alfred Adler:
The Interpersonally Creative Personality

As the father of Individual Psychology, Alfred Adler is popularly known as a kind of psychoanalytic thinker. His work has been described as a neo-analytic psychology, social psychological psychoanalysis, and (erroneously) neo-Freudian psychoanalysis. What is somewhat lesser known is that Adler was a highly original thinker who had an enormous influence on humanistic psychology. All of the humanistic "big four" (Abraham Maslow, Carl Rogers, Rollo May, and Viktor Frankl) were explicit about their indebtedness to Adler. They each in their own ways built upon his work and considered him to be an essential link in the historical chain that gave birth to the humanistic movement.

Developmental Foundations

Adler's personality theory is grounded in a theory of child development (DeRobertis, 2012) and begins with a simple observation: once born, human beings are in many ways quite helpless and are very dependent on others for a long time compared to many other living organisms. Without giving much credit to Adler, Erik Erikson (e.g., 1968) would build his psychosocial theory on this insight decades later (i.e., recall the issues involved in basic trust versus basic mistrust, see Massey, 1986). The basic fact of infant dependency struck Alfred Adler as both highly important and highly neglected in psychology, and it furnished him with a specific developmental insight: Personality development receives its initial impetus by the drive to overcome feelings of inferiority. As Vygotsky (2004) would later put it, "A creature that is perfectly adapted to its environment, would not want anything, would not have anything to strive for, and, of course, would not be able to create anything" (p. 29).

According to Adler (1992), there are certain factors that increase the likelihood that a child will be able to overcome feelings of inferiority. The first of these is a genetic factor: the inheritance of a healthy body. This provides a feeling of physical strength. The second factor concerns the child's environment: primary caregivers who can help them to manage life's challenges with increasing independence (Adler, 1958). This provides a feeling of emotional stability. The final factor involved in overcoming feelings of inferiority is the developing person's evolving creative power (Adler, 1958; Ansbacher, 1971). Through creative power, the child will eventually begin to envision and pursue a future wherein they are no longer weak or inferior (Nuttin, 1962). Adler called this vision the person's "final fiction," due to its origins in the creative imagination (i.e., "fiction" does not mean "false"). However, in order for this vision to provide genuine relief from feelings of inferiority, Adler insisted that the final fiction must be guided by community feeling or social interest, as he called it. For Adler, inferiority can only be truly overcome if a person looks outside the scope of their own self-interest for fulfillment throughout development. His understandings of growth and health were thus paradoxical in essence: The fulfillment of the self only comes about by way of the impetus to cooperate with others with a sense of genuine community feeling. Success in the pursuit of heightened independence ultimately results in the overcoming of the very need itself!

Holistic Orientation

Adler's (1979) entire approach to personality formation is emphatically holistic and field theoretical (i.e., context oriented). The integrative unity of the person is prioritized over any "part," part-process, or summation of functioning parts. In harmony with the theories of both Stern and Allport, the whole or Gestalt takes theoretical and methodological precedence. Alfred Adler expressed the fundamental unity of the person prior to any psychological analysis of parts with the term style of life or lifestyle. For Adler, lifestyle denotes the existential unity of the person and is superior to any psychological concept that would define the personality as a totality in the abstract. The term *lifestyle* is "existential" because it describes the child's burgeoning personality as a perpetual lived involvement in the surrounding world. This involvement is simultaneously bodily, affective, intellectual, and social.

In Adler's view, development is a matter of forming larger, more complex wholes, constructing relations between mind and body, over time, in the world with other people. Adler did not shy away from the very personal, very existential question of "who" develops (i.e., the question of the irreducible subject in integrative human becoming). Adler (1935) was unsatisfied with strictly behavioristic, psychosexual, and genetic explanations of behavior, and in his quest to avoid atomistic reductionism he asked who uses the raw materials of human development. As a result, he found *relational selfhood* to be an inescapable phenomenal reality of personality development.

In stark contrast to the misguided tradition of searching for the self in discrete psychic processes or physical localities, Adler (1979) used the concepts of self and lifestyle almost interchangeably. As Allport (1961) noted, the formation of a unique lifestyle is virtually synonymous with the integrative processes associated with selfhood (see also Hall and Lindzey, 1978; Heidegger, 1962). Adler maintained that psychology should be about relationship and not the isolated individual. The self is always a relational reality. Adler never used the concept of self as a convenient, elusive homunculus for explanatory purposes. The self is not "structurally absolute" in Adler's works (a sentiment that was later echoed by George Kelly, as we have seen). Adler envisioned the person as simultaneously shaping and being shaped by others. The person is an inherently social being, thoroughly socialized and subject to the imaginative dynamics of many minds. To state the matter more strongly, it is dubious to point to characteristics of a person and label them the mere results of heredity, for example, because all of a child's traits emerge in and through their concrete interactions with others. For Adler, what is innate via inheritance is never immediately visible but always intermingled with the mutual relation of self and other. Every tendency that might have been inherited has been adapted, trained, educated, and made over again in a field of worldly interactions. To be sure, Adler believed heredity to be an important, influential force in the development of a child. However, he also felt that inheritance tends to be overemphasized due to a neglect of the fact that heredity is always radically contextualized and made meaningful through environment, circumstance, concrete experiences, and personal history. Every aspect of a person's lifestyle is in contact with the world.

The intimate intertwining of selfhood and lifestyle in Adler's (1958) works gives his thinking on personality formation an unmistakably dynamic, transactional character. The self is meant to refer to the person moving in their uniquely creative manner toward relative integration within a sociocultural context. Integration is not presupposed as a primordial fact but as a relational emergent. Selfhood always denotes an interpersonally embedded, world-relating integrative tendency that is goal oriented. Although the person's organizing, integrating efforts begin early in life, Adler did not consider them to be fixed. Adler believed very strongly that goal setting is fluid and changeable throughout the lifespan. This fluidity is directly related to the creative power of the individual.

Teleo-Analytic Perspective

According to Adler (1998), the integrating efforts of the person are creative efforts. They hinge on the creative imagination of the interpersonally enmeshed individual. Nowhere does the uniqueness of a person's lifestyle appear more clearly than in the products of their imagination. According to Adler, the person uses their creative power in the formation of the goals that come to structure their lifestyle. Integrated human living emerges through the establishment and pursuit of existential projects or imaginative projections in time. The creative power of the self in Adler's work is not a mysterious, unscientific concept, but a self-evident characteristic of beings who live in a world that is partially of their own design. At the same time, it is critical to bear in mind that humans *co*-constitute their worlds with others. For Adler, interpersonally emergent creative power is the existential, experiential wellspring that gives rise to the initiation, direction, and modification of goal setting. Creative power is evident in the particular manner in which the person confronts the struggles of their set of worldly circumstances.

This confrontation implicates not only behavior but experience as well. Stated differently, how the person comes to strive and struggle toward personal unification throughout the lifespan involves interpretation and is therefore a matter of personal perception. For Adler, the individual's total style of life ultimately arises from the way they organize and perceive the world and from what therefore appears to them as success. The person does not experience pure circumstances; they always experience circumstances in terms of their personal meaning via an interpretive act. Interpretation enlists the creative power of the child, and the child's individuality is observable in both what they perceive and how they perceived it. Adler asserted that perception is a complex psychic function from which one may draw the most far-ranging conclusions concerning psychological life.

Adler defended the very humanistic notion that a person does not relate to the world in a purely predetermined manner but rather according to a creative appropriation of life's raw materials. Heredity and environment provide the raw materials of development, but they are insufficient in and of themselves to account for the course of personality formation. Although such sentiments would normally appear uninformed in an age of ever-expanding brain imaging technologies and high-powered genetic research, recent trends in psychology like dynamic systems thinking have been heading in this very direction for years now. For example, child psychologist Esther Thelen (1996) has made a convincing case that change throughout the lifespan is not the result of a genetic program or mere conditioning, but rather the result of improvisation. Years before anyone ever heard of dynamic systems thinking in psychology, Adler admonished that a person is not a calculating machine but an actively striving organism that tries out different alternatives to find satisfactory means for self-enhancement beginning in infancy. It was in this regard that Adler developed a deep respect for the importance of play in childhood. Adler believed that a child greatly benefits from having been given the time and space to play because in this space the child is empowered to freely develop creative power and practice goal setting. Through play the child imagines, creates, and practices self-expression with a comfortable, liberating distance from the preestablished meanings of the adult world.

Creativity and goal setting are perhaps the two most vital concepts in Adler's thinking on personal integration. For Adler, to say that a person is goal oriented means that they pursue immediate goals simply due to being an active, creative, purposeful organism as well as a final goal that is dimly perceived in its origin and worked out over time during the lifespan by way of intermediate goals. On the basis of its goal-directedness, Adler saw personality formation as teleological in nature, though he proposed no homunculus to account for this goal-directedness. Goals emerge from a field of embodied movement in time and space that is decidedly non-mechanistic; it is fundamentally different from the activity of a computer in that Adler never assumed that the pursuit of goals was always thematic, thought out, or even conscious. The consciousness of a person's goal is always relative and dynamic rather than the clearly conceived aim of an unsituated mental executive (Adler, 1992). Adler believed that considerations of a real-life person involved in their circumstances should be free of scientific projections. In advance of description, there should be no positing of static, unchangeable laws believed to govern behavior, thereby stacking the cards in advance of the person's actual striving. For Adler, the ever-present goal is always in flux. This is not to say that general principles cannot be derived by observing the behavior of a person. Rather, Adler's position was a polemic against biased observation that overlooks human behavior in all its intricacies. Unbiased observation, he believed, would account for the creative power of the individual to set into motion all the potentials and other influences intrinsic to their unifying, goal-setting efforts as they unfold over time.

Adler saw the pursuit of goals as arising from a lived sense of incompleteness (i.e., inferiority) that has its origins in embodied movement. Adler (1998) believed that movement stood at the heart of mental development. The ability and urge to move oneself, sensorimotor knowledge acquisition, acts as a foundation for the development of the finer details of consciousness. The power to move is, moreover, the very impetus for the development of motives. Self-movement founds the inclination toward goals, plans, and ultimately the creative discovery of meaning. Thus, physiology and psychology require one another. Furthermore, embodied action has a certain existential priority over intellection in Adler's works. Movement gives rise to attention, the creative impetus, intention, goals, and decisions, each of which unifies living, breathing person. For Adler, laws of movement and the language of the body provide more information about a person's direction in life than their words alone. A person's *organ dialect* consists of varied forms of meaningful bodily expression both prior to and alongside their words.

If it has not become obvious by now, Alfred Adler believed that humans are capable of free decision. He was opposed to the notion a human being has nothing original to contribute to the course of their development. As mentioned earlier, he opposed stacking the cards in advance of development and saw the evolution of personal freedom as beginning in childhood. This is one of the more controversial aspects of his work. A reason for this is that Adler (1979, 1992) tended to speak in extremes when making assertions that carry significant societal import. This writing style is perhaps best understood as a consequence of the priorities of Adler's own lifestyle. Adler's life was one of dedication to the welfare of humanity. He was deeply concerned with the welfare of children and how those children become the leaders of tomorrow. He was strongly invested in helping parents and teachers work efficiently and effectively with "pampered" and "problem" children. He was not as concerned with impressing academicians as much as he was interested in overcoming the deleterious effects of their folly. Consequently, he sometimes felt the need to express ideas in the manner of an impassioned battle call rather than a calm, cool, logical inference. Maintaining a clearly identifiable, consistent style of argumentation throughout his writings was, therefore, not always as much of a priority as was his desire to speak strongly and directly to those entrusted with the mental health of children.

Returning to the issue of freedom, one can find Adler asserting that children use their genetic endowment and environmental affordances freely, while elsewhere he will characterize the environment as the decisive factor in determining the child's lifestyle. He makes note that the behavior of a child is never causally determined, yet elsewhere he admits of self-created causality. This is sometimes confusing to readers who do not have a holistic grasp of his writing and its associated aims. Simply put, freedom and determinism are neither all-or-nothing issues in Adler's works; nor can his work be adequately characterized from within a dualistic freedom-versus-determinism conceptual framework. Adler advocated a position of limited (contextually situated or delineated) freedom with regard to personality. He felt this way about adults and children alike. Adler did not believe that human experience and behavior are utterly and completely determined until some point labeled adulthood, wherein freedom suddenly appears. Rather, Adler's view on the matter of freedom in childhood tended to mirror what is perhaps a commonsense view of the topic. Using the freedom-implies-responsibility model, we give children far more latitude to make mistakes than adults because we know that they do not possess the same degree of freedom as we adults but still assume that they are capable of some degree of burgeoning self-determination.

Against hard, biologically reductive determinism, Adler (1958) insisted that the brain is the instrument, rather than the origin of the mind. He foresaw the coming of enactive approaches to neuroscience (e.g., Varela, Thompson, & Rosch, 1991) inasmuch as he held that personal perception is not merely an anonymous, mechanistic process in the brain, but a kind of activity carried out by the person as a whole. For Adler, students of heredity misguidedly work backwards, as it were, deducing the cause of behaviors associated with a more or less finished product back to a single kind of precursor. This is fallacious reasoning through sloppy induction and hasty generalization. Adler was further aware that some forms of psychology advocate a hard determinism consisting of a purely materialist combination of both nature and nurture. He found this position equally untenable because this kind of interactionism is too often defended on the basis of statistical probability alone. To infer strict, materialist causality from statistical probability alone ultimately amounts to a non sequitur, meaning it does not logically follow of necessity. It requires a sound, reasoned theoretical argument that offers a logic in support of one's numerical data, which he found to be lacking. Thus, Adler rejected materialistic determinism because it glossed over the active, spontaneous, original contributions of the child as a potent force in the nexus of influences that constitute personality. Adler admitted of causal influence but not reductive, materialist causality. Adler acknowledged that both heredity and environment partly determine the creative power of the self, which is a little-known fact about Adler's worldview. When he spoke of self-created causality, he did so with the assumption that it emerges dynamically from within a network of meaningful influences. His was never a linear model of cause and effect coopted from Newtonian physics.

Adler's personality theory is a field-dependent theory. He stressed the fact that a person is born with a certain body and into a certain familial and cultural milieu that is not of their own choosing. In fact, Adler did not speak of freedom in relation to the very outset of development at all. Rather, he spoke of the child's body, the child's social position (including birth order), and the characteristics of those responsible for educating them as equal determinants of development. Freewill emerges from out of a context consisting of "alluring and stimulating" forces from both inside and outside the child's body. Of all these contextual forces, Adler was most impressed by the role of the child's social environment and their relationships with others. Adler constantly pointed to the critical role of the child's concrete circumstances throughout development, which he considered to be thoroughly interpersonal. In Adler's view, it is the responsibility of adults to first orient the child's innate creative power in the direction of social interest. At the beginning of personality development, the child looks to the adult for direction. It is the parent's job to help the child envision a final fiction on the basis of a lifestyle firmly rooted in social interest. According to Adler, any child born with a properly functioning brain and body has a natural inclination toward the development of cooperative relations with other people. However, this inclination is not an instinct or even a drive in the Freudian sense. There is no guarantee that a child will develop a tendency toward cooperation and community feeling (i.e., social interest). To reiterate, however, situations in and of themselves are not what Adler considered decisive for understanding personality, but the person's evolving interpretation of their circumstances. Adler analyzed developmental phenomena from a *teleo-*

analytic perspective (Nuttin, 1962; Sweeney, 1998).

Another reason why Adler's thoughts on freedom of the will are sometimes confusing to readers is that he considered freewill to depend on the relative health of the person. Thus, although he tended to argue in favor of the notion of freewill, one can find passages in his works where he opposes the notion of freewill. Adler (1958) held that there are many factors that can impede healthy personality development, such as pampering, exaggerated physical deficiencies, and various forms of emotional neglect resulting from defects in economic, social, racial, or family circumstances. Such factors can intensify feelings of inferiority and transform into an inferiority complex characterized by a compulsive need for personal superiority. In other words, they have the power to influence the person in the direction of deriving mistaken meanings concerning their relations with others, meanings that promote egotism and personal superiority while truncating social interest and cooperation. When a person becomes trapped by the allure of egotism, they habitually interpret social situations in a manner that is fraught with anxiety, giving rise to knee-jerk reactions designed to make them feel superior to others. Because of the "automatic" nature of these desperate reactions, the person's behavior is far less spontaneous and conscious than the behavior of a person with social interest. The personality will be characterized by a rigid, perfectionistic lifestyle that alienates others, increases isolation, and continually worsens inferiority. To be sure, Adler considered compulsive behavior to be a warning sign, an indicator of the beginnings of neurotic development. However, if a person's social context is welcoming, supportive, and nurturing, then personal freedom is more likely to emerge. The more experienced, better educated, and more properly supported the individual, the more likely one is to find compelling evidence of relatively free, relatively conscious self-determination.

Birth Order

Because Alfred Adler was so emphatic about the importance of social relations in the formation of the personality, he gave some attention to the role of birth order in child development. Unfortunately, this aspect of Adler's (1958, 1979, 1992) theory has been widely misunderstood and falsely exaggerated. According to Adler, birth order does have an influence on personality development, but it can only be properly understood on an individual basis. He would not have endorsed the formulaic versions of his study of birth order that are so often disseminated through today's textbooks. The reason for this is that the child's actual position in the family is not dictated by the chronological order of birth alone. In addition to the mere fact of birth order, the child's position in the family is the result of several factors, including one's style of attachment to primary caregivers, one's relationship to siblings, and the number of years between siblings. Adler insisted that there are no fixed rules concerning this complex aspect of social development. Nonetheless, he did point out some general trends concerning birth order under average circumstances.

According to Adler, an oldest child becomes accustomed to being the center of attention, but is then suddenly ousted from that privileged position. An oldest child will thus have to manage the feeling of no longer being special. If the parents do not prepare the oldest child for this feeling and then neglect them upon the arrival of the new child, certain detrimental outcomes may arise. For instance, the child may hold a grudge against the mother due to being pushed into the background, so to speak (again, "mother" was the default term in psychology for the primary caregiver). The child may then look to the father for companionship and emotional healing. The child may fight against being pushed into the background by acting out in disobedience. The child might even become a habitual "problem child." Through adolescence and into adulthood, such a child would be at higher-than-average risk of suffering from emotional problems or engaging in criminal behavior. On the other hand, if parents prepare the oldest child for the arrival of a new baby and continue to make the child feel secure, the occasion of the new arrival may simply pass without incident. In fact, Adler believed that if parents properly prepare the oldest child for the arrival of a sibling and ensure a feeling of being loved after this arrival, the oldest child might develop a notable talent for organization and a marked striving to protect others.

In Adler's view, only children are in much the same position as the oldest child. In addition, however, they are the most likely to display obvious signs of the Oedipal struggles noted by Freud. With no other siblings to intrude on their ambitions, only children are at risk for entering into competitive relations with parents.

Stereotypical second child behavior tends to occur when a child is born into a family with siblings who are relatively close in age. Adler believed the best spacing between children was approximately three years. When the spacing between children reaches four to five years and beyond the child will actually experience a blend of both a first and second child's predicament. For Adler, a second child is born into a less stressful situation than a first child, assuming that there is no rivalry forced upon the second child by a neglected first born. Being a second child presents certain advantages. It means having to learn cooperation early on in life. In addition, the second child already has a role model in the first born. The first-born child sets standards of excellence for the second child and provides a model for the means for meeting life's challenges. Adler was most optimistic about the situation of a second child on this basis. He considered the second child to have the greatest potential for success under average circumstances. He also considered the second child to be the least likely to become a problem child.

All things being equal, the youngest child is the most likely to be pampered or "spoiled" in Adler's view. Pampering prevents the child from learning what it is like to struggle against life's challenges and experience personal success. As a result, the child may come to lack mastery experiences, which then makes it difficult or impossible to feel independent in life. For Adler, the situation of a pampered youngest child creates an overinflated sense of ambitiousness that is made impotent by confidence problems and laziness. It is important to keep in mind, however, that none of this is certain. The ongoing dynamics of the child's interpersonal relationships and the influence of creative power in the formation of a personality make it impossible to predict developmental outcomes such as these in the abstract.

Reflection

Long gone are images of the person as managing the burden of having to adapt to prevailing biosocial conditions, and Alfred Adler plays an important role in overcoming this limited vision. It is of no small significance that Adler's theory transforms life's givens, like biology and environment, from forces of causal influence to raw materials harboring potentials to be actualized in the creative envisioning of goals and the integration of a lifestyle. A lifestyle that is founded on a goal structure that leads one in the direction of habitual competitiveness, the need to feel powerful, and the striving for personal superiority (to compensate for feelings of inferiority) is prone to personal and interpersonal conflict, thus making it relatively tenuous. In contrast, a lifestyle that is founded on a goal structure that leads one in the direction of social interest (i.e., true community feeling rather than cooperation for the sake of its "payoff") is freer and thus better able to take advantage of the integrative potential of one's creative power.

Obviously, Alfred Adler's Individual Psychology is anything but individualist in nature. Quite the contrary, it gives one a more empathically attuned understanding of the relational aspects of selfhood and goal setting in the process of personality integration. While his ideas are very harmonious with those of William Stern and Gordon Allport, Adler's theory provides additional insights into the origins of personality and the nature of the healthy developing personality. Adler drew from the infant's situation of relative inferiority the motivation to bond with others, grow, and achieve a unified lifestyle. If the individual can transition from being a near helpless child to an empowered adult with the assistance of their primary caregivers, their primary goal orientation will increasingly shift from overcoming inferiority to exploring the productive possibilities inherent in social interest and community. Adler highlights the intense degree to which the will and the creative impetus of the person are interpersonally emergent. Selfhood is seen as unbounded, meaning fully embodied and relational, making personality thoroughly interactional on the whole. In Adler's view, personality formation is a function of dynamic exchanges between the forces of inheritance, physiology, social context, social position (including birth order), and creative power. Though rooted in antecedents, personality is simultaneously self-determined and future-oriented. The personality is to be understood in terms of motivated movement, social interface, joint meaning-making, and personal perception.

Taking it Further: Food for Thought

Alfred Adler saw human beings as thoroughly social. In line with this view, he believed that the key to good education is the ability to foster community feeling in students. Stated differently, he considered cooperation to be the ideal outcome of a quality education. Education is only successful when the child feels valuable not only to themselves, but also to the "common welfare" (Adler, 1979, p. 304). At the same time, "real community" requires something more than mere tolerance or a blind conformity to social norms (Adler, 1979, p. 305). According to his concept of individual psychological education, students should be taught both subject matter and how to think for themselves simultaneously. In other words, the job of schools is to increase cooperation and facilitate character education at the same time, rather than focusing on intellectual growth alone. Education is responsible for not one, but two outcomes: intellectual development and interpersonal prophylaxis (i.e., the prevention of social ills), for which parents, educators and mental health professional must all work together (Adler, 2012). In his words, "We no longer wish to train children only to make money or take a position under the industrial system. We want fellow men [sic]. We want equal, independent and responsible collaborators in the common work of culture" (Adler, 1958, p. 157). In Adler's view, the issue of character cannot be underestimated. What Adler is implying is that it will not do to just go through the motions of being a cultured, civilized person. That amounts to little more than social adjustment and adaptation. The *genuineness* of the personality is a vital aspect of its integration. This issue will come to the fore in the next chapter with two thinkers who have drawn much inspiration from Adler: Karen Horney and Carl Rogers.

Make it Work!

Birth order has captured the imagination of laymen and some social scientists as well. Unfortunately, however, the complexity of Adler's views on birth order has rarely been properly represented in the research on the topic. This has made the study of birth order look like a wild goose chase to many. Still, interest in the topic remains, as birth order has made a resurgence in the area of evolutionary psychology (e.g., Salmon & Daley, 1998; Sulloway, 1996). Buss (2004) describes this new interest as follows:

> It has been proposed that the adaptive problems imposed by parents on children will create different "niches" for children, depending on birth order. Specifically, because parents often favor the oldest child, the first born tends to be relatively more conservative and more likely to support the status quo. Second borns, however, have little to gain by supporting the existing structure and everything to gain by rebelling against it. Later borns, especially middle borns, according to Sulloway, develop a more rebellious personality because they have the least to gain by maintaining the existing order. The youngest, on the other hand, might receive more parental investment than middle children, as parents often let out all the stops to invest in their final direct reproductive vehicle. (p. 223)

Where is your place in your family constellation? Does this description work for you and your siblings?

Key Concepts

Birth order
Creative power
Emotional neglect
Exaggerated physical deficiencies
Feelings of inferiority
Final fiction
Goal setting
Individual psychological education
Individual psychology
Inferiority complex
Interpersonal prophylaxis
Meaning-making
Mistaken meanings
Organ dialect
Pampered children
Perception
Personal superiority
Play
Self (creative/relational)
Social interest
Style of life/lifestyle
Teleo-analytic perspective

Chapter 10

Karen Horney and Carl Rogers: The Realizing–Actualizing Personality

This chapter focuses on the ideas of Karen Horney and Carl R. Rogers. Horney is known as a psychoanalytic thinker while Rogers is known as one of the founders of humanistic psychology. Nonetheless, there is extensive overlap between Horney's and Rogers's views of personality (DeRobertis, 2008). The holistic, social psychological emphasis of Horney's work makes her theory decidedly humanistic. Thus, Horney experts often note that Horney's mature theory is most similar to the kinds of viewpoints espoused by humanists. Conversely, Rogers (1951) cited Horney's ideas concerning the self-realization process as being similar to his understanding of the self-actualizing tendency.

This chapter takes up the theme of selfhood that has been developing throughout recent chapters. With William Stern and Gordon Allport, the self was identified with those aspects of the personality experienced as warm or otherwise personally relevant and value laden. The self was most closely affiliated with the synthetic unification or integration of the total personality. In addition, selfhood was seen as intimately connected to goal setting. These themes were present in Alfred Adler's personality theory as well, with Adler emphasizing the co-creative aspects of goal setting as a means toward the consolidation of a unified lifestyle. Adler identified numerous factors involved in stirring the individual's creative power into action, including inheritance, embodiment, self-movement, social position, cooperative social relations, feelings of incompleteness or inferiority, imagination, perception, and cooperative meaning-making.

In this chapter, Karen Horney and Carl Rogers will help us to become more familiar with another significant dimension of selfhood. Together, Horney and Rogers give one an appreciation of the extent to which the self as represented to oneself and others matches or mirrors (i.e., is harmoniously integrated with) the individual's embodied experience and reflects their innermost desires. Horney and Rogers address the realness, trueness, genuineness, or wholeheartedness of the personality in both its self-relatedness and relatedness to other people. The development of one's genuine or "real" self actualizes and optimizes the personality's potentials for integrative living. In contrast, self-alienation in personality formation embattles and erodes personality integration. The chapter thus introduces the reader to *the realizing–actualizing personality*. The word "realizing" derives from the term *self-realization*, which Karen Horney (1950) uses to refer to the development of the real self. The word "actualizing" derives from the term *self-actualization*, which Carl Rogers (1961) uses to refer to the tendency for human beings to activate and express their potentialities (optimally, in the direction of genuine self-ideals).

Karen Horney

Horney's reputation as a humanistic analyst stems in no small measure from her holistic orientation, which is exemplified by her emphasis on self-development. For Horney, selfhood is a holistic notion that is ultimately incompatible with the Freudian subdivided personality. Horney rejected the mechanistic, reductionistic view of personality presented in Freud's psychosexual theory. Horney's self does not refer to any kind of psychic apparatus like an id or ego; nor is her concept of self a homunculus. According to Horney (1950), the real self is the always unique inner force of growth in each human being. Being one's real self means realizing one's particular talents and living in accord with one's genuine wishes within a context of fulfilling interpersonal relationships. Whereas Freud's depiction of personality revolved around the ego's constant efforts to manage conflict, Horney saw the personality governed by the real self as integrated and at peace. The self is integrative and growth oriented, and this contrasts with Freudian theory, which is focused on conflict and the past.

Like Freud, Erikson, and Alder, Horney saw personality formation as rooted in a theory of child development. According to Horney, a child's relationships with their primary caregivers powerfully influence whether or not the real self will manifest during the course of personality development. A child's family is thus the most important aspect of their developmental milieu. This does not mean that early childhood development is the exclusive determining force in personality formation, however. Still less did Horney consider the evolution of selfhood to be a purely learned process in the manner outlined by behaviorism. Rather, she saw development as rooted in a set of *intrinsic potentialities* that emerge and are sustained in nurturing relationships. So, in her view, human beings are born with an innate drive to realize the true self, a process that she referred to as *self-realization* (Horney, 1950). Self-realization is guided by intrinsic growth potentials, but it does not occur in a vacuum, like some autonomous maturational unfolding. It requires supportive socialization in order to flourish.

To be more precise, self-realization actually represents a meeting point between genetic endowment and the powers of socialization without being totally reducible to either one. Even though inheritance and early socialization are both highly influential forces in the formation of a personality, they do not preclude the development of freewill except under highly adverse circumstances. The critically important job of primary caregivers is to meet the child's intrinsic potentialities in a welcoming, facilitating way that allows self-realization to proceed unimpeded. When that occurs, spontaneous, creative, participatory self-determination can thrive.

A health-conducive parental relationship is one that provides the child with proper parental love. Horney's belief concerning personality development is that the real self naturally emerges as an inherent part of human nature if the individual is allowed to grow and mature in an uncorrupted manner. In particular, Horney held that the child must have been accepted, embraced, and permitted to grow according to their individual needs and possibilities. Parents need to empathize with and understand the child as the particular individual they are. Empathy must be communicated to the child via genuine warmth and interest. The result of this loving warmth is that the growing individual will develop a deep and validating sense of belonging, or what Horney (1945) called *we-ness*. This sense of belonging, in turn, will bring out basic confidence. The person is emboldened by their nurturant social milieu, given a fundamental sense of adequacy and self-worth. These feelings of self-assuredness thereby stimulate the development of various positive, growth-facilitating qualities that Horney (1937, 1939, 1945, 1950) identified as hallmarks of self-realization. These qualities are listed below.

- The ability to be in touch with one's own wishes and desires
- Responsibility for one's thoughts, feelings, and actions
- A sense of vitality or "feeling alive"
- Acceptance and embracing of one's uniqueness
- A sense of belonging or "we-ness"

- Basic confidence in one's adequacy and value as a person
- Clarity and understanding with regard to one's feelings, thoughts, wishes, and interests
- The ability to tap resources and exercise will power
- The ability to actualize one's special capacities or gifts
- The ability to relate to others
- The ability to find one's set of values and aims in life
- Spontaneity of feeling and expression with others
- The ability to recognize one's limitations
- The ability to live in truth with oneself and others
- The ability to be oneself when alone and when with others
- A feeling of evolution in one's personal development

With the process of self-realization underway, the developing person is able to appropriate the model of behavior that supported the emergence of these qualities and "pay it forward," as the saying goes. Self-realizing persons are capable of showing other people that they are accepted, embraced, and permitted to grow according to their own individual needs and possibilities. Self-realizing persons empathize with and understand others as the particular individuals they are. As a result, self-realizing persons, according to Horney, are capable of cultivating sustained, fulfilling relationships.

Just as proper parental love facilitates a burgeoning self-realization process, inadequate parenting increases the potential for poor self-development. According to Horney, primary caregivers may truncate their child's self-development if they are unable or unwilling to somehow communicate loving affection and thereby emotionally bond with their child. The styles of behavior that constitute inadequate parenting are manifold for Horney. She believed that there were countless ways for parents to create an unsupportive, unhealthy childrearing environment. References to the varieties of behavior that threaten a child's self-development are strewn throughout Horney's works. For Horney, however, a particular parental behavior in and of itself may not necessarily constitute inadequate parenting. Rather, the more essential issue is the spirit in which parents care for the child and, correlatively, the way the child perceives their parents' attitudes toward them. In other words, the total affective atmosphere or emotional tone of the parent-child relationship ultimately determines the adequacy of parenting. Horney associated certain kinds of behavior with inadequate parenting if these behaviors block the child from attaining the fundamental warmth and security needed for self-realization. The danger, Horney (1945) felt, was that the child would perceive a lurking hypocrisy in the environment, by which she meant that that the child would see their parents' love as nothing more than pretense.

When the child does not feel adequately loved, the immediate result is that they feel helpless and conceive the world as potentially menacing. They feel alone in a hostile environment. We-ness is replaced by insecurity and hostility. Feelings of isolation and vulnerability create a desperate situation for the child, a basic lack of self-confidence. Horney (1950) called this fundamental lack of confidence *basic anxiety* and noted that in order to manage it, the child finds themselves forced to abandon self-realization. Lacking genuine warmth and interest, the child develops a feeling of not being valuable unless they are something they are not. In other words, if really being themselves results in basic anxiety, then the only viable alternative to quell their fears of abandonment is to avoid their real self. The individual feels that in order to be wanted and loved they must uphold some kind of image of acceptability, something that they feel others would expect them to be. As a result, they come to forfeit the "real me." Their genuine will, wishes, feeling, likes, and dislikes become paralyzed in fear. They gradually lose the capacity to fully comprehend their own values and become reliant on appearing acceptable according to the real or imagined views of others.

Thus, a parental relationship that arouses basic anxiety derails the individual's self-realization process. The real self is rejected, and a schism occurs in the personality. Once the real self has been abandoned, Horney (1950) observed that various coping strategies are adopted in an attempt to overcome one's fundamental sense of insecurity. In Horney's view, any particular attempt to manage basic anxiety can be classified as either a *moving toward, moving against,* or *moving away* strategy. The anxious person will develop a passive and dependent interpersonal style (i.e., moving toward), an aggressive and dominant interpersonal style (i.e., moving against), or a withdrawn and isolative interpersonal style (i.e., moving away). Each mode of comportment promises to help the person manage their deep-seated fears of abandonment and rejection. To be sure, these strategies are not adopted consciously and with full intention. They are desperate, "automatic" reactions to an unbearably painful and difficult relationship with one's primary caregivers and oneself (as Alfred Adler had shown). These coping strategies are thus defensively and tenaciously guarded.

Since the three basic coping strategies are mutually exclusive in style, Horney also noted that one style must be chosen as a predominant behavioral trend as a substitute for genuine personality integration. Thus, the anxious person will come to rely on one of the three styles more than the others. Moreover, the person will find that they can strengthen their defenses against their feelings of insecurity by creating an *idealized image* of themselves in their moving toward, against, or away from others (Horney, 1950). Consequently, they will lift themselves above others by forming an aggrandized mental representation of their particular mode of flight from the painful feeling of insignificance and vulnerability. This self-glorification gives the individual a feeling of significance and superiority over others. According to Horney, compliance is reinterpreted as goodness, love, and saintliness. Aggressiveness is reinterpreted as strength, leadership, heroism, and omnipotence. Aloofness is reinterpreted as wisdom, self-sufficiency, and independence.

Upholding a glorified image of oneself is, for Horney, a way for the person to prevent themselves from being crippled by feelings of shame and insignificance or the sense of being "thoroughly bad," as it were. Rigorously identifying oneself with a glorified, idealized self-image, promises to compensate for the depletion of the real self. Horney (1950) referred to the drive to actualize the perfectionistic goals of the idealized self as a "search for glory," which exists in opposition to the genuine strivings of self-realization. Rather than developing the characteristics of the real self, Horney noted that the individual searching for glory is compulsively preoccupied with appearing perfectly aligned with their particular (impossible) "solution" to basic anxiety. The fantasy of perfection creates egocentrism and a sense of entitlement on the whole. That this perfection is merely self-deception is evidenced by the prevalence of deep self-hate and palpable hypersensitivity in the personality. The person's defensiveness is indicative of the fundamental conflicts of their psychological life. These include their contradictory attitudes toward others and the rift between their idealized self and the hated real self, which is tied to basic anxiety and feelings of worthlessness.

Carl Rogers

Carl Rogers approached personality development in a similarly holistic fashion. Rather than making psychological constructs such as the id or ego the focus of his observations, Rogers sought an empirically verifiable theory of the whole person or total organism. Rogers (1951) tended to use the terms *person* and *organism* interchangeably. However, organism was the preferred term when he referred specifically to the body's "sensory and visceral equipment" (p. 500). The term *person* was favored when Rogers referred to the one's mental capacities, one's phenomenal field of experience, one's self-concept, and one's self-ideal (i.e., the more psychological dimension of existence). This emphasis on the self is in no way meant to imply that the person exists in isolation from the world with others. For Rogers, there is no possibility of a sharp limit or boundary between person/organism and environment.

According to Rogers (1959), the developing personality has a single sovereign motivational predisposition, which he called *the actualizing tendency.* The actualizing tendency is the innate tendency of the personality to develop all of its biological and psychological capacities in ways that serve to maintain or enhance itself. The actualizing tendency is present at birth and is observable in infancy.

As infancy progresses and the child begins to experience an increasing sense of autonomy and control over their body and surroundings, they start to develop what Rogers called a dawning awareness of the "I experience." At this time, a particularly significant dimension of the organism becomes manifest, which Rogers considered the earliest sense of selfhood or the self. According to Rogers, a major aspect of the actualizing tendency is the capacity of the individual, in a growth-promoting environment, to move toward increasing self-understanding and self-direction. Rogers's self is not a homunculus. As was the case with Horney, the self is but one expression of the general tendency of the personality to behave in those ways that maintain and enhance the person. The self is not the total organism either, but is rather the awareness of being, of one's functionally coherent acting and experiencing. *Self* and *self-concept* tend to be interchangeable terms for Rogers. In his view (Rogers, 1959), the self is an organized, consistent, yet fluid conceptual pattern of perceptions, characteristics, relationships, and values referring back to an "I" or "me" as its behavioral and experiential center. This is not to say that the self always remains within focal or conscious awareness. For Rogers, the self is more precisely merely available to awareness. The self is a fluid and changing Gestalt, a dynamic system.

As the self/self-concept evolves, the infant arrives at increasingly sophisticated understandings of themself in relation to others and their environment. This process is value laden, meaning that the child begins to see certain kinds of worldly and interpersonal relations as good, neutral, or bad. Under healthy circumstances, the child is allowed to positively value experiences that they perceive as enhancing their life and negatively value experiences that appear to threaten their development. Here, the self is said to be congruent with the genuine aims of the whole developing person or organism. As a result, a complementary self-actualizing tendency begins to develop in consort with the global actualizing tendency (Rogers, 1951).

Whether or not the child develops a healthy self-actualizing tendency in the direction of a genuine self-ideal has to do with the nature of their upbringing, especially their interactions with their primary caregivers. Healthy developmental conditions are those in which the child experiences unconditionally caring parental affection (i.e., unconditional positive regard). The result of these conditions is that the individual will most likely view themselves as good, as worthy of love. Unconditional positive regard refers to the genuine affirmation of a person's intrinsic value as a human being and as a unique individual. It does not altogether preclude a parent disapproving of "naughty" behaviors, for example. Rather, what it communicates to the developing person is that they never have to question whether or not they are truly loved and accepted for being themselves. The developing person who has been given unconditional positive regard will have an unwavering faith that they are an inherently worthwhile and loveable creature. They can experience fully and accept themselves. The person who was not threatened by the loss of love can be open to the full range of their organismic experiences.

The personality that results from unconditional positive regard would be realistic, based upon an accurate symbolization of all the evidence given by the individual's sensory and visceral equipment (i.e., the full array of available organismic experience). Thus, the self-structure of healthy developing individuals is integrated, whole, and genuine. This experientially open, congruent self actualizes its potentials in consort with its more global actualizing tendency in the direction of a particular self-ideal or ideal self. In Rogers's theory, *ideal self* is a term used to denote the self-concept that the individual would most like to possess, the one upon which they place the highest value for themselves. These individuals can let the flow of their experience carry them in a forward-moving direction toward tentative goals and ideals. Moreover, when the actualizing tendency of the organism is adopted by the self, the self-actualizing tendency orients the person's development in the direction of socialization, broadly defined. The self both develops in an interpersonal context and desires good interpersonal relations during the growth process. Rogers (1959, 1961, 1980) observed that the actualizing self has numerous qualities, such as those listed below.

- Perceptions and judgments that are down-to-earth, realistic, and grounded in facts
- Openness to experience without feeling threatened or being defensive
- Maturity and responsibility; owns one's feelings
- Acceptance of others as unique individuals
- Acceptance and prizing of oneself unconditionally
- Acceptance and prizing of others for who they are
- An internal locus of evaluation when judging oneself
- Willingness to be "in process"; tolerance of change and ambiguity
- Appreciation of the uniqueness of each moment of one's life
- Experience of oneself as "fully functioning"; a general sense of richness of one's life experience
- Spontaneity; displays unpredictable creativity
- Trust in oneself; confidence in one's skills, perceptions, and evaluations
- A life-affirming nurturance of all living things
- Ability to be open, expressive, flexible, and willing to take risks in relationships
- Independent, autonomous, self-motivated to seek fulfillment
- The search for enhancement over the maintenance of one's organism overall

When the child is not given unconditional positive regard, however, healthy self-development is jeopardized. For instance, should the child experience their parents as disapproving of certain behaviors that they enjoy or would otherwise value positively, they may (depending on the spirit of the parenting) perceive their parents as saying, "You are bad and you are not loveable when you behave this way." This threatens the foundations of their self-worth, their feeling of lovability as a person. There is, in Rogers's (1951) view, no greater threat to development. For this reason, the individual will take measures to survive this threatening situation. In particular, they will deny and/or distort their organismic experience. In order to guard against losing the sense of being loved, the individual finds themselves compelled to refashion and falsify their phenomenal field of experience to fit what they perceive their parents as wanting in exchange for their love. The individual warps their experience in order to conceive of themselves as a certain kind of person for the purposes of being perceived as "acceptable." Consequently, the values intrinsic to the personality are in some instances real, but are in other instances false. The personality comes to revolve around conditions of worth as a result of conditional positive regard from one's primary caregivers.

As the process of denying and distorting one's genuine experience proceeds, the self-concept becomes increasingly alienated from the total organism. Accurate representations of experience are not allowed to be made conscious. Experiences other than those that meet the personality's conditions of worth cause the individual anxiety because such experiences threaten their feeling of value and lovability. Instead of developing a healthy, maturing, congruent self, the individual with conditions of worth manifests an *incongruent self* that is at variance with their organismic experience (Rogers, 1951). A rift occurs between the actualizing tendency and the self-actualizing tendency. Self-actualization is no longer genuine, but rather a kind of unwitting deception that is confusedly alienated from the person's real feelings and desires. The individual's distorted self-concept prevents the personal evolutionary flow of unobstructed growth and optimized functioning.

Rogers noted that this falsified self-concept could exclude either positive or negative evaluations. That is, individuals may deny that they have a good or bad trait in order to preserve a distorted self-image. However, the general point is that incongruence creates a situation wherein the personality comes to be patterned in accord with false ideals. Real self-actualization is stunted or thwarted. Incongruence creates growth-obstructing inner tension. The self becomes defensive, rigid, socially maladjusted, and confused with regard to its own motives, feelings, and behaviors. Behavior is intellectually regarded as enhancing the self when no such value is directly experienced. Behavior is intellectually regarded as opposed to the enhancement of the self when there is no direct negative experience to corroborate this belief.

In the end, the person is left with a distorted sense of self and a poor self-image. This increases the likelihood that they will display insecurity in relationships with others.

Reflection

Transitioning from Alfred Adler's theory, the theories of Karen Horney and Carl Rogers add significant depth and detail to an understanding of how selfhood emerges from within the familial relationship. They alert one to the fact that qualities like warmth, empathy, genuine acceptance, and an overall spirit of unconditional positive regard (not to be confused with what Adler called pampering or over-indulgence) are critical in assuring the genuineness and associated structural integrity of the personality. Horney and Rogers both recapitulate the idea mentioned in reference to Erik Erikson's psychosocial perspective, that the primary caregiver needs to have a deep belief in the meaning of their parenting behaviors. In addition to merely providing for the child's physiological needs, the primary caregiver must carry themselves with an air of welcoming receptivity for the purpose of establishing an abiding emotional bond with the child. This bond provides the confidence and sense of value or self-worth that founds healthy personality development and social relationships.

Horney and Rogers bring into focus more of how selfhood is both a growth and health-oriented dimension of the personality, one that emerges from nurturant social relations. They each provided relevant data concerning how self-development can facilitate the formation of a personality with qualities like emotional stability, wholeheartedness, and overall vitality. Horney and Rogers provide a much-needed distinction between those instances when the self is being realized and actualized in accord with genuine desires and when the self is sent on a wild goose chase after a falsified, externally imposed idealized self. That is, they make an important distinction between "the real thing" and a mere facsimile when it comes to personality. Accordingly, their notions of growth and health highlight yet another paradoxical dimension of personality (already nascent in Alfred Adler's theory of the final fiction): that the genuineness of one's actual self in the present is judged against the genuineness of the not-yet-actualized self-ideal that one is pursuing.

Taking it Further: Food for Thought

Karen Horney is widely known as a pioneer of feminine psychology. Horney's perspective, while influenced by Freud, is also critical of what she considered a pervasive bias toward masculinity in psychosexual theory. She objected to the notion that the defining characteristic of female psychology was penis envy. While she did not reject the notion outright, she did insist that the phenomenon of penis envy was not the standard for understanding female psychology. The reasons for a phenomenon like penis envy are not biological, but social, economic, political, and historical. The fact is that any female child growing up in a male-dominated society can see the obvious benefits of being a male and the freedoms it affords boys (e.g., see Baumgartner & Tavris, 1983). In a social context where it pays to be male, penis envy is bound to occur, but that does not make it natural or inevitable. If anything, a close examination of male and female behavior would show that it is actually males who are far more preoccupied with possessing vaginas! Accordingly, Horney (1967) countered Freud's notion of penis envy with a kind of womb envy theory, wherein men secretly resent the female power over reproduction (the ability bear children). As a result, males compensate with an exaggerated focus on achievement, social power, and "success."

As it happens, Carl Rogers's daughter, Natalie Rogers, would eventually go on to become a humanistic pioneer of feminist psychology. As O'Hara (2016) wrote:

> Her first book, *Emerging Woman*, offers a candid and heartfelt description of the transition many women were making at that time, from a life defined by the expectations and needs of others to one that sprang from her own deep interiority. Hers was the voice of a generation of women who grew up in the claustrophobic 1950s who were expected to submerge their own potential in favor of their husbands'. (p. 561)

As you may be able to tell from the sound of this description, Natalie continued certain aspects of her father's work. While most people are aware of Carl Rogers' contributions to psychotherapy, his interest in the topics of learning and creativity are not as appreciated (e.g., see Rogers, 1969; DeRobertis, 2017). Rogers observed that creativity is most likely to occur when three "internal," psychological conditions are present: openness to experience, an internal locus of evaluation, and the ability to experiment with things and ideas. Rogers maintained that these three conditions are most likely to emerge in a social environment that promotes psychological safety and psychological freedom. Psychological safety results from a social environment that provides unconditional acceptance of one's worth, the minimization (though not the elimination) of external evaluation, and empathic understanding. Psychological freedom emerges in an environment where a person feels permitted to engage in self-expression without the fear of judgment.

Rogers's psychology of creative expression in particular has been extended by Natalie Rogers. To Carl Rogers's two contextual (environmental/social) conditions (i.e., psychological safety and psychological freedom), Natalie Rogers (1993) has added a third condition: offering the person stimulating and challenging experiences. Qualitative research on creativity supports Natalie's contribution (see DeRobertis, 2017), which illuminates the dynamic tension inherent in the creative person's efforts to operate within given situational parameters. Natalie has, moreover, brought both her father's insights and her own contributions concerning the real-world context of the creative process into the professional context of creative arts therapy. As she described it:

> Whilst the first two conditions [again, psychological safety and psychological freedom] may be viewed as providing the soil and nutrients for creativity, this third, external condition is offered by the therapist/facilitator in a more active way. The expressive therapist may offer suggestions to the client designed to stimulate and challenge. (Rogers et al., 2012, p. 35)

Together, Carl and Natalie further articulate Adler's basic insight that creativity lies at the heart of what it is to be human. To be fully human is to actualize one's creative potentials. Conversely, to live in a manner that is essentially uncreative is to be in some way alienated from oneself (Rogers et al., 2012). The actualization of one's creative potentials is a theme that will reappear in the next chapter, along with an intensified focus on the self-transcending potentials of the person to meaningfully appropriate a given life situation and find some form of fulfillment therein.

Make it Work!

Both Horney and Rogers place a lot of importance on the role of a specific kind of bonding with a primary caregiver to ensure that a child grows up with a stable sense of self-acceptance. They both see danger in the possibility of a child feeling as if certain standards have been imposed on their very acceptability wholly "from without," meaning that the caretaker lacked the proper empathic attunement to the child's individual needs in the process of advancing familial values. This is actually a controversial idea in psychology, as there are theorists (e.g., factor-analytic trait theorists) who see constitutional factors as far more important than "mothering" or childrearing. In your own experience, have you ever struggled to manage certain conditions of worth? Looking at the social conditions of your own development, does it make more sense to you that you were simply born vulnerable to these particular conditions of worth, or does it make equal or more sense that your parental relationships were "off" in certain critical ways? Is it a blend of both? Or, does it go beyond that, meaning that there are extended, complicating sociological conditions that have to be considered? As we will see in the next chapter, Viktor Frankl (1967, 1969) will call these *sociogenic* factors.

Key Concepts

Actualizing tendency
Basic anxiety
Basic confidence
Fluid self/ self-concept
Conditions of worth
Conditional positive regard
Congruent self
Female psychology
Genuine self-ideal
Idealized image/self-glorification
Image of acceptability
Incongruent self
Internal psychological conditions of creativity
Lurking hypocrisy
Moving against strategy
Moving away strategy
Moving toward strategy

Organism
Person
Real self
Search for glory
Self-actualizing tendency
Self-realization
Unconditional positive regard
We-ness
Womb envy

Chapter 11

Abraham Maslow and Viktor Frankl: The Transcending–Actualizing Personality

Abraham Maslow and Viktor Frankl come from two different branches of the third force—the humanistic, or human science, movement in psychology. Maslow is a founder (if not *the* founder) of the specifically American branch of humanistic psychology, while Frankl comes from the tradition of European existential–phenomenological psychology. This chapter presents ideas from Maslow and Frankl to introduce the reader to the transcending–actualizing personality. The word "transcending" derives from the term *self-transcendence*. The word "actualizing" derives from the term *self-actualization*. Self-actualization was previously discussed in relation to Carl Rogers's theory. This chapter brings self-transcendence into focus. It is an inherently paradoxical concept. The idea is that a person is more themselves when they are able to transcend themselves. While the seeds of this idea were already sown with the advent of Alfred Adler's Individual Psychology, Maslow and Frankl (both of whom considered Adler among their teachers) extend this line of thinking to further deepen and broaden its synoptic outlook and integrative capacity.

Abraham Maslow

Abraham Maslow (1970, 1993, 1999) constructed his personality theory by drawing upon three currents of thought: Gestalt psychology (e.g., Max Wertheimer), functionalism (e.g., William James), and psychoanalysis (e.g., Freud and Adler). From Gestalt psychology and functionalism Maslow derived the idea that a human being cannot be reduced to a collection of individual parts. The person's various organs, inclinations, and psychological capacities all work together to form a complex functional whole (Maslow, 1961). From psychoanalysis, Maslow took the idea that the functioning of the organism is dynamic, involving a wide variety of interactions between mind and body that are not always consciously understood. As a result, Maslow (1970) called his theory a *holistic–dynamic theory*.

Maslow's personality theory is grounded in a theory of motivation. Like Allport, Maslow held that the behavior of an individual has many determinants and many different kinds of needs, and thus cannot be understood on the basis of a single motive alone. Behavior may spring from many motives at once, as anyone who has been on a date knows. Something as simple as eating a meal can be a social affair as well as a biochemical affair. Moreover, Maslow proposed that the motives that govern the formation of a personality are rooted in an interactive, integrative hierarchy of needs and their accompanying motivational strivings.

Human beings have varied needs that emerge developmentally from within a loosely prioritized motivational hierarchy that can nonetheless reorganize responsively in the face of changing environmental demands. Maslow's ideas have profound developmental import (Bland & DeRobertis, 2020), though it is important to note that he did not advocate for a set of "stages" of child development. For Maslow, certain needs tend to have a global or generalized priority over others in personality functioning. When a need is satisfied, it loses its prepotent status as the primary motive and gives way to a new motive that tends to take precedence over the others. *Prepotency* is a concept that originates in evolutionary biology (recall that Maslow's theory has roots in this tradition, but in a more creative–progressive, personalistic way that deviates from the reductionistic style of David Buss, see Coonan, 2016). Contrary to popular belief, it is important to understand that Maslow's theory is in no way an all-or-nothing conceptual framework. Most people are partially satisfied and partially unsatisfied in the basic needs that Maslow discussed simultaneously. Need complexes emerge slowly and in relative overlapping degrees (Maslow, 1970). Moreover, while the satisfaction of needs generates new motivational trajectories, none of the needs that compose the hierarchy simply vanish. Well-satisfied needs simply become less potent motivational forces in the personality (Bland & DeRobertis, 2020).

In Maslow's view, there are certain needs that must be met if a human being is to be free of pathology. He called these "deficiency needs" or "basic" needs. All people everywhere share these deficiency needs. Therefore, Maslow (1970) made them the first needs in the hierarchy. Human deficiency needs consist of physiological needs, safety needs, love and belongingness needs, and esteem needs, respectively. Physiological needs are needs for food, water, oxygen, and so forth. Without the means to satisfy these needs, the organism would die. With the means to meet these needs satisfactorily secured, increased attention can be given to safety needs. The person will be motivated to seek a stable, secure environment in which to live. From here, the personality will begin to revolve increasingly around the desire for intimacy, affiliation, and affection with other human beings. Paradoxically, a strong sense of attachment, especially early in life, supports and facilitates the further actualization of one's potentials for self-regulation and a willingness to approach unfamiliar situations with curiosity and interest (Bland & DeRobertis 2020). Having achieved a satisfactory sense of love and belonging from others, the individual can confidently turn toward an interest in comprehending their intrinsic value as a person through accomplishments, achievements, and other demonstrations of competence (i.e., esteem needs). With the adequate satisfaction of physiological, safety, love and belongingness, and esteem needs, Maslow believed the individual will have avoided those threats to human health that would result in pathology as traditionally conceived. In addition, the satisfaction of these needs readies the personality for the potential satisfaction of self-actualization needs (self-actualization is not universally pursued).

When deficiency needs are not met, they lead to the development of neurotic needs (Maslow, 1970, 1999). Neurotic needs are compensatory impulses rooted in the lack of satisfaction of normal human needs. So, for example, a person who has not had their safety needs met might find themselves compelled to pursue goals designed to compensate for feelings of insecurity. A person who has not had their belongingness needs met might find themselves compelled to pursue goals designed to compensate for feelings of isolation and loneliness. There is no obvious limit to the ways in which these compensatory behaviors might manifest themselves.

Self-actualization needs are not needs in the sense of what has been discussed thus far in that unsatisfied self-actualization needs will not result in neurotic needs. It is more the case that the person will not be as fulfilled in life as they could be. Maslow referred to self-actualization needs as *meta-needs*, indicating a positive striving or desire to fulfill ideals perceived to be valuable to one's being (one's unique personality) rather than a need in the ordinary sense of an urging to satisfy some specific lack that is species-typical (Maslow, 1999). So, to cite a simple example, Maslow distinguished between *deficiency love*, or D-love, wherein one needs the other as a means to personal ends (e.g., security, esteem, etc.), and *being-love*, or B-love, wherein the other person is treated as an end with intrinsic value rather than a means of any kind. Meta-needs are also referred to as *being-values,* or *B-values.* Below is a list of fourteen common B-values.

1. Autonomy
2. Truth
3. Beauty
4. Goodness
5. Wholeness
6. Aliveness
7. Uniqueness
8. Perfection
9. Completion
10. Justice
11. Simplicity
12. Totality
13. Effortlessness
14. Humor

Meta-need satisfaction is not as orderly as deficiency need satisfaction. As you might imagine, not all optimally functioning, thriving individuals would be equally invested in each B-value. Some might be held in higher esteem than others, depending on the self-actualizing person in question. Meta-needs are the most autonomous of all the needs and they are the least stereotyped. This is because self-actualizing is a highly individualized process, yet it bears a conspicuously paradoxical quality about it, which Maslow (1999) described as follows:

> Authentic or healthy [individuals] may be defined not . . . by [their] own intrapsychic and non-environmental laws, not as different from the environment, independent of it or opposed to it, but rather in environment-centered terms. . . . Self-actualization . . . paradoxically makes *more* possible the transcendence of . . . self-consciousness and of selfishness. It makes it *easier* for [one] . . . to merge as a part in a larger whole. (pp. 199, 231)

Thus, individuals are both more externalized and ego-centered at the lower end of the needs hierarchy, whereas at the higher end they are both guided by more idiosyncratic/intrinsic aims and more self-transcendent (Bland & DeRobertis, 2020).

According to Maslow (1970, 1993, 1999), there are a number of traits that are more common among self-actualizing people than non-self-actualizing people. Fifteen of the traits identified by Maslow are broken down below under their typical category headings comprised of awareness, honesty, freedom, and trust.

Awareness
1. Penetrating perception of reality
2. Freshness of appreciation (wonder, awe)
3. Higher likelihood of intense "peak experiences" of fulfillment
4. The ability to discriminate between means and ends

Honesty
5. Social interest (as described by Alfred Adler)
6. Humility, and respect, ethics (profound interpersonal relations)
7. Democratic character
8. A non-hostile sense of humor

Freedom
9. Spontaneity
10. Need for solitude
11. Autonomy
12. Creativity

Trust
13. Acceptance of self, others, and nature
14. Problem-centeredness (rather than ego-centered)
15. Resistance to blind enculturation

However, one of the more important things to bear in mind about Maslow's research on self-actualizing persons is that his results can never be understood on the basis of a mere summative list of strengths, virtues, meta-needs, values, and so forth. To make this error would inevitably result in a superficial misunderstanding of the self-actualizing orientation to life, which is a highly paradoxical Gestalt. Maslow's study of self-actualized persons often leads to seemingly contradictory conclusions which, if translated into a mere list of items, would appear to lack internal consistency. So, for example, Maslow had learned that self-actualizing people are more attuned to both the good and the bad in themselves, others, and the world than non-self-actualizing people. At one moment (depending on the real-life context), the self-actualizing person may appear extraordinarily resilient and positive but at other moments appear so anguished and disappointed that other people perceive them to be a walking contradiction. This has prompted Winston (2016, 2018) to note that Maslow's concept of psychological health is bound to be misrepresented and misinterpreted when approached linearly. Self-actualizers are not contradictions; they are expert paradox negotiators. Note, however, that "negotiation" in this context does not refer to the merely adaptive quality of living in moderation. Rather, expert paradox negotiation denotes an outstanding integrative ability that is creative in nature. As Winston (2018) so aptly put it:

> Self-actualizers' integration of polarities, however, does not imply that they are a lukewarm average of polarities. Instead, they are both hot and cold. They do not belong at the center of the normal distribution curve; they belong at both ends. (p. 167).

Self-actualizers are at once more childlike in their wonder and appreciation of life and the most somber or "adult" in their sense of personal responsibility for the way they engage their social and natural environments. Pfaffenberger (2007) has made similar observations of Maslow's view of health, noting:

> [Rollo] May (1958) and Maslow (1954/1970) consider maturity as being associated with greater complexity and the ability to tolerate paradox. Growth is not necessarily seen as being easy; individuals may have to leave comfortable, familiar circumstances behind to embrace a new reality and express their potential. Both theorists emphasized the dynamic aspects of maturity; it is a process of becoming . . . . (pp. 507–508)

It is equally important to note that Maslow's theory is not a trait theory. Self-actualization is not a mere accumulation of various psychological characteristics. Self-actualization is a lifestyle, a perpetual work in progress, and not an end state (Maslow, 1999). A personality can never be said to be self-actualized "once and for all," so to speak. Self-actualization entails living life to one's full potential, being oneself, and pursuing one's ideals irrespective of what anyone else expects or demands. Self-actualizing people have an insatiable appetite for life, for learning, and for becoming exactly who they feel they ought to become. While this may sound appealing, Maslow believed that it is not easy to come by. Throughout life, people are faced with family expectations, peer pressure, and societal demands to conform and obey. Achieving great things is often met with jealousy, even by people once thought to be friends. Thus, people do not automatically move on to the last level of the hierarchy.

Fortunately, unmet meta-needs (i.e., unfulfilled B-values) do not result in the emergence of neurotic needs. But unmet meta-needs can result in *meta-pathology*, or emotional distress resulting from the absence of meaning and fulfillment in life. One form of meta-pathology is called the Jonah complex or the evasion of growth (Maslow, 1993). This represents the fear of being one's best, if for no other reason than the envy, jealousy, and hostility one encounters from others when living life to one's fullest potential. The Jonah complex can also be elicited by the fear of the intense emotionality (e.g., the ecstatic joy) that comes with being one's best. Another form of meta-pathology is *desacralization*, which refers to the loss of a sense of the important, the precious, and the special due to a deep sense of social disillusionment and a pervasive mistrust of values and virtues (Maslow, 1993).

Having realized that it can be difficult to lead a self-actualizing lifestyle, Maslow specified certain ways that people move toward embracing B-values and addressing their meta-needs. What follows is a sample of these transitional phenomena.

- Experiencing things, events, situations, and others with full absorption, vividly, and selflessly
- Choosing growth opportunities rather than habitually opting for adaptive functioning or maintaining present securities
- Becoming self-aware
- Being honest
- Learning to trust one's judgment and one's ability to make good life choices
- Working at doing things with excellence and mastery
- Abandoning and avoiding egoic defensiveness
- Relishing in (rather than retreating from) peak and plateau experiences.

Of the items presented above, peak and plateau experiences have special import for Maslow's mature theory of personality (Maslow, 1993).

Peak experiences are moments of self-actualization wherein the person feels more whole, more integrated, and more aware of themselves and the world. They experience unprecedented clarity of thought and feeling as well as a loving acceptance of others. These periods can be highly constructive and highly creative as well. Plateau experiences are similar to peak moments but have a more enduring character, as if the person has learned to live life in general in the aura of the transcendent vision characteristic of the peak experience. Gruel (2015) explained this as follows:

> Prior to his plateau experience, Maslow had stated, "The greatest attainment of identity, autonomy, or self-hood is itself, a going beyond and above selfhood" .... His plateau experience appears to have provided a deeper embodied understanding of this ultimate existential paradox that he spent the final months of his life seeking to philosophically apprehend. (p. 44)

The reader versed in mystical or Eastern spiritual traditions will likely find the language of peak and plateau experiences vaguely familiar. With these insights, Maslow was pointing to the possibility of a future psychology called *fourth force* or *transpersonal psychology* designed to handle the self-transcendent, spiritual aspects of human psychology. Transpersonal experiences are those wherein an individual's sense of self extends beyond the individual and integrates with a wider, more comprehensive reality. Since some self-actualizing individuals appear to be more open to transpersonal experience than others, Maslow made a distinction between pragmatic self-actualizers and transcending self-actualizers. The latter group, he believed, had a more profound sense of humility and a deeper appreciation for the sacred, the ambiguous, the awe-inspiring, and the mystical or transcendental (Maslow, 1993).

Viktor E. Frankl

Viktor E. Frankl was an Austrian psychoanalytic psychiatrist who came under the influence of two currents of thought that originated in philosophy: existentialism and phenomenology. Existentialism began as a reaction against what was perceived to be a pervasive bias toward abstract, hyperrational thinking in Western culture. Søren Kierkegaard

(1954, 1962), who is thought to be a modern founder of the movement, insisted that philosophers focus more of their efforts on understanding those things that matter the most to human beings: their decisions in life. From an existential point of view, life is in large part a series of impassioned decisions that a person must make. The message is not to mistake existence itself for thoughts about or theories of existence. Do not identify life itself with intellect or reason alone, because it is routinely far more complex and ambiguous than sterile logic can comprehend. *Phenomenology*, in Frankl's works, refers to a qualitative method of data collection created by the German philosopher Edmund Husserl (1977, 1999). A phenomenological approach to research in psychology involves inquiring as to the meaning and qualitive structure of human behavior (including mental processes) as experienced first-hand by the individuals under study. A phenomenologist would not begin research on depression, for instance, by making the assumption that the condition is nothing but the side-effect of an anonymous neurological irregularity. Rather, a phenomenological approach to data collection would begin by asking what "being depressed" is (what it means) for the depressed person, including a faithful description of how it structures or shapes their efforts to live and cope in the world with the condition on a daily basis.

Frankl (1967, 1969, 1978, 1986, 2006) ingeniously combined these two traditions of thought by creating an approach to personality that focuses on the uniquely human search for meaning in life. Frankl joined the existential focus on life decisions and the phenomenological focus on meaning to create a view of personality that envisions human beings as creatures who thrive on discovering opportunities for creating a meaningful existence. Thus, the relative/situated freedom of the will, commitment and responsibility, and the feeling of purpose all play a central role in Frankl's thought.

According to Frankl (1967, 1969), personality development is stratified, with formative influences emanating from at least four different points of origin. As a psychiatrist, Frankl held that there are *endogenic* factors (meaning organic forces within a system) involved in personality formation, referring to the kinds of life-shaping influences discussed in biology (e.g., evolution, genetics, biology, anatomy and physiology, endocrinology, biochemistry, and so forth). As a psychiatrist trained in Freudian and Adlerian versions of psychoanalysis, Frankl also held that personality is subject to the influences of *psychogenic* and *sociogenic* forces as well. Psychogenic factors are those most commonly studied and discussed in the context of developmentally oriented psychology and the psychology of individual functioning in general, while sociogenic factors are those most closely associated with social psychological, sociological, and cultural-anthropological research. For Frankl, the fourth set of formative life influences comes from the mind of the individual themself, envisioned as irreducible to the other dimensions of the personality system. This resulted from his philosophical training in existential phenomenology. Here, Frankl spoke of a *noögenic* aspect of the personality. The individual human being is a creative influence in their own right in the unfolding of their personality formation, particularly by way of the fact that interpretive meaning-making is required for personality formation. Frankl referred to this as the "spiritual" aspect of personality, which he considered to be a dimension of meaning. The endogenic, psychogenic, sociogenic, and noögenic aspects of the personality form an integrative system or Gestalt, a *unitas multiplex* (recall this term from William Stern, though Frankl traces the concept back to the philosophy of St. Thomas Aquinas, see Frankl, 1969). All aspects are intertwined and interdependent, yet no aspect is reducible to another.

Like Maslow, Frankl's (2006) approach to personality is rooted in a theory of motivation. Individual personalities may be more or less mature depending on the motives that characteristically underlie their decision making and life goals. According to Frankl, human beings seek to satisfy three kinds of motives in life: *the will-to-pleasure*, the *will-to-power*, and the *will-to-meaning*. As Freud, Skinner, and many other psychologists have noted numerous times, human beings seem to be naturally drawn toward the attainment of physical pleasure. Inasmuch as this plays a formative role in the development of a personality, Frankl referred to this as a person's will-to-pleasure. In addition, human beings want to feel empowered in life. They want to feel competent, strong, and independent. Hence, a young child might exclaim, "I'm three *and a half*," while an adolescent might try cigarettes in order to look more mature. This is the person's will-to-power at work. These are the motivational strata that dominate traditional, mainstream psychology. However, for Frankl, personality development need not stop here. Frankl considered a genuinely mature, optimally functioning, and resilient personality to be motivated by the will to meaning, which he considered to be a self-transcending tendency. People motivated by the will-to-meaning are not focused on the attainment of pleasure or power. Rather, their primary aim is to devote themselves to the welfare of something or someone outside themselves (relate this to William Stern's *heterotelie*, but with more emphasis specifically on the dimension of life meaning). Self-transcendence is thus a value-rich orientation toward life.

Frankl's emphasis on self-transcendence places paradox at the center of his entire approach. His basic understanding of what it means to be human is a kind of transparency of self:

> Consider the eye, an analogy I am fond of invoking. When, apart from looking in a mirror, does the eye see anything of itself? An eye with a cataract may see something like a cloud, which is its cataract; an eye with glaucoma may see its glaucoma as a rainbow halo around the lights. A healthy eye sees nothing of itself – it is self-transcendent. (Frankl, 1978, pp. 38–39)

To illustrate his viewpoint in terms of concrete behavior, he reminds his readers of the crippling nature of self-consciousness when, for example, someone is attempting to engage in a performance task. Imagine being at bat, but then being self-conscious that people are staring at you. Self-consciousness as reflectiveness is typically lauded as a good quality, and it is. But it makes us forgetful of everyday embodied activity and how the default state of consciousness is an intentional directedness away from itself. It is only through this directedness that consciousness could ever become informed, robust, and operational in allowing for the possibility of rich inner lives (the theme of intentional directedness will come up again when we discuss Rollo May's theory).

Armed with this insight, Frankl took to the clinic and used his self-transcendent orientation to create an approach to psychotherapeutic intervention. He devised a style of doing meaning-focused therapy called *logotherapy*, the aim of which was to help clients connect to a more self-transcendent lifestyle (Frankl translated the Greek word *logos* as "meaning"). He is perhaps most famously known for the techniques of *paradoxical intention* and *dereflection* (Frankl, 1978). Where a patient appears to be held in the grip of a self-defeating cycle of anxiety and inner turmoil, Frankl employed paradoxical intention to loosen the person from this grip and return them to the ability to engage the world in a poised, competent manner. As he described it:

> To understand how paradoxical intention works, take as a starting point the mechanism called anticipatory anxiety: a given symptom evokes on the part of the patient the fearful expectation that it might recur. Fear, however, always tends to

bring about precisely that which is feared, and by the same token, anticipatory anxiety is liable and likely to trigger off what the patient so fearfully expects to happen. Thus a self-sustaining vicious circle is established . . . . How then is it possible to break up such [a] feedback mechanism? And to begin with, how can we take the wind out of the individual fears of our patients? Well, this is precisely the business to accomplish by paradoxical intention, which may be defined as a process by which the patient is encouraged to do, or to wish to happen, the very thing he [*sic*] fears . . . The pathogenic fear now is replaced by a paradoxical wish. The vicious circle of anticipatory anxiety is now unhinged. (Frankl, 1978, pp. 130, 133–134)

Similar results are achieved by the use of dereflection, where a cycle of anxiety that prevents optimal performance is broken by redirecting the patient's attention outward to its intended objects rather than being focused on their own striving, efforts, or desire. Here, to "heal" the patient entails working with them to see self-concern dethroned by *self-commitment*.

Logotherapy is not mere a set of techniques, however. It is an entire approach that is focused on the aim of self-transcendence as a meaning-centered way of living. According to Frankl (2006), life can be made meaningful by three broad means. First, one can create works or do good deeds. Second, one can experience something or encounter someone lovingly. By love, Frankl means the impetus to enable the beloved person to actualize their potentials. Finally, one can take a meaning-oriented attitude toward life's unavoidable times of pain and sorrow. Frankl's approach to personality reminds us that we all need a reason to get up in the morning and persevere through the hard times. He considered the will-to-meaning to be a wellspring of strength in the face of adversity. People are capable of enduring unimaginable suffering, Frankl (2006) noted, when they believe that the suffering has a meaning or value. Thus, as a therapeutic recommendation, Frankl always admonished that the patient take a creative attitude toward unavoidable suffering to make it meaningful. In fact, it was partially due to his contact with Frankl that Maslow began to increasingly include an emphasis on transcending motives in his characterizations of self-actualizing people.

At the same time, it is worthwhile to note that Viktor Frankl added a measure of controversy to the humanistic movement with his particular introduction of a self-transcendent will-to-meaning in personality. Viktor Frankl was once a prisoner of war and spent time in Nazi concentration camps. During his time in the camps, Frankl observed that there were people who crumbled like a Maslowian house of cards upon the denial of their basic needs. The personalities of these individuals seemed to be driven by lower, deficiency needs in day-to-day behavior. Yet there were people in the camps who were able to tap into strengths that they would have never discovered about themselves were it not for the adversity that they had come to endure. These individuals (and he counted himself among them) did not seem to move down the hierarchy. Rather, Frankl believed that a different kind of motive had strengthened these individuals and provided resistance to their adversity, a motive that he felt Maslow did not articulate clearly, forcefully, or thoroughly enough in his early writings on the hierarchy (Frankl, 1967, 1969). Frankl considered this motive to be the self-transcendent will-to-meaning. People who were able to focus their attention on a commitment to something or someone other than themselves, something or someone meaningful that needed their devotion, were provided a reason to persevere. Frankl had much faith in the possibility of appealing to a person in a meaning-focused cognitive manner to make alterations in a personality structure, potentially making radical changes to the hierarchy in any given circumstance.

Having said this, Frankl regularly qualified his criticisms of Maslow. He insisted that it is only to the extent that a person has fulfilled the meaning of their existence that they will also have fulfilled themselves, and that this "is in no way contradictory to the theory of self-actualization as presented by Abraham Maslow" (Frankl, 1967, p. 54). Frankl simply maintained that self-actualization is the result of a self-transcending orientation rather than "the other way around." Human potential is best tapped through an outward-focused attention to things, others, events, situations, projects, and relationships that are perceived to be meaningful or valuable. To unlock potentials, one must prioritize devotion to something other than one's own self-actualization. If one looks at Maslow's characterization of self-actualization, one will note that he was careful to emphasize things like social interest, problem-centeredness, acceptance of others, and the like. Maslow's account of the self-actualization process was never devoid of a self-transcendent aspect, and as his theory matured it became increasingly pronounced. Moreover, Maslow (1970) did allow for exceptions to his hierarchy.

In the end, this theoretical battle amounted to a lover's quarrel and a difference in emphasis at best. What is important to learn from this debate is that humanistic psychology is not a self-centered tradition of thought, as some contemporary currents of "positive" psychology have suggested. Quite the contrary, Frankl (1967, 1969, 1978) saw the self-transcendent aspects of human personality as a guard against the dangers of subjectivism and pure relativism. As he noted, popular writers calling themselves existentialists sometimes neglect the relative objectivity of human meaning and value. These writers, he held, repeat ad nauseam that personality must be understood on the basis of being-in-the-world, but forget to mention that meaning is also in-the-world and is thus not a merely personal, merely subjective aspect of reality. Meaning is more than self-expression or a projection of the self onto or into a world of dead matter, and this is a message that most positive psychologists have yet to process

In recognizing the need to preserve the integrity and "otherness" of meaning in its own right, Frankl was sensitive to the call of responsibility that comes from respecting differences. As he put it, if meanings and values were just something emerging from a "subject" rather than something stemming from a sphere beyond *and* above the individual, then they would instantly lose their *demand quality*. This bears a direct relationship to the interpersonal, ethical, and moral aspects of personality formation. For Frankl, self-transcendence is equally implied whether a person transcends through general meaning fulfillment or through loving encounter where an expressly interpersonal meaning is fulfilled. Loving a person reveals their essential uniqueness, which is a core aspect of both personhood and personality according to Frankl.

Similar to Maslow, Frankl believed that there can be deleterious consequences for not satisfying higher human needs. If a person lacks or has lost a sense of meaning in life, this will give rise to what Frankl (1967) called *noögenic neurosis*, by which he referred to the emotional distress and dysfunction that result from a lack or loss of meaning-in-life (i.e., an unfulfilled will-to-meaning). For Frankl, the movement toward a self-transcending orientation is a natural process in human personality formation. When this tendency is blocked for some reason, a painful form of self-consciousness can result. This sort of self-consciousness can manifest itself in many forms, such as feelings of anxiety, chronic boredom, depressive states, and compulsive behaviors. In all instances, the individual is focused on their own discomfort rather than on the things and people around them that would otherwise bring happiness into their lives. For Frankl, this is the hidden meaning behind Freud's now famous claim that the aim of therapy is to return a person to their capacity for love and work.

In effect, whereas Maslow's use of the term self-transcendence tended to have the connotation of an exceptional state of consciousness (more likely of a self-transcending self-actualizer), Frankl saw self-transcendence as pervasive throughout day-to-day living as well. When Frankl referred to the search for life meanings embedded within the fabric of daily existence, he spoke of a *secular logos*. When he referred to the search for higher, more sacred or religious sorts of life meanings (i.e., something a bit more akin to Maslow's peak experiences), Frankl spoke of an *eternal logos*. But, in the end, this was more of a superficial difference in linguistic style between Frankl and Maslow. Maslow (1961) also used the term *transcendence* to refer to the more mundane fact that human living cannot be adequately understood as a mere adjustment to external conditions, as has been mentioned repeatedly throughout this text.

Reflection

With Maslow and Frankl, personality theorizing becomes more motivationally well-rounded. For Maslow, self-development and personality formation are motivated by physiological, safety, love and belongingness, esteem, and self-actualization needs. Frankl considered the will-to-pleasure to be roughly equivalent to what one finds in Freud's psychosexual theory, which would make it a parallel to Maslow's physiological needs. Frankl's will-to-power referred to the individual's striving for strength, competence, and self-enhancement, which is well represented by Maslow's other needs, like safety, belonging, and esteem needs. Frankl's most original contribution came in the form of the self-transcendent will-to-meaning, which is also represented in Maslow's mature theory. Maslow and Frankl each made original contributions to the notion of self-transcendence in human personality.

Maslow and Frankl leave the early developmental periods of human becoming and concentrate on the more advanced stages of personality formation. In their respective emphases on the transcending–actualizing aspects of personality, both Maslow and Frankl highlight a realm of human existence that is highly paradoxical. The transcending–actualizing aspects of personality are the ultimate expressions of individuality, yet Maslow and Frankl also considered them to be universal needs among human beings rather than merely individualistic. In the absence of their satisfaction, one is at risk for diverse forms of meta-pathology, to borrow Maslow's term.

With their respective emphases on the self-transcendent dimension, Maslow and Frankl bring the transpersonal in personality formation into focus. First used by William James, the term *transpersonal* is used here to refer to that which occurs through, across, and beyond the individual person. This theme will take center stage in the next chapter on Carl Jung, who spoke of things like the collective unconscious and archetypes. From this view, the strict individuality of the person as a standalone ego is an illusion, as it is always a kind of participatory engagement occurring within a wider contextual reality. This idea had been steadily developing since the chapter on George Kelly's personal construct theory, but with Maslow and Frankl it has come into relief. By their particular transcendent orientations, Maslow and Frankl bring us into contact with the myriad diversifying, differentiational potentials that can nurture the integrative process. In doing so, they orient personality theory toward limitless vistas of meaningful world-relatedness and optimal states of fulfillment. Yet, their views maintain a macro-integrative imperative that systematically rejects exclusionary thinking. The personality, as *unitas multiplex*, is now embraced as a bio-psycho-social-spiritual Gestalt.

Taking it Further: Food for Thought

Maslow has seen a prolonged period of professional criticism based on misunderstandings of his theory. There seems to be a never-ending desire to take up Maslow's hierarchy as the whole of his personality theory and, moreover, to oversimplify the hierarchy as linear and unidirectional, as involving an all-or-nothing need satisfaction process, as impervious to cultural diversity, and even as implying that the goal of human growth is to become some sort of Nietzschean superman. In striking contrast to this trend, Bland and DeRobertis (2020) have shown how Maslow's thought has been unwittingly and vicariously supported by various lines of research within the area of lifespan development for years. In the process, Bland and DeRobertis highlighted a number of Maslowian principles that are usually overlooked in the process of oversimplifying his viewpoint.

For example, with regard to physiological needs, Maslow (1970; Maslow & Mittelmann, 1951) also noted that healthy growth and development involves not only gratification of the basic needs but also the ability to withstand reasonable deprivation. Safety needs, which have been confirmed over and over again in the areas of attachment theory and parenting styles, are also more complicated than is usually acknowledged. To illustrate, Maslow (1999) suggested:

> It is necessary in order for children to grow well that adults have enough trust in them . . . [to] not interfere too much, not *make* them grow, or force them into predetermined designs, but rather *let* them grow and *help* them grow in a Taoistic rather than an authoritarian way. (p. 219)

Similar things can be said of love and belongingness needs. Maslow (1970) conceptualized love needs as "giving *and* receiving affection" without which one "will hunger for relations with people in general—for a place in the group or family—[because] the pangs of loneliness, ostracism, rejection, friendlessness, and rootlessness are preeminent" (pp. 20–21).

Esteem needs, which are almost always cast in an exclusively self-serving manner, appear different when one reads all of Maslow rather than selected parts of his texts. What is regularly missing is the distinction between the deficiency aspects of esteem (i.e., D-esteem) and its prosocial dimensions (i.e., B-esteem). B-esteem is more decidedly transactional, interpersonal, and conducive to the more self-transcending orientation that typifies the transition to a self-actualizing lifestyle. Finally, far from implying a superman, "Self-actualization does not mean a transcendence of all human problems. Conflict, anxiety, frustration, sadness, hurt, and guilt all can be found in healthy human beings" (Maslow, 1999). According to Bland and DeRobertis (2020):

> Maslow's description of self-actualizing people is consistent with R. Walsh's (2015) conceptualization of *wisdom*, which involves the following: (a) people's abilities to "more deeply and accurately . . . see into themselves, reality, and [their] existential challenges and limitations" and to embrace "ethicality and benevolence [as] appropriate ways to live"; (b) the motivation to benefit others; and (c) operating on the awareness that "the deeper the kind of benefits they can offer . . . the more skillfully they may offer them (p. 289)." (p. 947)

One might further add that this description is not unlike certain descriptions of self-realization as found in the works of Carl Jung, to whom we turn next.

Make it Work!

Frankl (2006) once noted that there is a kind of malaise, even depression, that befalls some people when the rush of a busy week is over. Their minds left idle, people suddenly become aware that there is a void or existential vacuum in need of filling. They see that they have been habitually preventing themselves from making life meaningful by distracting themselves with the myriad tasks of day-to-day functioning. Borrowing from the psychoanalytic psychologist Sandor Ferenczi (2013), Frankl called this *Sunday neurosis*. Sunday neurosis does not have to happen on Sundays, of course. Consider how down time has affected you in any given situation. Have you ever experienced anything like Sunday neurosis? Sunday neurosis is a kind of wakeup call. How have you responded? Did you hear the call?

Key Concepts

Being
Being-love
Being-values or b-values
Bio-psycho-social-spiritual gestalt
Deficiency love or d-love
Deficiency needs
Dereflection
Desacralization
Endogenic
Esteem needs
Eternal logos
Existential vacuum
Existentialism
Hierarchy of needs
Holistic–dynamic theory
Jonah complex
Logos
Logotherapy
Love and belongingness needs
Meta-needs

Meta-pathology
Noögenic
Noögenic neurosis
Paradox negotiation
Paradoxical intention
Peak experience
Phenomenology
Physiological needs
Plateau experience
Pragmatic self-actualizers
Prepotency
Psychogenic
Reasonable deprivation
Safety needs
Secular logos
Self-actualization
Self-actualization needs
Self-transcendence
Sociogenic
Sunday neurosis
Transcending self-actualizers
Transpersonal psychology
Will-to-meaning
Will-to-pleasure
Will-to-power

Part IV

Macro-Integrational Theorizing: Spanning the Horizons of the Irreducible Relationality

Chapter 12

Carl Jung: The Ancestrally Nested Transcending Personality

Next to Sigmund Freud, Carl Jung is arguably the most famous psychoanalyst who ever lived. Jung's school of thought is called *analytic psychology*. Like Alfred Alder, Jung believed humans to be motivated by both past events and future goals. In contrast to Freudian determinism, Jung maintained that humans constantly develop and achieve a more balanced, more complete form of personality. Unlike Freud, Jung was not a reductionist in his interpretation of the past or the unconscious. Themes revolving around unfulfilled desires and aggression do not have universal priority in the Jungian view of the unconscious. The unconscious may just as easily be seen as a great reservoir of untapped potential for growth.

Jung (1961, 1964) created a personality theory that utilized some basic Freudian concepts, but he altered their meanings to suit his own viewpoint. The ego, for example, is a rational structure of the personality for Jung, just as it was for Freud. However, there is a stricter identification of the ego with the conscious mind in Jung's work. For Jung, the ego is the very center of the conscious mind.

In Jung's work, the unconscious now has two meanings: There is a personal unconscious and a collective unconscious. The personal unconscious resides just below the conscious mind and occupies a place like Freud's preconscious mind. For Jung, there is more mutual interaction between the conscious mind and the unconscious than what one finds in Freud's theory. The personal unconscious houses what Jung (1961) called *complexes*. A complex is a dense cluster or node of emotionally charged images, ideas, values, and memories that occupies somewhat larger than average space in the mind of the individual. A complex refers to any aspect of psychological functioning that has far-reaching associations with the rest of one's psychology. Complexes color more of who a person is than other aspects of psychological life. So, for example, it would be quite natural for one's cognitive functioning to involve more connections to one's maternal relations than say one's favorite food. Jung would thus expect a person to display a mother complex, and that would be normal. In everyday language, we have become accustomed to thinking that anything identified as a complex is pathological. This strict identification of complexes with pathology is not present in Jung's work, though he did believe it was possible for any complex to over-inflate in terms of its overall significance and take on a pathological character. In other words, it would be normal to have a mother complex; however, it would not be normal for one's mother complex to become so exaggerated that one's life decisions are habitually and compulsively tied to images of one's mother. Since complexes are in the personal unconscious, the person is typically only vaguely aware of their existence, but they can become more aware of them with the right kind of effort or assistance.

For Jung, a complex can be the result of personal experiences. Thus, a person could have a pathological complex about the size of their nose from personal experiences of being teased at school. However, Jung believed that some complexes, like the aforementioned mother complex, are actually the combined result of personal experiences and the collective experiences of many human beings over the course of our development as a species. So, here we see a novel, creative return to the importance of evolution. Any experience that is powerful and universal to being human is in contention for having created the prototype for a complex. Since all people everywhere have formed in the womb of a mother and been "mothered" by someone, it makes sense to Jung that there should be a mother complex. At this point, Jung asserted that there must be a level of unconscious functioning that is deeper and more mysterious than Freud ever suspected. There must be a level of mental functioning that is tied to the collective experiences inherent in our evolutionary history, which Jung called the *collective unconscious*.

The collective unconscious houses the prototypes of species-wide complexes, which Jung (1961, 1964) called *archetypes*. An archetype is an archaic impression that is emotionally charged and inclined to incite arousal, action, or forms of experience in a member of a species. Archetypes are not innate ideas, but rather innate tendencies to react holistically in a particular way to certain kinds of phenomena. They are powerful, implicit racial memories, not in the sense of bearing all the details of past experiences but in their essential meaning or core sense. Archetypes are emotionally charged iconic images rooted in our ancestral past that predispose us to perceive and behave in more or less species-typical ways. They operate like a lived, implicit, non-conceptual background knowledge that provides the substructure for the eventual development of higher forms of understanding. The core sense (not the final product in all its detail) is similar for people in all cultures, whereas the final product is culture specific. Thus, archetypal research has to engage in interpretations of cross-cultural forms of expression, especially in its highly symbolic forms, sometimes referred to as a kind of hermeneutic research.

An archetype is vaguely similar to a universal human instinct or drive, but it is more psychological than biological in nature. Archetypes are responsible for the many myths, legends, and spiritual and religious beliefs that human beings have created. They represent the universal imagery that you find repeatedly reemerging in great literary texts, enduring political documents, seemingly timeless movies, plays, musical lyrics, and so forth. Staying with the example of one's mother, it was Jung's belief that the intense joy or reverence (or hatred) that a person has for the image of their mother is not explained on the basis of personal experiences alone, but on the fact that throughout history people have experienced their mothers as protectors who can nonetheless punish, hurt, or destroy them. Accordingly, the age-old mother image or *great mother archetype* is a frequently appearing cultural symbol. Think of phrases such as "mother earth," "mother ship," and religious images of "the Madonna" and of goddesses.

At first these reaction patterns are not very vivid or clear, but over time as they are repeatedly associated with certain iconic images (rather than just unreflective reactions), they become more identifiable and qualify as full-fledged archetypes. Archetypes represent the common ground that psychologically binds us together as members of the same species. In the Jungian world, they are the most important contextualizing dimension of psychological life, founding and explaining why diverse and seemingly dissimilar humans can identify with one another in a deep and profound manner. Archetypes are the deepest aspects of the mind and the most difficult to comprehend. In fact, Jung (1969) recommended reading Christian mysticism and Indian philosophy as preparation for archetypal discourse.

When a personal experience corresponds to an archaic, ancestral impression, an archetype is "activated." The archetype cannot be directly represented by the intellect; it can only be activated. Thus, only a handful of archetypes have evolved to the point where they can be clearly conceptualized. This is not the stuff of standard issue logical discourse, which is the purview of the ego. Linear, logical thinking falls short of being able to think archetypally, if for no other reason than archetypes are fundamentally paradoxical in nature. As we will see momentarily, they always involve antinomies that give rise to contrasting, dialectically shifting, oscillating meanings and images. In Jung's (1964) words, "The unconscious can only be approximately described (like the particles of microphysics) by paradoxical concepts. What it really is 'in itself' we shall never know, just as we shall never know this about matter" (p. 383). Moreover, not only does every archetype tend to evoke another archetype embodying a contrasting theme, but each archetype itself can manifest in contrasting ways. To use Jungian terminology, every archetype has its shadow (Jung, 1964). This intense complexity explains why things like dreams, fantasies, and delusions are so problematic and confusing for the logical, linear, analytical mind. For Jung, archetypes express themselves most forcefully through dreams, fantasies, and delusions. Dreams were Jung's (1964) favorite hunting ground for archetypes. He found that in dreams we envision motifs that often coincide with scenes and ideas that were important to and illustrated by ancient peoples in their cultural forms of expression.

Archetypes, appearing in opposing pairs, represent both contrasting tendencies and potentials inherent in human psychological life. Jung (1964) sometimes refers to them as *paradoxical personifications*. So, for example, Jung (1961, 1964) considered the human psyche to have both a masculine and a feminine nature. This is universal and present throughout our evolutionary history as constitutionally bisexual organisms. Human beings have both masculine and feminine characteristics embedded within their biology (e.g., men still have nipples but produce no breast milk). Men and women have always had to relate to each other and achieve some kind of mutual understanding. Thus, Jung believed that there is a masculine aspect present in the female psyche, which he called the *animus*. Conversely, there is a feminine aspect within the male psyche, called the *anima*. The animus represents the rational, pragmatic tendency in humans, whereas the anima represents the more emotional, empathic, caring side of humans. His ideal vision of healthy human functioning involves striking a functional balance between these two tendencies. For instance, a male who represses and denies his feminine side altogether might be inordinately cold, possibly aggressive, yet deeply insecure about his sexuality. On the other hand, over-identification with the feminine aspects of the psyche might make for an emotionally unstable male who may also display insecurities about gender or sexual identity. What the personality needs in both instances is a workable balance and harmony. Below is a list of some of the other, more commonly identified archetypes.

- *Persona*: The profile of the personality that people show to the world, which tends to abide by social norms. The persona does not represent the whole personality and should not be mistaken for the Self.
- *Shadow*: The deviant, dark side of the personality, which is more likely to be seen as morally objectionable. The shadow side of the personality can nonetheless house constructive and creative potentials that we might be reluctant to face.
- *Great Mother*: The archetype associated with both the positive and negative feelings related to mothering (i.e., both nourishment and the power of reprimand).
- *Wise Old Man (Senex, Sage, or Sophos)*: The striving for wisdom and meaning-in-life, the wise old man symbolizes our innate sense of the mysteries of life. Politicians and those who speak authoritatively in order to sound sensible and be influential try to access this archetype.
- *Puer Aeternus*: The eternal boy in us all.
- *Trickster*: Sometimes identified with the *Puer* archetype, the trickster represents the impulse to disobey rules and contradict conventional behavior. The trickster can be a villain (e.g., The Trickster in The Flash comics, The Joker in the Batman comics), but since this personification can sometimes incite humor, the trickster can be depicted as a buffoon, jester, joker, or clown. The trickster can act as a catalyst for positive change or simply become a villain.
- *Hero*: The part of the personality that fights against the odds to vanquish an enemy of mankind and overcome darkness, evil, and so forth.

When viewing this list, bear in mind that Persona and Shadow are applied across archetypes, complexifying the psyche exponentially. The Great Mother has a Shadow in the image of a witch or evil stepmother. The Wise Old Man has a Shadow in the jaded, rigid old man stuck in his ways. The Trickster, as noted above, can be a buffoon or a villain. Heroes have their flaws and dark sides as well, if they dare recognize it, and if they cannot muster up that humility, it increases the likelihood of their undoing.

Because Jung saw such diversity within the human psyche, he believed that human health is dependent upon psychic balance and harmony. Jung's (1961) emphasis on balance can be seen in his characterization of other personality structures, such as character orientations and psychological functions. Human personalities display two opposing character orientations: introversion and extraversion. Introverts have a bias to turn inward to one's own flow of experience, whereas extraverts tend to turn outward toward interactions with other people and the world at large. Psychological functions comprise two sets of opposites: thinking and feeling, sensing and intuiting. Thinkers rely on passionless intellectual analysis to adapt to the world, whereas feeling people tend to rely more heavily on emotionally colored conviction and value judgments. Sensing people adapt to their surroundings by relying on sense perception. They need to see it with their own eyes to believe it. Intuitive people go beyond what is present to the senses and rely on gut feelings or hunches. In Jung's view, sensation tells you that something exists, thinking tells you what it is, feeling tells you whether it is agreeable, and intuition tells you both where it comes from and where it is going. Together, character orientations and psychological functions combine to make psychological types. There are eight types found in Jung's works: extraverted thinking, introverted thinking, extraverted feeling, introverted feeling, extraverted sensing, introverted sensing, extraverted intuiting, and introverted intuiting.

Jung (1961, 1964) believed that each archetype, character orientation, and psychological function is capable of playing a growth-oriented role in human personality when engaged in a balanced manner. Since there are people who achieve a healthy, balanced lifestyle in the world, Jung needed to identify some aspect of the personality associated with the achievement of order and the growth potential of the personality. As is to be expected, he found the psychic tendency toward balance and harmony in an archetype, which he called the Self (Jung, 1980). The Self is the innate tendency to move toward growth, balance, completion, and "perfection." According to Jung (1969), the child image is often the iconic representation of the Self archetype because the Self is a wholeness that transcends consciousness, ordinarily conceived as a kind of rationalized awareness. The child, like the Self, is a kind of receptive flowing into an unknown future fit with dangers and potentials. The way Jung described it, the child image appears paradoxical in the sense that their particular life potentials are seen as already existing, yet they are simultaneously in the process of being put together or synthesized. For Jung, the image is both invincible and powerless unto itself, going beyond what adults can fathom on a logical, linear basis.

The Self stands between the conscious and unconscious minds, as well as all the opposing extremes of the personality (e.g., anima–animus, introversion–extraversion, etc.). The Self is symbolic of the wholesome and the hardy. It, not the ego, is the true core of the personality. Achieving an understanding of this goes hand in hand with the development and subsequent harmonization of one's many opposing psychological tendencies. This is what Jung called *self-realization*, which is the ultimate goal of personality development in his theory. Self-realization depends upon an individuation process, whereby the various aspects of the personality (i.e., archetypes, character orientations, characteristic functions, life experiences in general) are fully developed. These, in turn, have to be synthesized over time into a well-functioning whole. This synthetic process is referred to as *the transcendent function*. In other words, self-realization is dependent upon an unfolding dialectic of differentiation (i.e., individuation) and integration (i.e., the transcendent function). Accordingly, it would be a mistake to interpret this language of Self and individuation in the spirit of stereotypically Western individualism. For Jung, *Self* and *individuation* are terms for describing a fuller, more complete fulfillment of collective human potentials and our uniquely human possibilities for realizing psychological maturity (Jung, 1999). In fact, Jung's theory of neurosis is precisely that a conflict has arisen between the opposing attitudes of the presumptive individual ego and the deeper unconscious layers of the psyche. Psychosis reverses this trend: The will of the ego cannot control the free flow of powerful personal and collective unconscious fantasies and, the Self cannot harmoniously integrate the person's array of complexes.

The developmental character of self-realization prompted Jung (1961) to carve out various stages of the lifespan to complement his personality theory. These stages include childhood, youth, middle age, and old age. Childhood is the time for coming into being. It is when the initial structuring of the ego emerges. Youth is the time when the striving for independence appears. During youth, the individual is collecting evidence to support the establishment of a belief system and characteristic lifestyle. Middle life is a time for crisis (since the lifespan is half over) and is characterized by a need to revise one's personality along the lines of a more conscious individuation process. If accomplished, individuation can lead to an unambiguous impetus toward harmonious synthesis and self-realization. Finally, old age is the time for reflection, the development of wisdom, and preparations for death.

Reflection

Carl Jung's personality theory situates personality within an evolutionary context, but not in the biologically reductive manner that we first saw in connection with factor-analytic trait theorizing. Rather, Jung's approach to personality is quite holistic in emphasis and bears direct relevance to the psychological world of the person. For Jung, evolutionary history is born into the personality and maintained through the progression of cultures, their myths, their symbolism, their artistic forms of expression, and so forth. Jung gives one a sense of the sheer plurality inherent in personality and the vital need for balance, harmony, and integration for healthy human functioning.

For Jung, experience and behavior are always nested within an ancestral past that only manifests itself in specific cultural contexts. Individual personalities are inextricably connected via the common threads embedded within the collective unconscious. The transcending-realizing tendencies of the self are still viewed as involving socially mediated processes of differentiation and synthesis, but are examined simultaneously in a broadened evolutionary and cultural light. By seeing personality as a function of a culturally endowed environmental context, Jung's theory calls attention to two formidable currents of thought that have recently emerged in psychology. These are the multicultural and ecopsychological viewpoints to be discussed next.

Taking it Further: Food for Thought

Jung's thought is rarely discussed outside of the areas of personality and psychotherapy. On the whole, his name is perhaps just as likely to be heard in literature and the arts as it is in psychology due to the nature of archetypal research. And yet, despite the very "high," occasionally ethereal (if not psychedelic) sound of his theory, it would be too convenient to discount his work as merely obfuscating. It must be remembered that Jung's work acts as primary undergirding for what is currently the most popular and influential form of personality theorizing in the field to date: factor-analytic trait theory! The push to reduce the vast expanse of potential trait descriptions down to a precious two or three characteristics of temperament involved words like introversion, extraversion, neuroticism, psychoticism, and superego, all of which figure prominently in Jung's writings. Extraversion and neuroticism remain as part of the Big Five. What is interesting is that this way of thinking has jettisoned the extended array of concepts and insights of Jungian thought. The real meat of Jungian thought, so to speak, has to do with the way in which all the various aspects of the personality are integrated throughout the ever-unfolding processes of individuation and synthesis. This is simultaneously unique to the person, not as a self-contained individual but as a member of the human race embedded within a cosmic ecology. Further, contemporary analytic psychology tends to reject the notion that the fundamental bases of personality can be found in specific genetic codes as espoused by contemporary factor-analytic and evolutionary theorists (Roesler, 2012).

Jung's analytic psychology also remains a vibrant source of inspiration for transpersonal psychology, with its emphasis on higher forms of consciousness, optimal functioning, and different conceptions of psychospiritual development. Jung was interested in the psychologies inherent in religion, mysticism, alchemy, and wisdom traditions. He was deeply troubled by the loss of numinous experience in contemporary society, having been supplanted by mere churchgoing and religious fanaticism. Jung was not afraid to inquire as to the deep meaning and cultural diversity of various paranormal and occult phenomena. His intellectual development spanned the globe, integrating Eastern thought in novel ways into Western psychoanalysis. As Heisler (1973) put it:

> Advanced stages of a person's individuation must transcend ... personal psychology and reach into the realm of the transpersonal. From this point of view, Freud regarded the unconscious as a repository of the person's repressed personal contents. While Jung acknowledges this phenomenon, he sees the unconscious as much more than that. Jung brings the unconscious to life as a vital and primordial source out of which the ego has differentiated as a little island in a vast and dynamically moving ocean. Within the single individual, the self carries the inherent, unique identity that distinguishes this person from all other persons, but the self also transcends his unique identity and connects him with the universe of which he is a portion and an aspect. (pp. 337–338)

Moreover, Jung's work has also been taken up as a way of reconnecting human psychology with the earth itself, meaning the whole of the natural world as the universal setting of diverse cultures. In Perluss's (2012) words:

> What modern man [sic] has considered to be a more "civilized" higher state of consciousness has been wrongly equated with ego-consciousness, thus resulting in a limited understanding of the unconscious psyche. The way beyond the "cult of consciousnesses" is to attend to that which the rational mind does not understand: dreams, symptoms, and the presence of archetypes. By doing so, the Western heroic ego, along with its need to dominate and control nature, is dismantled, opening the door for a participatory relationship with both psyche and nature. (p. 181)

For Perluss, drawing on Jung, optimal personal becoming entails developing a penchant for attending to what we do not understand within ourselves, civilization at large, and all of nature. She calls this "the paradoxical path toward a depth ecopsychology" (p. 181). These themes will be discussed further in the next chapter.

Make it Work!

Archetypes like anima and animus, persona and shadow are relatively easy to relate to. Each one of us can see ourselves as more pragmatic and analytic at times or more emotional and caring at other times. Each one of us knows a little something of what we show to the world and what comes out in private. But what about an archetype like the hero? Psychological literature on heroism has been growing for some time now (Franco, Allison, Kinsella, et al., 2016; Franco, Efthimiou, Zimbardo, et al., 2016). Is there any part of you that is inclined toward being a hero to others? Whether yes or no, how do you think this archetype was activated? Taking your analysis one step further, is there any way in which you have had to be or have considered being a hero to yourself? Don't stop there. Is it possible that there are "villainous" forces within yourself, perhaps some strangely self-destructive, anti-heroic trickster? After all, psychoanalysts are famous for pointing out human potentials for self-sabotage and self-destruction. If the answer is yes, how do you think this archetype was activated?

Key Concepts

Analytic psychology
Anima
Animus
Archetypes
Character orientations
Childhood
Collective unconscious
Complexes
Depth ecopsychology
Ego
Extraversion
Feeling
Great mother
Hero
Individuation
Intuiting
Introversion
Middle age
Mother complex
Neurosis
Numinous experience
Old age
Persona
Personal unconscious
Psychological functions
Psychological types
Psychosis
Puer aeternus
Self
Self-realization
Sensing
Shadow
The transcendent function
Thinking
Trickster
Wise old man
Youth

Chapter 13

Personality as Multiculturally and Ecologically Nested

This chapter does not present a unified theory of personality. Instead, it introduces cultural diversity as relevant to the differential–integrative process of personality formation. Since the issue of culture has resurfaced with considerable force in the discussion of Jung's theory, an extended consideration of the topic is now imperative.

Cultures are always operative in personality dynamics, typically in the background on an unreflective basis, and sometimes enduringly so where a person or persons are not presented with cross-cultural encounters that throw them back on themselves. Culture is paradoxical in this way. As Hall (1977, 1990a, 1990b) once observed, a person can only really experience and affirm their true cultural self once they have experienced another, different cultural self and seen it as valid (see also, DeRobertis & Bland, 2020; Husserl, 1999, 2001). Intercultural experiences can provide insights into boundaries and contours of self-knowledge that would be seldom seen under normal conditions.

With this in mind, it seems obvious that the issue of culture (or better, cultures) cannot be ignored. As Ruth Benedict (1934) once noted, human culture is personality writ large. At the same time, the reader is reminded that one can take up the issue of culture in different ways. Were one to adopt a highly micro-integrative approach, the personality would be seen as determined by the forces of culture. At best, the personality would thus be seen as a cultural adaptation. In this chapter, culture is not introduced in order to revert back to a focus on the micro-integrative processes of social adjustment. It is, rather, an attempt to further the macro-integrative view that culture is part of the relational matrix of self-development and personal becoming.

Multiculturalism and Psychology

Cultural psychologists hold that culture, experience, and behavior are inherently interconnected. Thus, cultural psychology is an attempt to understand how culture, experience, and behavior interact. Cultural psychology does not assume in advance that theory and research about something like personality from one culture would necessarily be applicable to all cultures. The branch of cultural psychology that focuses on comparisons and contrasts between cultures is called *cross-cultural psychology*. Cultural psychology on the whole relies on data from both within and between cultures.

Cultural psychologists David Matsumoto and Linda Juang (2013) define culture as a unique meaning and information system, shared by a group and transmitted across generations, which allows the group to meet basic needs of survival, pursue happiness and well-being, and derive meaning from life. As clean and thorough as this definition is, the psychological study of culture is nonetheless an extremely complicated affair due to the vast array of life factors that can influence the formation of unique and shared meaning systems. To be sure, there have been many attempts to identify the core constituents of culture creation throughout history. For example, below is a list of items that have been considered crucial to an understanding of culture by numerous authorities from within the social sciences.

- Ability/disability
- Age
- Artistic forms of expression
- Beliefs
- Common sense
- Education level
- Ethnicity
- Folk psychology
- Gender
- Geographic location
- Ideology
- Languages
- Marital status
- Nationality
- Norms
- Organizations
- Parental status
- Religion
- Self-definitions
- Shared attitudes
- Social organization and status hierarchies

- Social roles
- Socioeconomic status
- Values

Given the size of this non-exhaustive list, it is obvious that cultures can take an amazing variety of forms. It is further obvious that all human beings are of necessity multicultural. Many cultures coexist within a given society, and cultures also exist as nested systems within other (broader) cultures. Hence, we have a diversity of terms for describing cultures, including *co-culture*, *subculture*, and even *counterculture*.

Varieties of Individualism and Collectivism

Since it would be impossible to consider such a formidable spectrum of factors in relation to personality within the confines of a small textbook chapter, the current discussion will begin with a focus on a broad cultural dimension that implicates most of the above-noted factors, especially values. This chapter will introduce *the individualism–collectivism continuum* to demonstrate how culture relates to personality. This continuum has remained a prominent cultural consideration in research and theory on selfhood and personality, even though it has evolved to be more nuanced over time.

For example, the individualism–collectivism continuum has played an important role in the research of Geert Hofstede (1997) in the area of organizational studies. According to Hofstede, individualism refers to the degree to which individuals in a culture are expected to be more autonomous versus more integrated into groups. In individualist-leaning cultural settings, the connections between individuals range from flexible to tenuous. Individuals are expected to look after themselves and those close to them. Collectivism, on the other hand, refers to the degree to which individuals in a culture are expected to be more connected to strong, cohesive groups, even extending outward to include distant relatives or non-relatives.

Many social scientists believe that Western cultures tend to include personalities that are more indicative of the individualist end of the individualism–collectivism continuum. Countries like the United States, Australia, the United Kingdom, the Netherlands, and New Zealand tend to rate very high in individualism. In contrast, South American and Eastern cultures tend to include personalities that are more indicative of the collectivist end of the individualism–collectivism continuum. Guatemala, Ecuador, Panama, Venezuela, and Colombia rate very high on the collectivism side of the continuum. It is interesting that most research and theory pertaining to collectivism tend to focus on Asian cultures. For instance, places like Indonesia and Taiwan also rate very high on collectivism. However, it must be noted that collectivist tendencies in personality are by no means exclusive to those regions of the world. For that matter, individualist tendencies are not exclusive to places like the United States, Australia, and the UK. To illustrate, consider the following results from a 2002 meta-analytic study of individualism and collectivism:

> European Americans were found to be both more individualistic—valuing personal independence more—and less collectivistic—feeling duty to in-groups less—than others. However, European Americans were not more individualistic than African Americans, or Latinos, and not less collectivistic than Japanese or Koreans. (Oyserman et al., 2002, p. 3)

As you can see, people the world over show diverse mixtures of individualistic and collectivistic tendencies. Such subtlety has prompted some authors to distinguish between varying styles of individualism and collectivism. For example, Sampson (1988) drew a distinction between *self-contained individualism* (which is more stereotypically Eurocentric) and *ensembled individualism,* in which the boundary between self and others is not as sharply demarcated and others can be considered part of the fabric of the self.

The English-speaking world is generally more accustomed to self-contained individualist values. In the United States, the term "rugged individualism" has been a commonly used phrase since President Herbert Hoover coined it. Rugged individualism refers to the belief that individuals should be able to manage their affairs independently. According to Harry Triandis (1995), a pioneer in cross-cultural psychology, collectivist-leaning cultures maintain a very different value system with regard to the behavior of individuals. In collectivist-leaning cultures, the self includes more group-linked references. In other words, individual identity is strongly linked to social context.

Along similar lines, Edward T. Hall (1977, 1990a, 1990b) noted cultural differences in context-relatedness in the area of intercultural communications. To express these differences, Hall introduced the terms *high-context culture* and *low-context culture*. In a high-context culture, a speaker assumes in advance that the listener already understands all sorts of things from the context of their communication.

Speaker and listener are highly embedded within a social structure placing high value on family and community. Thus, the speaker does not assume the need to spell out many of the details of their message. There is a strong reliance on nonverbal communication. Meanings are likely to be implicit, requiring the listener to actively make sense out of a message. In a low-context culture, little is taken for granted by the speaker, so more explanation is expected in an interpersonal exchange. In a low-context culture, messages are regularly overt, explicit, simple, and clear to compensate for an implicit sense of disconnect. Thus, the message and the task at hand must have communicative priority over the relationships that contextualize the interpersonal exchange.

For some psychologists, these contrasting forms of communication are reflective of global differences in cognition or thinking style among individuals from contrasting cultures. In the area of social cognition, Richard Nisbett (2003) has noted differences in thinking style related cultural context. According to Nisbett, people who have been born and raised in individualistic-leaning cultures tend to have a more analytic style of thinking in comparison to those who have been reared in collectivist-leaning cultures. Analytical thinking is more abstract. Analytical thinkers separate things from their contexts in order to place them into discrete categories based on their distinct characteristics. In contrast, people from collectivist-leaning cultures tend to think more holistically. Holistic thinking is sensitive to the context or "field" as a whole. Holistic thinkers pay more attention to the dynamic relationship between things and their environments.

To be sure, Nisbett's line of inquiry demonstrates just how complicated it can be to apply individualism and collectivism to a population, and how much caution needs to be taken when doing so. As an example, Western psychology (especially American psychology) has been explicitly dominated by the analytic (atomistic) impulse to think in highly individualistic terms, ranging from emphases on self-serving motives to the search for the "internal" causes of behavior. More relatively "molar" or holistic theories (like those we have been covering since George Kelly) and areas of inquiry (like personality!) have always had to fight for respect and remain a part of scientific discourse. But this is due to a simultaneous implicit collectivistic value system embedded within scientific cultural identity (van Kaam, 1961). The discipline of psychology has always preferred aggregate data and the analysis of large groups to the relative neglect of approaches, methods, and content that seek to be mindful of the concrete life of persons beyond the collective (hence, the seemingly unrivaled popularity of factor-analytic thought in personality). In other words, the culture of psychology shows a complex blend of both highly individualistic and highly collectivistic trends.

Differences between individualist-leaning and collectivist-leaning cultures are also evident in the area of self–other relations. Love and marriage provide relevant contrasts. In individualist-leaning cultures, it is typical that romance or feeling in love with another person is central to the decision to marry. People in individualist-leaning cultures tend to experience more self-focused emotions in general when compared to people from more collectivistic backgrounds. Traditionally, there has been less emphasis on the "feeling in love" component of the marriage decision and more emphasis on things like family obligation and community expectation in collectivist-leaning cultures. In fact, the Chinese even have a word for filial piety—*xiao*. For the reader familiar with the theatre, you may recall that the tension between the desire for passion and family duty was portrayed in dramatic fashion in the play *The Fiddler on the Roof*.

Returning to selfhood, Hazel Markus and Shinobu Kitayama (Markus & Kitayama, 1991) have noted differences in *self-construals* between individualist-leaning Americans and many Asian cultures. Self-construal refers to the ways in which individuals interpret, perceive, and understand themselves in relation to the world around them. Self-construals form the basis of self-definition, which is codified in terms of *self-schematics* (i.e., "knowledge structures developed to understand, integrate, or explain one's behavior in a particular domain") that collectively form a total *self-system* (Markus et al., 1982, p. 38). Markus and Kitayama have held that contrasting self-construals account for differences in individual experience, cognition, emotion, and motivation. Self-construals in many Asian cultures are based on the assumption of a fundamental relatedness between individuals. The societal emphasis in these cultures is on attending to others, fitting in, and achieving harmonious interdependence. In contrast, the general norm in the United States is the development of self-construals that value independence from others and the expression of one's unique inner attributes. Again, however, caution must be taken not to see the issue in black-and-white terms. There is a rather explicit way in which Americans tout their freedom and independence. Yet, who could deny the existence of collectivistic trends in the United States after January 6, 2021, when hordes of people seeking to "save democracy" attacked their own capital in protest of an election that was characterized as the most secure in American history by their leader's own political appointees? Clearly, an all-or-nothing conceptualization would not do justice to the complexity of the issues at hand. This duality with regard to freedom as an American cultural value will come up again in the next chapter on Erich Fromm's theory.

Recently, neuroscientific studies have lent support to Markus and Kitayama's views on self-construal. Activity within the anterior rostral portion of the medial prefrontal cortex (loosely, the midsection of the frontmost portion of the cerebral cortex or MPFC, for short) is thought to reflect the neural correlate of self-knowledge. Thus, cultural neuroscientists are questioning whether the self-construals that activate this region of the brain differ depending upon where one falls along the individualist–collectivist continuum. For example, there is some evidence to support the idea that individuals from collectivist-leaning backgrounds demonstrate MPFC activation even when presented with trait descriptors referring to someone close to them. To this end, Joan Y. Chiao (Chiao et al., 2009) tested the possibility of cultural variations in neural activity when making trait judgments concerning self and others using functional magnetic resonance imaging (fMRI). Chiao used American and Japanese participants to examine whether collectivist-leaning personalities would show a greater response to context-dependent (i.e., relational) self-descriptions within the MPFC. Her results supported the notion that self-relevant processing within the MPFC does vary as a function of culturally related self-construal.

These findings concerning the self make sense when considering the fact that highly contextualized notions of self are pervasive among non-Western spiritual (value) traditions. For example, in the Hindu tradition emanating from India, the word *Ātman* is used to refer to the self. Ātman is the *true* self of an individual, which exists beyond superficial attachments and identifications with things. To achieve knowledge of the true self means realizing that Ātman is identical with *Brahman*. Brahman is the supreme, universal spirit that is the origin and support of the universe. In Sufism, which is the mystical tradition of Islam, the self is referred to with the word *nafs*. Nafs is a graded phenomenon spanning various manifestations of self-development, from egocentric to self-transcendent. Examples of such manifestations are provided below.

- Inciting nafs (an animalistic, impulsive self, that incites evil)
- Inspired nafs (a self with the impulse to do good)
- Self-accusing/regretful nafs (a self with strong conscience)

- Nafs at peace or serene nafs (a non-materialistic, content self)
- Pleased nafs (a self that lives in the moment, accepting God's will)
- Pleasing nafs (a soft, tolerant self)
- Pure nafs (a self completely surrendered to God)

Finally, in the teachings of Zen, which is a school of Mahayana Buddhism that originated in China during the 6th century, there are diverse views of self, some of which deem the notion to be conceptually bankrupt. This view posits that there is only a dynamic stream of consciousness that links life with life, a *bhava* or continuity of consciousness from moment to moment. There are, however, views that are more paradoxical in nature, representing a middle path between the opposing extremes of the ruggedly individualistic self and no self at all:

> In the Buddhist view of self, the ultimate goal is to reach an understanding that the self is an illusion or empty. This often is viewed as a cognitive understanding or assent to the idea that the self is not real. The Buddhist conception, however, goes much deeper than the cognitive realm. A better analogy is that the Buddhist seeks to achieve a letting go of the illusions of the self at an experiential level. It is the experience of no-self. Additionally, many Buddhist perspectives do not advocate that the no-self ideal is something that individuals should directly seek to accomplish. In other words, denying oneself will not yield the experience no-self. It is helpful, if not necessary, to maintain a conception of the self along the way (Epstein, 1995; Hoffman, 2008a). Using the analogy of the middle path, the journey to no-self avoids the extremes of excessively holding on to conceptions of the self and the extreme of denying oneself. (Hoffman, et al., 2009. p. 149–150)

In sum, these considerations allow one to briefly characterize the opposing ends of the individualism-collectivism continuum. On one end, there are low-context, socially independent characteristics. On the other end are high-context, socially interdependent characteristics. The characteristics that dominate each end of the spectrum are as follows.

Low-Context/

Socially Independent Characteristics
- Achieving self-consistency and individual identity
- Being autonomous
- Being direct
- Being unique
- Engaging in self-expression
- Engaging in self-gratification
- Focusing on internal processes, private states, and personal needs
- Having control
- Savoring personal freedom
- Supporting one's own needs for inclusion and appreciation
- Valuing separateness
- Thinking analytically

High-Context/
Socially Interdependent Characteristics
- Being appropriate
- Being flexible
- Being subtle and indirect
- Belonging
- Feeling connected
- Fitting in
- Fulfilling expected social roles
- Promoting others
- Promoting social harmony
- Relating
- Respecting other persons' needs for freedom or privacy
- Supporting other's needs for inclusion
- Thinking holistically

Because of these distinctions, it is critical for the reader to realize that the above-noted characteristics can become part of a personality, but do not represent preestablished personality types. Following Ruth Benedict, no well-informed cultural scientist would assume that individuals are automatons mechanically carrying out the decrees of their culture. Moreover, the distinctions made above refer more to values than geographic locations (which, as noted above, are two different aspects of culture). Thus, for example, in Chiao's neuropsychological studies, she found that participants' cultural values of individualism or collectivism modulated their neural responses within the MPFC during self-judgments, and not merely their cultural affiliation.

Edward T. Hall (1977, 1990a, 1990b) made the relative distinction between values and geographic location long ago. For Hall, cultures display a mix of characteristics from both ends of the spectrum when it comes to individualism and collectivism. That is why I have been referring to an individualism-collectivism *continuum*. Again, there are both individualist and collectivist values distributed throughout the United States in differing degrees (Oyserman et al., 2002). There are various reactionary movements against the dominant rugged individualism associated with the Caucasian, Anglo-Saxon, Protestant male ethos. For example, currents of feminist thought do not hold linear logic and independence in the highest esteem but rather value community, connectedness, egalitarian process, sharing, and holism as well. The feminist ideal for the healthy personality is a balance between individual empowerment and relational competence. Feminism rejects the prevailing trend of labeling relational difficulties resulting from individualistic social norms "dependency issues" (Shaw & Proctor, 2005). Similarly, Afrocentric thought seeks to counter the trends of Eurocentric individualism with a conscious commitment to social connectedness and spirituality rather than self-determination and individuation. Molefi Kete Asante (1980) has advocated a philosophy of *African personalism* that emphasizes the active devotion of life energy for the purpose of achieving harmony in one's personal and interpersonal life. Afrocentric thought emphasizes a communal cognitive will and the fundamental connectedness of all things, such that there is no individualized self, only a community of extended selves. Moreover, ethics and aesthetics (e.g., highly symbolic communication, musicality, and so forth) have ontological or top priority for the Afrocentric personality.

As a further demonstration of the cultural plurality found within societies, one need only return to the more interpersonal, holistic theories covered in this text, which have all been created by Westerners. By their very nature, these theories represent a countercultural force within Western psychological science, which accounts for their relative marginalization. As Calvin S. Hall and Gardner Lindzey (1978) have noted, personality theorists, especially those of the more holistic variety, have always been the rebels of psychology. In fact, because of its inherently relational, synoptic thrust, the field of personality theorizing as a whole has often failed to achieve the respect of mainstream psychology.

In light of the diversity inherent in cultural contexts, personality must inevitably be conceptualized in multicultural terms. All personalities are always multiculturally nested. In essence, multicultural personality theorizing is a sort of inversion of the factor-analytic tradition of thought. The factor-analytic tradition of research has sought to carve out a bare-bones basic core of personality, a skeleton on which to hang the flesh of the personality, so to speak. A genuinely multicultural approach to personality moves in the opposite direction. It illuminates the intense plurality involved in personality formation because of the many factors that form the basis of those meaning and information systems used by groups to meet their various needs. At the same time, and this is critical, self-construal ultimately resides in the hands of the irreducible person and should not be buried beneath the rhetoric of bald cultural reductionism/cultural determinism (as George Kelly noted long ago), cultural relativism, or societal adaptation.

The Culture of Place:
"Eco" Considerations for a Psychology of Personality

Having highlighted the distinction between values and geographic location, it must be noted that location or place can nonetheless be a powerful contextualizing force in culture creation and personality formation. To be sure, insights into the power of place have given rise to numerous "eco" orientations to psychology. The history of this kind of thinking in psychology can be traced back to Kurt Lewin's *field theory*. Lewin (1935, 1951) is considered to be a seminal figure in the emergence of social psychology. Field theory emphasized the idea that behavior is a direct function of the person's interactions with their environment, resulting in the heuristic formula, $B = f(P, E)$. However, Lewin focused on the "field" interpreted as the psychological environment of the person, the environment as interpreted and perceived as an actional life-space, rather than the "objective" behavioral setting in its own right. Lewin did feel that the study of the extended environment was important and noted that a psychology that would move into that area of investigation would be called a *psychological ecology*.

Readers familiar with the work of James J. Gibson (1986) and his wife Eleanor J. Gibson (1969) will note Lewin's influence on their respective "ecological" theories of perception and development. This is most easily illustrated via their work on *perceptual affordances*. From a Gibsonian point of view, perception is intimately bound to possibilities for environmental interaction. The perception of a given object or environment involves more than the apprehension of their readily obvious visual characteristics. It also involves an immediate grasp of what the object or environment affords in terms of possibilities for meaningful interaction.

Lewin also had an influence on Urie Bronfenbrenner (1981), who would go on to develop *ecological systems theory*. For Bronfenbrenner, the individual human being functions as a system nested within various other interactive systems. Bronfenbrenner identified five such systems, each of which is briefly characterized below.

- *The Microsystem:* The immediate interactions that occur between the individual and their family, school, religious institution, neighborhood peers, and so forth.
- *The Mesosystem:* Communicative relations that hold between two or more aspects of the individual's microsystem (e.g., parent–teacher communications).
- *The Exosystem:* Linkages involving individuals and/or social settings that are rarely experienced directly but have an influence on the individual (e.g., what goes on in the Mayor's office or at a parent's place of work that can impact the life of a child).
- *The Macrosystem:* The culture in which the individual lives (e.g., the above-noted individualist and collectivist value systems).
- *The Chronosystem:* The historically unfolding events and transitions that occur over the individual's lifespan, including the sociohistorical circumstances within which their life is unfolding.

The ecological focus on trans-individual behavior settings is still more pronounced in Roger Barker's (1968) *ecological psychology* and the *ecopsychology* of individuals like Theodore Roszak (1995). Barker's ecological psychology focuses on the relationship between physical settings (otherwise known as *non-psychological inputs*) and behavior in general. Barker was explicit about his interest in the ecological environment beyond the psychological life-space of the individual human being and insisted that the study of the literal material setting of behavior would make unique and indispensable contributions to psychology. As an example, he noted that one can learn about being a first baseman from a focused, concrete examination of that particular player's firsthand experiences and interactions on the ball field. However, remaining at this close range of study, one would never learn about the deep structure of the rules of the game to be played in that literal physical space, both of which structure and govern the first baseman's overall tendencies and general repertoire of behavior as well. To acquire this kind of knowledge, one would need to shift one's attention to a more general ecological viewpoint. In Barker's view, environments in the modern world change so fast and endure so much duress due to things like industrial–technological advances that the development of an ecological perspective has become imperative.

This sentiment is pervasive throughout ecopsychology as well. Ecopsychology, though very similar to ecological psychology, is a psychological application of *Gaia theory*. In ancient Greek mythology, Gaia was the goddess or personification of the Earth (i.e., Mother Earth). Thus, ecopsychology focuses on behavior settings with an emphasis on nature or ecology in the popularly used senses of those terms while allowing for the possibility of highly advanced and diverse interpretations of such concepts. Gaia theory holds that the organic and inorganic components of our entire planetary ecosystem are part of a single living, self-regulating system. Disturbances or perturbations in one part of the system can affect other parts of the system. Moreover, human beings are held to be an integral part of the living environment. From this point of view, human personality exists as nested within the flux and flow of the ecosystem at large. A healthy, thriving environment is correlative to healthy, thriving personalities. At the level of human nature, there is no separate, encapsulated self, only selfhood as part and parcel of the living Earth. The growing feeling of alienation from oneself, others, and the world that has been written about since at least the middle of the twentieth century stems in part from our failure to realize this inherent interconnectedness. Thus, journalist Richard Louv (2008) has coined the term *nature-deficit disorder*, while psychologist Allen D. Kanner (1998) has introduced the concept of *Mount Rushmore Syndrome*, which refers to an attitude toward nature that is grandiose, entitled, distant, dominating, manipulative, hyper-independent, and empty. An ecologically informed approach to personality proposes a new model of health that revolves around the concept of *biophilia*. Biophilia is a concept that was first introduced by the humanistic psychoanalyst Erich Fromm (1955, 1956, 1986) to designate the love of all living things.

Can things like environmental temperature, an abundance of living things (e.g., plants and animals), physical space, color, or aesthetic beauty affect personality? If so, in what ways might they affect personality? These are critical questions for an ecopsychological approach to personality. Consider the following research findings and related questions. Laboratory rats grow more rapidly in cool environments (i.e., 55° F.) than hot environments (i.e., 90° F.) (Moore, 1944). When it is very hot and humid, do you find yourself moving slower or getting agitated more easily? Studies have shown that induced alterations in body temperature can have an effect on things like speed of performance on cognitive tasks, alertness, and irritability (Holland et al., 1985). Is your mood affected by changes of season? The *Diagnostic and Statistical Manual of Mental Disorders* includes a specifier for major depression called seasonal affective disorder, which is diagnosed with varying degrees of frequency in numerous countries. Alternatively, can caring, thoughtful interactions with the natural world be health-conducive? Psychologist Crystal-Helen Feral (1998) has developed an ecological connectedness model of psychotherapeutic treatment for emotionally at-risk children. Feral has found that thoughtful, involved interactions with natural settings can promote the development of qualities like self-esteem, happiness, perceptual skills, self-efficacy, and empathy.

What about the perception of physical space? Ethologist John B. Calhoun (1962) coined the term *behavioral sink* to describe the behavioral deterioration that results from overcrowding. Overcrowding produces a whole host of negative behaviors ranging from miscarriage, to sexual deviance, to cannibalism in laboratory animals. Along related lines, psychologist and professor of architecture Alton De Long (1981) has shown that the size dimensions of physical space have a direct effect on time perception and also on the speed of neural and cognitive processing.

Does something as simple as color affect mood or behavior? A recent study of twenty-five seasons of NHL hockey found that teams were penalized more when they wore black jerseys (Webster et al., 2012). Have you ever noticed that jails and schools are regularly painted in "soft" colors? A favorite in jails is what has become known as "drunk tank pink." This is Baker-Miller Pink, and it is used in hopes of calming prisoners. Businesses are careful about which colors they choose for their interior architecture and design (Alter, 2013). In fact, some mental health professionals use color exposure for therapeutic purposes, a practice referred to as *chromotherapy*.

Could it be that a polluted, dilapidated environment lends itself to certain patterns of behavior as opposed to a clean, aesthetically pleasing environment (Maslow & Mintz, 1956)? In school settings, studies have found that students in "beautiful" rooms have better attitudes and greater achievement motivation than students dwelling in "average" or "ugly" rooms (Phillips, 1997; Taylor & Gousie, 1988).

These are all very controversial ideas, to be sure, but they do give one pause to consider the interconnection between environmental ecology, the sense of self-world relatedness, self-construal, and personality. At present, there is no systematic body of literature to represent a unified ecopsychological theory of personality. However, its prospects are promising (see DeRobertis, 2015), as long as ecology is not artificially isolated from its conceptual connection to culture. The potential effects of color on personality provide a clear illustration of the interconnection between the environment and culture, as colors have highly symbolic meanings that can shift and change from culture to culture, person to person. Thus, Gaian-inspired thinkers have recently begun to use terms like *transpersonal ecology* and *transpersonal ecopsychology* (Davis, 1998). Similarly, psychologists Shigehiro Oishi and Jesse Graham (Oishi & Graham, 2010) have advocated for the development of *socioecological psychology*. Finally, moral philosopher Mary Midgley (2005) has made a convincing argument that Gaian thinking leads us away from the atomistic, mechanistic, reductionistic cultural ethos of Western science and the rugged individualism nascent withing the popular works of Western thinkers like Jean-Paul Sartre and Ayn Rand.

Reflection

This chapter featured significant cultural factors that contribute to the differential–integrative process intrinsic to personality formation and the evolution of healthy human personalities. What has been discussed here brings individualistic, low-context personality characteristics and collectivistic, high-context personality characteristics into relief. Inasmuch as personality is nested within a context, ecologically situated multiculturalism provides a means for appreciating the sheer diversity of personality as well as the relative health of the personality. Human environments, in terms of both regional ecology and shared meaning systems, are remarkably diverse, and some are more conducive to thriving than others. The material in this chapter not only places selfhood within a socially and symbolically mediated ecosystem;

it also provides a vision of optimal personality functioning based on the love of the total environment of which each of us is an integral part and that Erich Fromm (covered in the next chapter) dubbed *biophilia*. For Fromm, the cultural issues of political and economic context are of prime concern for people living in the present age due to the increasing tendency among many cultures (especially American culture) to interpret all of life in terms of resources to be consumed. Fromm thus spoke of the biophilic personality as an alternative to the self envisioned as an isolated, alienated, superficial, ego-driven consumer.

Taking it Further: Food for Thought

When I was in college, the term *hermaphroditism* was used in my physiological psychology class. Today that term is no longer used. *Intersex* is the preferred term. In biology, hermaphroditism refers to the condition of having both male and female reproductive organs and capabilities. There are creatures in the animal kingdom whose reproductive habits are not neatly divided in the form of distinct binaries (i.e., the male and the female, strictly speaking). This term was carried over for use when speaking about human beings whose biological sex was made ambiguous in some way, but there are many ways that this judgment can be made. "True" hermaphroditism among humans was eventually reserved for those with both ovarian and testicular tissue. But even in these cases there is diversity, and these individuals cannot reproduce like those species in the animal kingdom for which the term hermaphroditism was created in the first place. Sometimes the tissue is separate, and sometimes it is fused, giving rise to more or less differentiated forms of "true" hermaphroditism. The problem becomes more complicated when looking at the causes of intersex presentation and the sheer diversity of "non-true" hermaphroditism. There is a wide range of form when it comes to sexually relevant characteristics (i.e., primary and secondary sex characteristics) in human beings, involving diversity in genetic codes, general anatomy and physiology, including glandular functioning, neurology, and their associated cultural interpretations and meanings.

Psychoanalytic psychology, in spite of the venom that is usually cast at Freud, has always been a trailblazer in this area. Beginning with Freud himself, the psychoanalytic tradition has been famous for conceptualizing sex and gender along a continuum, refusing to see and think in strict black-and-white terms (Stortelder, 2014). Jung's anima and animus as complementary archetypal pairs can be seen as lending itself to this idea. Outside of psychoanalysis, George Kelly's thought also allows one to think about gender as bipolar, as a social construct. Today, psychological theory is witness to a revolutionary movement seeking to transition away from gender binaries in the form of *queer theory*. At present, queer theory is in its infancy, and it would be impossible to pin it down to a singular form. It arose largely from the areas of critical literary theory and LGBT studies, but often clashes with LGBT theory over the issue of heteronormativity. Queer theorists have a tendency to look upon those advancing LGBT rights as accepting a default priority on traditional heterosexual cultural norms (or heterosexism), with all the conceptual rigidity, lack of understanding, and prejudice (e.g., homophobia, transphobia, etc.) that these norms have a tendency to transmit. Queer theory is also partner to the women's movement in its quest for liberation from male dominance. What does the future hold for queer theory in relation to our understanding of human personality? It is too early to tell, but the implications are that one must be careful about assuming that someone's personality is defined by terms like male, female, heterosexual, and homosexual, let alone their traditional meanings. Queer theory asks us to question just how central these concepts are in the wider realm of living as an incarnate being, or at least how they are understood to the degree that they are important to us as a species. Is it not interesting that there is no societal prejudice against those who choose to be celibate, disavowing the realm of sexuality, but when one merely refuses to "take sides," hatred ensues? Queer theory points out that the essential meaning of being a human animal may be far more complicated than you think. The meaning of human embodiment itself has to be revisited and rethought in terms of its relationship to *eros*.

Make it Work!

From George Kelly, Hazel Markus, and Shinobu Kitayama, we learned that self-construals form the basis of how we define ourselves with respect to our surrounding world. What do self-construals produce? As we saw back in Chapter 6, Kelly (1963) spoke of a bipolar self–other construct nested within one's broader personal construction system. In their approach, Markus and Kitayama (1991) spoke somewhat analogously of self-schemas nested within one's broader self-system, which can be more relatively independent or interdependent. Toward the end of this chapter, we took these highly relational approaches to self-definition into the arena of ecopsychology, speaking to the personality's relative degree of connectedness to or alienation from its surrounding ecosystem. Looking at the physical environments that you have lived in, can you identify any significant ways in which they have played a role (positive or negative) in influencing how you have engaged in self-construal? Is it possible that the kinds of places that you have inhabited in your life have played some overlooked role in shaping the way you tend to think, feel, perceive, value, and behave with respect to yourself and other people? If someone lives at the beach, in the mountains, in an ironbound city, in a thriving suburb, or a run-down ghetto, how might these habitats contribute to the processes involved in defining themself? If need be, narrow your focus and consider the environment of your block, your apartment complex, your home, your living room, or your bedroom. If nothing comes to mind, try a change. Make alterations to your daily living space and notice what kinds of effects these alterations have on your experience and behavior. You may be surprised how much you can learn about yourself and others simply by becoming more aware of the dynamics involved in human–environment relations. (If you need inspiration, consider the contrasting musical approaches of The Beach Boys and Black Sabbath, and then consider where they came from—southern California in 1961 and Birmingham, England in 1968, respectively).

Key Concepts

Affordances
African personalism
Analytical thinking
Ātman
$B = f(P, E)$
Baker-Miller pink
Behavioral sink
Bhava
Biophilia
Brahman
Chromotherapy
Cultural psychology
Culture
Ecological psychology
Ecological systems theory
Ecological theory of perception

Ecopsychology
Ensembled individualism
Feminist thought
Field theory
Gaia theory
Hermaphroditism
Heterosexism
High-context culture
Holistic thinking
Individualism–collectivism continuum
Intersex
Life-space
Low-context culture
Medial prefrontal cortex (MPFC)
Mount Rushmore syndrome
Nafs
Nature-deficit disorder
Non-psychological inputs
Psychological ecology
Rugged individualism
Seasonal affective disorder
Self-construals
Self-contained individualism
Self-schematics
Self-system
The chronosystem
The exosystem
The macrosystem
The mesosystem
The microsystem
Transpersonal ecopsychology
Xiao

Chapter 14

Erich Fromm: The Politically and Economically Nested Biophilic Personality

In order to attain a proper theoretical understanding of personality, Erich Fromm (1947) believed that one must first become cognizant of the human condition as such. One must begin one's approach to personality by starting from the fundamental predicament that all human beings find themselves in. This would provide the "ontological" (referring to one's very being and becoming) structural housing, so to speak, for the development of the myriad unique lifestyle variations we call personalities. In other words, Fromm insisted upon grounding his ideas about personality in an *anthropologico-philosophical concept of human existence*. For Fromm, human beings have evolved beyond the more decisive, more thoroughgoing union within nature that one finds among the rest of the animal kingdom. Human beings are one step removed from their animal nature and, as a result, they are unable to wholly rely on innate biological mechanisms like instincts to guide the development of their personalities. Even more so than Freud, Fromm (1947, 1955) was skeptical of the notion of human "instincts" in the strict biological sense of the term (the term is used in various ways in psychology, see DeRobertis, 2017). Traditionally, the criteria for something to qualify as a genuine instinct have been formidable. Instincts are inborn or innate, triggered more or less automatically, species-wide, rather inflexible across members of a species, and relatively complex in that they involve many actions (i.e., they are not mere reflexes but fixed action patterns). For a species as diverse as ours, that is a tall order to fill. Fromm is not opposed to the idea that human beings have drives or rely on a genetic and biological endowment. Rather, he points out that human beings and human personality formation are far more reliant on learning, reason, imagination, decision making, and self-reflective knowledge than any other creature on the planet.

This situation has evolved for productive reasons. Human beings are far more efficient and effective at adapting to diverse environments than other animal species. This is so much the case that the human population keeps growing while something on the order of one hundred and fifty to two hundred species of plant, insect, bird, and mammal become extinct every day (about one thousand times the "natural" rate of extinction). Thus, the sheer flexibility inherent in human adaptability clearly has drawbacks as well.

Moving far beyond the confines of adaptability, Fromm points out that self-reflective knowledge makes it possible for human beings to confront certain mysteries, riddles, or paradoxes that become apparent upon the development of conscious awareness. Fromm (1955) referred to these paradoxes as *existential dichotomies* because they are fundamental contradictions inherent in human existence. In Fromm's view, all human beings are alike in the sense that they share the same basic human predicament and the same existential dichotomies; however, they are each unique in their specific ways of dealing with these shared conditions, and that is the foundation for his approach to personality.

Fromm's first existential dichotomy results from the fact that self-reflective, conscious awareness bequeaths human beings a heightened appreciation for life. However, this very appreciation makes the sting of death all the more painful. A human being can savor their life in a deep and meaningful way, but all the while they know that the life they so relish must be taken from them.

The second existential dichotomy relates to the fact that human beings must orchestrate their lives and cooperatively create their personalities by making decisions. This brings with it a desire to fulfill one's potentials, to imagine and envision an ideal toward which one would work over the course of the lifespan. As Alfred Adler showed, human development is rooted in the desire to feel ever more complete and fulfilled. However, human beings are both fallible and limited in terms of their abilities and resources. In effect, reflective awareness brings with it the exhilarating perception of possibilities for realizing skills, talents, hopes, dreams, and aspirations, but these are never fully realizable. Human existence always bears the mark of a fundamental incompleteness. There will always be stones unturned, potentials untapped, risks not taken. There will always be more to see, more to learn, more to do. Fulfillment must always be provisional and, therefore, at least somewhat disappointing.

The third and final existential dichotomy arises from the realization that we are all part of an ancestry and a cosmic ecology (as we have seen over the course of the last two chapters). Human beings come to realize that they live among others and among nature. During peak experiences (recall Maslow), this feeling of being connected to the whole of the living universe is highly pronounced. Yet, at the same time, all humans feel the undeniable reality of our fundamental aloneness from the outset of human development (e.g., think of Erikson's basic anxiety). Individuality cannot simply be abandoned, hard as one might try. Reflective awareness and decision making give human beings the ability to become independent, which is often experienced as exhilarating. But it is equally true that human beings detest isolation and loneliness, not to mention feelings of rejection (recall the theories of Horney and Rogers).

According to Fromm (1947, 1955), the disharmony inherent in the human condition (i.e., the difficulties created by the lack of life-governing instincts) generates a need for human beings to creatively restore unity and equilibrium between themselves and nature. To this end, human beings develop a striving for personality integration in the form of "unified character." Character orientations provide an organized means for finding tentative "solutions" to existential dichotomies and allow people to live a fulfilled life in spite of the fact that existential dichotomies cannot be simply eradicated. For Fromm, answers to the problems of existence will inevitably be sought in strategic attempts to satisfy five human needs. These are the need for *relatedness*, the need for *transcendence*, the need for *rootedness*, the need for an *identity*, and the need for a *frame of orientation*. Like the striving for integrated character, Fromm believed that these needs also arise from the basic human situation of being dislodged from nature.

In Fromm's view, the patterned ways that human beings go about searching for answers to the problems of existence (i.e., their character orientations) are a function of how they engage their total sociocultural context, including its political and economic conditions. In this chapter, I will discuss the five human needs identified by Fromm and how they address existential dichotomies, followed by an outline of Fromm's thoughts on the political and economic context of contemporary character development. I will conclude with an overview of several character orientations mentioned in Fromm's works.

Fromm (1955, 1956, 1986) considered the need for relatedness and rootedness to be particularly effective at managing the pain of separation and aloneness. Relatedness is the desire for union with the world and other people. In unhealthy people, this desire manifests itself in the form of either submission to others or the impulse to have power over the world and other people. Submissives and power mongers seek a symbiotic relationship with the world around them and can be said to be in denial concerning the impossibility of erasing the existential dichotomy implicated in human individuality. Furthermore, they are inherently narcissistic in their inability to care for others as distinct individuals. This is not so for healthy people. The healthy person seeks relatedness through love, which does not seek complete merger, but authentic relationship (1956).

Love comes is several forms, including brotherly love, motherly love, erotic love, genuine self-love (which is the opposite of selfishness), and the love of God (Fromm, 1956). But love, according to Fromm, is not something we merely acquire like an object or product, and this is too often overlooked in a marketing culture such as the contemporary United States. Rather, authentic love is something we cultivate through active concern, dedication, and effort like the mastery of an artform. Love is a kind of awakening to and cultivation of one's fundamental relatedness to others that cannot be captured in linear, analytic discourse of any kind. The love of God, for example, requires linguistic devices that can speak truth in "paradoxical logic," since God's essence cannot be known by the intellect (p. 77). Paradoxical logic embraces contradictions as mutually complementary rather than strictly opposed or dualistic (p. 76). God, for example, represents ultimate reality, but is supernatural. Alternatively, consider how Christianity speaks of God (in the singular), but with the pluralistic description of the Father, Son, and Holy Spirit. The profundity of genuine love can only be approximated in symbolic discourse and ultimately in altruistic action (not words). The realization of the self is, paradoxically, a turning toward the other (and all of creation) in non-judgmental compassion, which is simultaneously the realization of genuine spiritual and religious experience (not mere churchgoing, empty obedience, or fanaticism), which Fromm (1966) calls *x experience*.

Rootedness is the desire to feel connected and at home in the world. Unhealthy individuals shy away from the challenges inherent in laying down roots somewhere and making a home. Instead, they remain *fixated*, by which Fromm means an incestuous, passive reluctance to move beyond the protective home environment provided by one's mother or primary caregiver. In healthy circumstances, people play an active role in creating warm, welcoming environments like a home.

Fromm (1955) considered transcendence and identity to be particularly efficacious at handling the problem of human incompleteness. Transcendence is the desire to rise above a passive, accidental existence and enter the realm of productive freedom and purpose. It is the urge to be a creator rather than just a creature. In the unhealthy person, the inherent striving to create is somehow or other thwarted. When this happens, the urge to create is transmuted into the urge to destroy. Fromm is clear that the striving toward death and destruction and the striving toward life and creation are not total and complete opposites, since both creation and destruction are forms of active involvement in the world. In both instances, the individual can feel gratified that they took good advantage of the possibility of doing something that was their own, even if the project was not completed.

Identity refers to the capacity to become aware of oneself as a unique individual. A person with an identity has a sense of personal responsibility for their own values, beliefs, emotions, actions, and so forth. In spite of the inability to complete oneself, there is a sense of gratification associated with the active exploration of life's many opportunities and the feeling of owning one's life. Unhealthy people do not have the resilience and perseverance to do the soul searching needed for identity formation. Instead, they opt to live life via a herd-like conformity and a blind obedience to authority.

Finally, a frame of orientation provides an additional tool for dealing with the problem of incompleteness, as well as a means to lessen the sting of death. To have developed a frame of orientation means that one has sketched out a mental schematic or narrative for interpreting and making sense out of life. The world, with all its complexities, ambiguities, and dichotomies, cries out for meaning and sense. Fromm (1955) held that human beings can use reason and imagination to put one's incompleteness in perspective and thereby make the problems of life feel that much less overwhelming and unmanageable. A frame of orientation is also a global philosophy of life and the relationship of life to death. Healthy people seek out reason and apply it in an embodied, impassioned, imaginative way to make sense out of their lives and eventual deaths. Unhealthy people avoid reason and consciously or unconsciously maintain irrational views of human life on earth.

All in all, there is no guarantee that a person will find adequate answers to the problems of human existence. Again, for Fromm (1941), much depends on how one engages one's total sociocultural predicament. In particular, Fromm was keenly aware of the difficulties intrinsic to healthy personality formation in a society where the individual is faced with adversity that is political and economic in origin. The United States of America provides a particularly clear example of the adversity that Fromm had in mind.

Americans are put in a rather precarious situation by virtue of the fact that we live amid two very powerful, yet incongruous social forces. On the one hand, Americans enjoy unprecedented freedom and embrace this freedom as a top value at the level of political ideology. America is, after all, "the home of the free." At the same time, marketers are free to bombard us with a constant stream of messages telling us who we ought to be. Americans live amid both high levels of political freedom and a commodity market capable of powerfully influencing not only our economic activity but our entire manner of social relatedness. Politically speaking, we enjoy much freedom from rules, regulations, dictates, and so forth, but this is just one aspect of freedom, and it is not enough to facilitate fulfillment and healthy personality formation. Freedom must be used productively in the interest of love, creativity, establishing roots, identity formation, and the development of a frame of orientation in order that a robust sense of self may be realized. However, rather than being part of a concerted effort to put our freedom to positive use, Americans live under the constant pressure to have and consume the "right" kinds of products. Corporations have increasingly worked to commandeer our cultural and personal freedom to be and replaced it with a mere freedom to have and expend. As a result, many people feel inexplicably uneasy in the face of their freedom.

According to Fromm (1941), modern capitalism seeks masses of complaisant people who will habitually consume according to standardized tastes that can be easily influenced and anticipated. It needs people who only believe they are free but who are in reality quite ready to follow anyone who might appear to have a remedy for the anxiety associated with freedom without productive purpose. As life becomes less about cooperative being and more about competitive having, freedom comes to feel more and more like a burden (though few would readily admit this, especially in a political climate like the United States). The result is that human beings in highly consumeristic social climates have become increasingly alienated from themselves, others, and nature. Self-realization remains elusive. The rock band The Rolling Stones captured the emotional conflict of this predicament in their song *(I Can't Get No) Satisfaction* with the lyrics, "When I'm watchin' my TV and a man comes on to tell me how white my shirts can be, well he can't be a man 'cause he doesn't smoke the same cigarettes as me."

Before moving forward, it should be noted that Fromm was careful to single out modern capitalism, which has become highly corporatized and consumeristic, rather than all capitalism for his critiques. He considered the exercise of untainted political and economic freedom to be important for self-realization. Fromm was no less willing to admit of the positive attributes of cultural individualism inasmuch as individualism can promote the uniqueness and dignity of the individual. Fromm did, however, oppose the superficial, empty, rugged individualism that modern capitalism produces. He believed that modern (i.e., corporatized, consumeristic) capitalism lends itself to the development of various non-productive character orientations.

As noted earlier, human beings develop organized strategies in an attempt to find answers to the problems of human existence, which Fromm (1947) referred to as integrative character orientations. Some attempts to develop unified character are productive and healthy, while others are non-productive. Fromm identified several non-productive character orientations that he believed were a reflection of the political and economic cultural conditions described above. For example, those who display *receptive character* feel that all that is good comes from outside themselves. Accordingly, their primary concern is with receiving things (e.g., love, gifts, even personal style and ideas). Those who display *exploitive character* are similar to receptive individuals, but they do not expect to be given things, so they aggressively take what they want from others. People with *hoarding character* orientations seek to save what they have gained and not let anything go. They are the misers of the world, and their preoccupation is with keeping things inside the walls of their protective psychological stronghold. Individuals who display a *marketing character* orientation are a direct reflection of modern commerce. These people see themselves as commodities on the market. Their personal value is felt to be dependent on their ability to sell themselves.

Receptive, exploitive, hoarding, and marketing character orientations are more or less garden variety attempts to achieve personal integration. However, Fromm also identified three unification strategies that he considered regressive or pathological character orientations. The first of these is called *necrophilia*, by which Fromm meant the love of death and destruction in all of its forms. The second regressive orientation is called *narcissism*, meaning an intense attachment to oneself or one's groups that distorts rational judgment. The third regressive orientation is called *incestuous symbiosis*, which is a condition wherein a person remains so attached to their mother or primary caregiver that self-development is more or less abandoned.

In contrast to these character orientations, Fromm (1947, 1986) described what he called a *productive character* orientation. The productive character orientation refers to the healthy personality. This orientation is associated with the rational and imaginative employment of positive freedom. That is, people who display the productive orientation use their freedom to create, to innovate, and to be generative, but in a deeply meaningful, aesthetically, and ethically cultural sense foreign to the corporate–consumer mindset. Fromm held that human beings are not merely rational and social; they are also creative and productive. For him, productiveness is the quintessential realization of human potential. Productiveness is gauged by a person's loving dedication to the mutual flourishing of self, others, and the whole of the natural world. Only through this biophilic style is a human being capable of experiencing deep, robust personality integration and the qualities of psychological health described in previous chapters.

Reflection

Erich Fromm's personality theory reminds us that neither the human condition nor the political and economic context of human affairs can be ignored in personality theorizing. Fromm's theory provides novel insights into the nature of both unhealthy and healthy personalities. His socially informed critiques outline several compelling ways in which consumeristic culture can impede optimal personality development (i.e., his non-productive and pathological character orientations). Indeed, the current popularity of American reality television programs that require individuals to "sell" themselves, as well as those that focus on human hoarding, give one a sense that Fromm was ahead of his time.

Fromm's focus on both a universal human condition and the total sociocultural (political and economic) context of personality formation constitutes a refutation of bald, unchecked cultural relativism. Fromm is clear that cultures can be healthy or sick depending on their ability to help human beings find answers to the fundamental problems of human existence and, in the process, achieve unified character (i.e., relative integration). For Fromm, the relative health or sickness of a culture can affect the lives of the individuals who live in that culture. Contemporary corporatized cultures take *Homo sapiens* and turn them into *Homo consumens*, says Fromm. On a mass scale, the members of modern capitalism suffer from what has recently been dubbed "affluenza" (de Graaf et al., 2005). Though it might be tempting to interpret Fromm as saying that the contemporary preoccupation with having and consuming is the result of selfishness, Fromm would have found such an interpretation a bit superficial. He believed that people lack genuine self-love and have been emptied of all substance to make way for an overriding consumer impulse. Fromm saw that human beings on a mass scale have become progressively alienated from the depth, meaning, and harmony of a biophilic lifestyle by the tantalizing, stimulating lures of habitual consumption. In the process, the integrity of personality integration has become increasingly compromised. In fact, according to Fromm, the alienation inherent in contemporary society has become so pervasive that we no longer possess the linguistic competency to reach our own experience. Hence, "selfishness" does not quite strike at the heart of the matter. As Rollo May (1953) phrased it:

> We have an excellent vocabulary for technical subjects, as Erich Fromm has pointed out; almost every man [sic] can name the parts of an automobile engine clearly and definitely. But when it comes to meaningful interpersonal relations, our language is lost: we stumble, and are practically . . . isolated. (p. 56)

Humanistic psychology has attempted to overcome this problem by drawing on philosophical traditions like process philosophy, personalistic philosophy, phenomenology, and existentialism. It has also sought to access the humanities and use cultural forms of expression as sources of data (e.g., Cushman, 2012; Romanyshyn, 1989). These strategies are a major point of convergence with Erich Fromm's thinking. Like Jung before him, Fromm saw the need for large-scale cultural therapeutics by way of a rekindling of our appreciation for those symbolic forms of communication that have been cast aside in favor of the technical language of reductionist, scientific, and social materialism. In particular, Fromm (1951) believed that there was healing power in the possibility of reeducating ourselves, as a society, in the language of fairy tales, dreams, and myths. These manifestations of language force us to think in ways that maintain close contact with the visceral, emotional, and imaginative dimensions of human existence and can thus counterbalance the progressive depersonalization and dehumanization of contemporary discourse in both science and life. Rollo May (1953) picks up this theme in the next chapter:

> Dr. Erich Fromm's recent book, *The Forgotten Language*, points out that dreams, like myths and fairy tales, are not at all a

foreign language, but are in reality part of the one universal language shared by all . . . . (p. 99)

Taking it Further: Food for Thought

How prophetic was Fromm? Juliet Schor (2004) would later observe that marketers in the United States have taken stage-oriented developmental psychology and "reconceptualized the process of growing up as a process of learning to consume" (p. 43). From birth to two years of age, marketers see a stage of observation and beginning exploration because they want to get the child's attention and frame the parameters of their imaginative possibilities. It is not until three to seven years of age that marketers see a stage of burgeoning autonomy and creative fantasy because they now see clear product-related opportunities to capture the child's imagination and facilitate the impulse to consume in a relatively autonomous manner. Between eight and twelve years of age, marketers see a stage of role formation and the beginnings of "tween" identity because they want to influence the child's inherent sociality in a manner that will allow them to profit from it as soon as possible (Schor, 2004, p. 55). By the time the child reaches thirteen years of age, marketers want to be in a position to sell them the component parts of an independent identity, one that had its glimmerings during the tween years.

The segmentation of childhood into phases of life, each with its own cluster of stereotyped (consumer) behaviors, amounts to a homogenization process that erodes the individualized, creative aspects of the human integrative process (DeRobertis, 2012). As Kersting (2004) noted, the increasing use of "identity-oriented branding" in child marketing encourages the rejection and disapproval of anything or anyone different (p. 61). This homogenization process hijacks the child's imagination, making it more difficult than ever for the child to consolidate a thriving personality. At each stage of development, the child's creative impulse is redirected toward predetermined consumer aims, impeding the integration of a self-structure that is consonant with one's own unique potentials and "ownmost possibilities," to borrow Heidegger's (1962) language. The contemporary child is force-fed a limited range of consumer-oriented possibilities for being-in-the-world-with-others-alongside-things via the relentless onslaught of corporate advertising. As Sipiora (1991) put it, "The constellation of television conditioned imagination and consumption-oriented lifestyles results in a forgery of genuine psychological experience in which the self is disfigured and its transcendent possibilities are repressed" (p. 158). This is, in essence, exactly what Fromm warned of.

Fromm was hopeful, however. Following Alfred Adler, Fromm maintained that social change was not only needed, but possible by way of pedagogy and educational reform. For Fromm, to truly educate is to bring out potentials for self-realization and promote authenticity. Increasingly, however, educational systems appear to be making automatons, functional cogs in the big machinery of corporate culture. Instead, it should be helping students respond to the world with their senses in a meaningful, skilled, productive, active, and shared way. Fromm (1955) calls this outcome of education *collective art*, since our language currently has no word for such a state of being. Here, Fromm is again taking a lead from Adler, who once noted that to attain a proper understanding of a child's lifestyle requires that one develop an artistic manner of thinking and perceiving.

Fromm felt that students should learn to become skilled with their hands, as Maria Montessori once noted, so that there is a balance of both mind and body in the learning process. It is important to feel the value of creative production with one's own hands, which is a phenomenological insight relating to the fact that touch provides the most meaningful and intimate form of contact with the world (see DeRobertis, 2012, 2017). Good pedagogy, Fromm held, was vital to the development of the sane society. Fromm believed that there are those among us who can see through the trappings of consumer culture and can help others live productively. Similar to Alfred Adler before him, Fromm believed that what matters most is how each person interprets and appropriates the raw materials of self-development and personality formation provided by their environmental context.

Make it Work!

In the contemporary United States, we are everyday barraged with identity-based marketing. The products and services that a person can purchase are explicitly and implicitly brought to you as part of what defines you as a person. Consider the five most expensive purchases you have made in recent times, or perhaps you may just want to consider the five purchases that you rely on most. Then look at the way those products or services are marketed. Can you see any ways that the marketing wants you to construe yourself for having made those purchases? If not, look at the broader context of American consumer culture. What are the implications of those purchases in terms of what they mean in the eyes of others regarding the kind of person you are?

Key Concepts

Affluenza
Anthropologico-philosophical concept of human existence
Biophilic style
Collective art
Consumer homogenization process
Consumeristic capitalism
Existential dichotomies
Exploitive character
Fixation
Frame of orientation
Freedom to be
Freedom to have and expend
Hoarding character
Homo consumens
Identity
Identity-oriented branding
Incestuous symbiosis
Love
Marketing character
Narcissism
Necrophilia
Non-productive character orientations
Productive character orientation
Receptive character
Regressive character
Relatedness
Rootedness
Self-alienation
Symbiotic relationship
Symbolic communication
Transcendence
Unified/integrated character
x experience

Chapter 15

Rollo May: The Narratively Nested Destining Personality

Rollo May belongs to the same theoretical tradition of thought as Viktor Frankl. Both are existential psychologists who have had occasion to engage in phenomenological description as well. To review, existentialism is an intellectual movement that stresses the fact that human beings are not solely or even primarily thinkers. Rather, humans are first and foremost caring, choosing, and acting beings. This does not mean that humans are not thinkers, of course. Quite the contrary, thought is very important to existentialists since thought is vital to individual accountability and responsibility. Perhaps one could say that rather than claiming, "I think, therefore I am," existentialists claim, "I am, therefore I think." To existential thinkers, like Martin Heidegger (1962), for example, a human being is not a detached observer of the world, but rather a feeling, desiring *being-in-the-world-with-others-alongside-things*. All of these hyphens are meant to denote the fact that self, others, and the things of the world together form an intimately intertwined dynamic system. There is no separation of mind from body or person from world. Human beings always find themselves ahead or out in front of themselves, as always already caught up in worldly affairs as the default state of their being. Thus, one of the great challenges of being human is to be able to catch sight of this pre-reflective involvement so as to subject it to a conscientious assessment of its authenticity.

For groundbreaking existential philosophers like Heidegger (1962) and Kierkegaard (1954, 1962) before him, questions of authentic selfhood and personal identity were of utmost importance. Existential thought traditionally emphasizes the importance of taking ownership and responsibility for one's life, committing oneself to courses of action that demonstrate a belief in the personal meaning of one's behavior, and thoughtfully examining the impact of one's actions on oneself, others, and the world. Human beings have the power to redefine themselves and expand their scope of awareness through devoted, attentive action. This process leads to the development of traits like conscience, integrity, and resoluteness.

Rollo May (1981) takes this template and extends it by saying that this process of personal transformation allows human beings to find and fulfill a destiny. Before moving on, however, it is important to note that destiny is not fate. Existentialists do not believe in fate. Life is viewed as a project to be carried out. The final form of the lifespan is not given in advance of individual involvement. Rather, the task of every human being is to actively address and answer a question within a question. The first of the two interpenetrated questions is, "Why is there something rather than nothing?" This question, taken up by Heidegger, can be traced back to philosophers throughout history ranging from Parmenides to Gottfried Leibniz. The second question (the question within the first question) is, "What is the meaning of the life that I have been given?" The first question calls attention to the radical contingency of all of creation. Nothing *must* exist, but we have a universe populated with diverse existents, nonetheless. Things regularly come into being. They emerge, evolve, and are swept away into non-being (death) as a regular part of the circle of life. Life implicates death and vice versa. It is a paradox at the heart of all of creation. Since we are all part of creation, this is thus one of the main paradoxes of our lives.

Accordingly, the second question implicates one's own existence as nested within this more global radical contingency. There is a constant dialectical interplay of being and non-being at the core of human psychological life and, by default, personality. Death is ever present (embedded in widely varying levels of awareness) to remind us of how delicate and fleeting life is. I do not have to exist in this particular form, time, and place, but here I am. Consider the odds of my words on this page, having been written by me, and being read by you against the backdrop of all of the events throughout the history of time that have had to occur to make this possible. Since the beginning of time and until the end of time, there has never been another me or you, and there never will be again. And yet, this is happening! Here we are, *for now*. Unforeseen events can occur, and without warning, you or I could be gone. So, here, the second question poses itself with considerable urgency (to those who would open themselves to such profundity). Given the radical contingency of my life, what is the meaning of this? Here I find myself against staggering odds. Why so? What's it for? What is its meaning in the grand scheme of things? To address this question is to address the issue of one's destiny. Destiny is the true purpose of one's life, one's personal mission or calling. It is what you are going to do with it (this life) to make it significant and answer the question within the question. Destinies are fulfilled by way of an inspired dedication or commitment that creatively brings about the growth and fulfillment of oneself, others, and the world at large (i.e., the entire structure of being-in-the-world-with-others-alongside-things). In other words, a real destiny cannot be selfish in any of the pejorative senses of that word.

Given the fact that destiny is not fatalistic, one can immediately see that in May's thought there has to be a preference for the language of freedom rather than determinism. But while there is a truth to this (he is not a determinist in the strict sense), it would be a mistake to interpret his theory one-sidedly on the basis of freedom only. Bearing in mind the nature of life's radical contingency, consider that people do not get to choose the time, place, and conditions of their birth (sometimes referred to as the *thrownness* of existence, see Heidegger, 1962). Throughout life, there are many things that one cannot choose or control. Thus, one does not create a destiny willy-nilly. One has to hear a call from within one's total life situation. And, in the process, commitments have to be made that will immediately close doors to other potential courses of action. Freedom, in other words, is only activated by choices that narrow the range of action within which it operates. Freedom and limitation thus have a paradoxical relation, an ongoing interplay in finding and fulfilling a destiny.

Still other paradoxes emerge as well. Despite the curtailing, channeling effect that commitment has on freedom, one does not feel less free. One actually experiences an opening effect, wherein suddenly there are avenues available for unleashing one's powers of creativity. To illustrate, think about a time when you were presented with a restaurant menu that was gigantic. Sometimes, a smaller menu makes life easier, and you can go ahead and begin custom tailoring your order to your specifications. Choice is limiting, but it is also structuring and constructive. With life choices, one can begin a creative expansion where previously one might have floundered in confusion. Of course, there will be times of confusion and fear in life. The threat of non-being is never vanquished, and this makes it inevitable that there will be moratoria and periods of relative constriction. Life sometimes involves stopping, recoiling, rethinking, reconsidering, even sticking one's head in the sand or regressing (depending on the severity of the situation). The processes of expansion and constriction thus constitute a basic developmental paradox inherent in personality formation (see Schneider, 1990).

Yet another paradox of human personality is its potential for both good and evil. May (1991) finds traces of this paradox in Freud's proto-archetypal notions of *eros* and *thanatos*. May interprets these as contrasting expressions of the vital, dynamic life energy that emerges from and is sustained within human social relations. May speaks of this as a *daimonic* core at the heart of human motivation. It typically manifests as a mixture of creative and destructive tendencies. Creation begets destruction; just consider the fact that your sustained existence entails destroying and consuming other things, like plants and animals. Ideally, one's creative potentials lead the way. But excessive frustration, confusion, and recoil from the process of finding one's destiny can have destructive consequences to varying extents. In those instances where a person cannot find a path to destiny, the daimonic does not inevitably become inert. It tends to distort, and this distortion can turn decidedly evil. Acts of evil, ironically, have a way of giving a person a substitute sense of purpose where no productive purpose reveals itself. So, just as the struggle to grow into a lifestyle that is meaningful and fulfilling will inevitably involve periods of relative expansion and constriction, there will also be opportunities to learn about and exercise one's potential for good and evil.

To live creatively, in accord with one's destiny, is the quintessential expression of healthy personality formation in May's works. For May (1953, 1969, 1979, 1991), there are a number of basic human potentials that make the process of finding and fulfilling one's destiny possible. These include intentionality, care, love, will, and myth. Together with one's destiny, these constituents form an integrative edifice for the development of the personality.

May does not use the word intentionality the way that Albert Bandura and others in psychology typically use the term. Intentionality does not mean merely that human beings sometimes do things on purpose, as it were. May's concept originates in the works of Edmund Husserl (1977), the father of phenomenology. May (1969) referred to intentionality as "the structure which gives meaning to experience . . . our imaginative participation in the coming day's possibilities" (pp. 223–224). For May, the word intentionality denotes the fact that the human mind is always connected to the world in a meaningful, interactive manner. The fact that human beings are intentional, in this sense, means that they never live within the confines of their own skulls with nothing but a mass of worldless, anonymous "sense data."

Intentionality is the oriented "aboutness" or directedness of subjectivity, the primordial connectivity that makes it possible for human beings to truly live in and with a coherent world of things and other people. Accordingly, phenomenological intentionality is the subjective foundation upon which acts done on purpose are able to emerge and evolve in the first place.

In addition to being intentional, May (May et al., 1958) noted that human beings display the characteristic of care. Here, May drew inspiration from Martin Heidegger. Again, care, in this context, means something more fundamental than the commonsense and popular psychological notions of gentleness and devotion. By care, May meant to highlight a fundamental characteristic of human intentionality, which is its mooded, emotionally invested nature. As May conceptualized it, care is a state in which things matter (and there are many ways in which they can matter). Human beings are not involved in worldly affairs primarily in the form of an intellectualized, rationalized detachment. Human beings are not first and foremost fledgling scientists, as some developmental psychologists might have it. It is our nature to be both intellectually and affectively caught up in-the-world-with-others-alongside-things. Meaningful involvement in the world, in other words, means something more than just data transfer and information processing. Human beings are engaged in projects and relationships that implicate their very being, their self-development as such. Drawing inspiration from Heidegger (1962), May held that care, when properly conceived, ultimately implicates selfhood, even if only in the most implicit of ways.

Optimally, love and will are added to intentionality and care. May (1969) defines love in general as a delight that one experiences in the presence of another person while affirming their inherent value. However, May believed that there are four different (though not mutually exclusive) manifestations of love in the world of human affairs. First, there is *philia*, friendship, or brotherly love. Second, there is sex, lust, or *libido*. Third, there is *eros*, which is the drive to love, create, or procreate with others. Eros refers to cooperative involvement aimed at achieving increasingly creative forms of relational being. Fourth and finally, there is *agape*, which is love that is primarily devoted to the welfare of the other, the prototype of which is the love of God for humanity.

According to Rollo May (1969), love breeds and feeds acts of *will*. The love of something or someone is unparalleled in its ability to mobilize potentials for organized, deliberate action. Thus, May defined will as the capacity to organize one's personal resources so that movement toward a certain goal may take place. Willing is care and love in action and the embodied actualization of intentionality. As May phrased it, willing is caring made free. By caring, willing is liberated. It is let loose on the world, unleashed, and set into motion. Thus, will is sometimes referred to as freewill and goodwill.

Myth, in Rollo May's works does not mean a falsehood, as it does in everyday discourse. May's (1991) usage is truer to the original meaning of myth as *mythos*, which is also used in other disciplines like anthropology and sociology. For May, myths are the linguistic housing of a culture's beliefs, values, attitudes, and so forth. He calls them the "narrative patterns that give significance to our existence" (p. 15). Myths are the stories that dispatch time-honored truths to the members of a culture across space and time. Healthy personality formation requires structure, direction, and an integrative framework of meanings and values to operate within. Human beings, as Fromm had also noted, need inspiration, hope, guidance and life perspective. In short, the achievement of optimal personality functioning requires access to templates or schematic prototypes for finding and fulfilling a destiny. The idea is that shared stories found personal life narratives. In this sense, May's concept of destiny is a more contemporary version of Alfred Adler's *final fiction*, which May (1991) readily admitted in his book on myth:

> Adler radically opposed the gospel of exclusive self-love; he preferred to speak of self-esteem or integrity, or, to use his special term, "social interest." He was radically opposed also to the kind of therapy which overemphasized independence and egocentricity. He would have been as critical of the "all-for-me," narcissistic view of the self as Bellah or MacIntyre. Perhaps the reason he has been so often overlooked in the evolution of therapy in America is that he does not fit our intoxication with narcissism and the ego-centered self. Adler developed his central concern with the "guiding fiction," which is a synonym for "myth." It refers to a significant event in one's early childhood that the person remembers; the event is turned into a myth which the person keeps as a guide for one's way of life, whether it is fictitious or not. One knows oneself through this myth. (p. 69)

Myths are integrative unifiers at both the social and personal level. Myths inspire the courageous search for personal identity and destiny, even in the face of hardship (e.g., think of David and Goliath or the trials and tribulations of your favorite superhero, for that matter). To call a cultural myth a falsehood or say it is just a story is to miss its core meaning entirely. Myths house explicit and implicit belief systems that provide perspective and give meaning to social and personal struggles. Myths are like the support beams of a house. They are the grand narratives that unite groups and societies and, under ideal conditions, direct their actions toward growth-oriented aims. To have words and sense-making narratives is to be deeply empowered. Words and narratives help human beings achieve stability, balance, purpose, and fulfillment in a complex, confusing, and often challenging world.

Unfortunately, Western society has seen a progressive breakdown of long-held myths, like biblical narrative, which saw a quickened deterioration after World War II. World War I was idealistically called "the war to end all wars." World War II unfolded, nonetheless, and the sheer magnitude and destructiveness of that war left Westerners at large with an unprecedented sense of doubt that there could ever be a God who loves us. But the need for myth remains, and where there is such a vacancy, people will desperately opt for virtually any kind of narrative to make them feel as if their lives have sense and purpose. Compounding the situation, many contemporary, industrialized and post-industrialized societies have pit positivistic and spiritual narratives against one another, as if one kind of *mythos* is necessarily right and the other simply false. People are torn apart as they feel that they must choose between narratives for God or science, for example. One side must be considered fact, while all other narratives would be deemed mere stories (and thus false) by default. On the one hand, how can one live as a rational person in contemporary society and turn a blind eye to science? The denial of science can have disastrous results, as the climate crisis and COVID-19 pandemic are showing us. On the other hand, a bald reliance on science alone creates its own set of difficulties. Positivism, because of its rationalist nature, seeks only the facts (or, better, its unilateral version of the facts). The ideal of positivistic science is to be *value-free*. Thus, positivism offers a highly technical *mythos* that provides much intelligence but very little wisdom, much knowledge but little to comfort the striving, struggling, suffering soul.

In addition to its claim of value neutrality (which, incidentally, is far from certain), positivistic science interprets human beings as so much biological machinery. A human being is a bio-machine, no different from any other *thing* in the natural world in any substantial way. This implicates another of May's paradoxes, the paradox of being both a subject and an object for oneself in the process of becoming. Natural science one-sidedly emphasizes the objective body, but it covers over the subjectivity that houses the profound power to participate in life in a meaning-bestowing manner. If something like personal subjectivity is granted in some measure, that subjectivity is viewed as locked within the cranium of the individual in question. This has come to be compounded by the fact that human beings are increasingly looked upon as human resources or human capital in the industrial and post-industrial ages (van Kaam, 1961). Moreover, our growing reliance on and fascination with technology means human beings are becoming incidental, if not altogether obsolete, to societies' sources of mass production.

All of these factors have led to the gradual erosion of the edifice of healthy personality integration described by May. Intentionality appears to yield pointlessness, absurdity, and insignificance. Care is being replaced by isolation, loneliness, boredom, and apathy. Love is being replaced by lust and narcissism. Will is being replaced by irresponsibility, helplessness, indecisiveness, and aggression. Myth is being replaced by resignation and a burgeoning interest in mass-media driven tribalism and cult membership. Finally, destiny is being replaced by confusion and anonymity. These cultural changes prompted Rollo May (1991) to refer to contemporary times as both an age of narcissism and, more generally, an age of melancholy.

May, following philosopher Paul Tillich (1980), believed this melancholy to be rooted in the spiritual anxiety of emptiness and meaninglessness. May further felt that this anxiety has become so powerful and overwhelming that it is giving rise to increasing levels of neurotic anxiety. Rollo May made a distinction between normal anxiety, which he believed to be associated with the typical challenges of living, and neurotic anxiety. Normal anxiety is a sign of eustress and the fact that one has a substantive, meaningful life full of valued projects and relationships. In an imperfect world, the failure of any of one's projects and relationships is always a possibility, but one perseveres nonetheless out of a dedication to that which is valued. Normal anxiety is productive in that it sharpens the senses and opens one up to the world-with-others-alongside-things. However, neurotic anxiety is destructive; it is akin to a form of panic wherein one is closed off to the world. In a state of neurotic anxiety, insight becomes elusive. If left unresolved, feelings of isolation, depersonalization, and apathy set in.

As a result of the pain associated with it, May noted that people seek shelter from neurotic anxiety through self-deception (e.g., defense mechanisms) and by relying on distractions that temporarily cover over the emptiness and meaninglessness in which neurotic anxiety is rooted. Things like promiscuous sex, drugs, television, food, alcohol, and the Internet provide temporary relief from the crushing realization of one's global psycho-spiritual impoverishment. Unfortunately, however, when a person avoids making choices that promote the discovery of a destiny and the development of an authentic identity, they only feel increasingly impoverished and existentially guilty. Existential guilt is a guilt that implicates one's entire choice of lifestyle. It is rooted in the unavoidable knowledge that life is time limited, but despite the fact that every moment counts, one is squandering these moments. Thus, what is called for is a cessation of avoidance, a refusal to succumb to the tantalizing lures of a culture that prefers automatons to human beings. What is called for is a renewed commitment to the task of creating a life narrative that promotes the emergence of authentic selfhood, lovingly in-the-world-with-others-alongside-things. For Rollo May, this kind of commitment is what distinguishes the healthy personality from the unhappy, unfulfilled personalities of our times.

Reflection

Rollo May outlined a holistic, systemic foundation for personality theorizing through his particular psychological interpretation and application of Martin Heidegger's notion of being-in-the-world-alongside-things. Because he was primarily a psychologist rather than a philosopher, May's application of existential thought allows one to address issues pertaining to the relative health of human beings. Healthy personality integration rests on a dynamic, world-relating foundation of intentionality, care, love, will, and myth, through which individuals and entire cultures find and fulfill their destinies.

For May, one cannot properly understand personality integration without accounting for the worldly context within which the individual lives. A crucial feature of this context is the narrative structures or stories that human beings live by. May did not consider contemporary industrialized and post-industrialized cultures to be particularly conducive to psychological health, and he noted that they have become devoid of reliable narratives to support human becoming. As a consequence, the present age is increasingly giving rise to phenomena like pointlessness, absurdity, insignificance, personal isolation, loneliness, boredom, apathy, lust, narcissism, irresponsibility, helplessness, indecisiveness, aggression, confusion, resignation, blind obedience, anonymity, emptiness, meaninglessness, depression, and neurotic anxiety. Along with Fromm, May highlighted the pressing need for social reform on a large, culture-wide scale.

Like Fromm, May emphasized the need for human beings to resist socializing forces that are not only unhealthy but homogenize human beings, strip them of their potential for authenticity, and make them unreflective herd animals or bio-mechanisms. Stated differently, Fromm and May both underscored the importance of what Abraham Maslow called *resistance to enculturation*, and both called for cultural reform. For May, this reform would involve the creation of revitalized cultural supports through a renewed value on narrative and storytelling, including a rehabilitation of the original meaning of myth. Both Erich Fromm and Rollo May reserved primary places for the dedicated study of love in their respective theories, especially what Maslow (1993) would call *being-love*. Both theorists felt that any discussion of personality would be incomplete without addressing the varieties of love and noting the central organizing importance of love for personality integration. All in all, it seems that both theorists perceived there to be an intrinsic connectivity between the authentically personal personality, the loving personality, and the healthy human personality. As May once observed, narcissism and unbridled self-interest actually destroy individuality, as contradictory as that might seem on its surface. Finally, fear not, Star Wars fans. Much in the spirit of Jung (and Freud before him), Fromm and May each give the proverbial dark side of human personality ample respect. (For more on this, see *Humanity's Dark Side: Evil, Destructive Experience, and Psychotherapy*, Bohart et al., 2013.) No vision of human health is offered without amply acknowledging the human capacity for destructiveness (Fromm, 1973; May, 1991). For that matter, both Fromm and May admonish that the entire structure of human existence and personality development is pervaded by paradoxical relations such as this, all of which must be creatively negotiated.

Taking it Further: Food for Thought

Rollo May brings the importance of myth as a critical medium of personality integration to the foreground, but it has been slowly simmering throughout this text. It was first mentioned in Chapter 4 with respect to trait theorizing, where we noted that the FFT reserved a place for personal myths in personality formation. However, it made an implicit appearance before that with Freud's metaphorical reference to the Ancient Greek play, *The Oedipus Rex*. George Kelly's attention to the formation of culturally embedded construction systems and Adler's notion of final fiction both orient personality theory toward the critical role of narrative and mythologizing as well. The mythological impetus virtually exploded in the analytic psychology of Carl Jung, and this has been adopted by the post-Jungian analytic psychology called *archetypal psychology*. As Hillman (1993) describes it, "The primary, and irreducible, language of . . . archetypal patterns is the metaphorical discourse of myths" (p. 3). In his view, this language orients archetypal psychology toward "the cultural imagination" in which personality is held to be embedded, rather than keeping personality theory strictly within the purview of either impersonal/mechanistic or strictly personal (as in individualistic) forms of analysis (p. 19).

From within Rollo May's own existential–phenomenological tradition, Edward L. Murray (1986) has unpacked this line of thinking to show how metaphor, symbol, and myth together form what is perhaps the imagination's most powerful integrational network. Murray refers to the metaphor as the midwife of integration, allowing us to suddenly see new meaningful relationships. Scientific metaphors in psychology provide a relevant example; all we need to do is reflect on where we have been in this text. For behaviorism, the mind was like an opaque "black box," and so it was largely off limits as far as scientific explanations were concerned. Freud compared the mind to a hydraulic energy system. From the evolutionary perspective, the human mind was to be compared to a kind of living fossil, a collection of mechanisms from days long past. With the advent of cognitive perspectives, the mind was no longer like a black box, it became more like a biological information processor or CPU. George Kelly used the metaphor of the person as an incipient scientist. As the text pressed onward, we also saw metaphors of improvisation, art, fluidity, and so forth. Metaphors drive science! In Murray's (1986) words:

> The metaphor is an imaginative leap that enables a person to arrive at a destination, so to speak, even before setting forth. The metaphor cuts a swath or path for the person. It blazes a trail for us, opening up a way of imagining our lives in some sphere or other in a manner that was hitherto unspeakable— unspeakable because it was hitherto unimaginable. It is in the light of these realizations that one can aptly say that the metaphor is not the cart of artistic tabs or stickers that one drags through life and periodically places upon some act or other. The metaphors are rather the horse that leads the way, and upon which we ride into the future with all that we possess. (pp.115–116)

Metaphors, however, have a limited range of convenience (to use George Kelly's term) and limited semantic reverberation. A metaphor can easily become sedimented, stagnating, and even imprisoning over time. "One can be victimized by his [sic] own metaphors, as can an entire people. Metaphors are not quickly abandoned" (Murray, 1986, pp. 116–117). So, once having reached the limits of the metaphor, human beings turn to symbols, which Murray calls a *multum in parvo* (a great deal in a small space). Symbols have meanings that extend to more of life's dimensions. They are composed of a larger network of meaningful associations:

> Complexities of life still confront us, and to meet them it is necessary that we effect larger amalgamations, syntheses than the metaphors allowed. At this point we have recourse to symbolizations. The symbol takes up the challenge and builds on the achievement of our metaphorizations. This is the function of our symbolic thinking, thanks to which we are able to tap the interpersonal, sacred, and historical depths of our lives in greater and more meaningful syntheses of life issues. These make possible for us to deal at once with the present situations as well as the historical antecedents that have preceded our situation, and orient ourselves toward the futurities that are our lot, indeed our principle lot. Symbols must take cognizance of our particular selves, whether we speak of the individual self or our people. It must partake of our unique times . . . . The "throwing together" must reverberate in all such respects . . . . (Murray, 1986, pp. 150–151)

Finally, the integrative process is brought to fruition when metaphors and symbols are consolidated into narrative form with the advent of mythologizing:

> The myth constitutes a story endowed with its own unique time and place and extended over some stretch of primordial time in drama fashion. It comes to grips with the human situation, the human issues, by following them back into a primordial time and casting them into the larger-than-life *dramatis personae* . . . to offer mankind [*sic*] the sought-for plentitude or wholeness that is missing from the lived human life. In short, the myth expresses dramatically ambiguous drama that is the human life. Human beings love their stories if for no other reason than that they are always living one. (Murray, 1986, p. 169)

Progress is made, but life goes on. Even symbols and myths can lose their productive potential. Even they can turn into a prison, at which point the imagination must temporarily loosen the reins on its integrational process to become creative by way of critique, to seek divergent meanings, to establish differentiating inroads that recruit the powers of new (or at least renewed) metaphorizations, symbolizations, and myths. Such is the way that narrative acts as a fulfillment of the power of the imagination. Such is the way that the imagination itself acts as *the unity building power of the personality* (Murray, 1986). And yet, imaginative thinking does not (and cannot) operate alone. Self-criticism and the construction of new narratives require the cooperation of logical, analytical, calculative thought as well. Accordingly, Murray (1986) observes:

> It is a proper human accomplishment to live both logically and imaginatively, and it may well be that the greatest human achievement of all lies in the experiential realization of genuine poetic living, thus optimizing the strong presence of both kinds of thinking in human existence. (pp. 36–37).

Are we now at a point where poetry has supplanted science? The question is a loaded one, based as it is on a rigid, preconceived conceptual bifurcation. So, before you rush to judgement, consider Siegel's (2001) observations in the area of contemporary neuroscience:

The structure of the narrative process itself may also reveal the central role of integration in states of mental health and emotional resilience. Within the brain, the neural integration of the processes dominant in the left hemisphere with those dominant in the right can be proposed to produce a "bihemispheric" coherence that enables many functions to occur. The left hemisphere functions as what has been called an "interpreter," searching for cause-effect relationships in a linear, logical mode of cognition. The right hemisphere is thought to mediate autonoetic consciousness and the retrieval of autobiographical memory. Also dominant on the right side are elements of the mindsight module of information processing. Coherent narratives can thus be proposed to be a product of the integration of left and right hemisphere processes: the drive to explain cause-effect relationships (left) and to understand the minds of others and of the self within autonoetic consciousness (right). In this manner, we can propose that coherent narratives reflect the mind's ability to integrate its processes across time and across the representational processes of both hemispheres. (pp. 86–87)

In the life of the unique person and the science of personality, the construction of coherent (micro-integrative and macro-integrative) narratives through the dialectic cooperation of rational and imaginative thought optimizes the growth process.

Make it Work!

Rollo May makes much of the concept of destiny. Describe your journey and progress toward finding and fulfilling your destiny up to this point in your life. Include material pertaining to your past and present. May also makes much of the sobering awareness of life's finite nature (i.e., that we all have a limited time here on Earth). Compare the progress you have made to what you would want your future obituary to say. When you are done, analyze it using concepts use from May's theory.

Key Concepts

Agape
Age of melancholy
Age of narcissism

Archetypal psychology
Authentic selfhood
Being-in-the-world-with-others-alongside-things
Bihemispheric coherence
Care
Cultural reform
Daimonic
Destiny
Eros
Expansion and constriction
Intentionality
Libido
Love
Metaphor
Myth/mythos
Narrative
Neurotic anxiety
Normal anxiety
Paradoxes of personality
Philia
Poetic living
Radical contingency
Resistance to enculturation
Spiritual anxiety
Symbol
Thrownness
Will

Epilogue

This small textbook has provided the reader with a sampling of theories that expose significant aspects of human personality. My aim was to show that each theory has made valuable contributions to the development of a holistic, synoptic, integrative understanding of personality. The text began with behavioral theories, which spoke to some of the mechanics intrinsic to the groundwork or soil out of which personalities emerge. They demonstrated that repeated exposure to specific environmental contingencies can create conditioned responses. They further noted the impressive power of reinforcement and punishment in the ongoing processes involved in giving shape to behavioral regularities. Stability and change in patterns of behavior were seen as the correlates of stability and change in environmental contingencies. As for the relatively integrated structural form or "dynamic organization" that undergirds the individual personality, behavioral theory offered an ambiguous conception of self-control lying somewhere between illusion and genuine adaptation.

By giving the power of pleasureful and aversive stimuli a central place in their thinking, the behaviorists established theoretical common ground with Sigmund Freud. Freud offered a similar approach to personality integration, emphasizing the managerial, self-regulatory work of the ego, conceived as properly modulated self-control lying somewhere between illusion (or self-delusion) and genuine adaptation. Freud's theory painted a more dynamic picture of the personality. The constitutional striving for pleasure (*eros*) is joined by aggressive drives (*thanatos*, which extends far beyond pain avoidance), and both have to be counterbalanced by ego and superego development if an individual is to coexist with others. Freud's articulation of these forces introduced the intrapsychic depths involved in personality formation, primarily in its frustrated, conflicted, and pathological aspects. It widened our view of the endogenic factors that are brought into, worked on, and given shape within specific environments. It also introduced culture as a factor in the formation of personality by way of the reality-confronting aspects of the ego and superego, as well as the taboo relational dynamics of the Oedipus complex. Thus, with Freud, personality integration was bequeathed both depth and enhanced breadth.

The more constitutional, evolutionary biological focus of Freud's theory was then taken up as the basis for a foray into the world of factor-analytic trait theorizing. Here, genetic endowment was seen more in terms of providing the basis of temperamental predispositions that have to be adapted to environmental conditions, and this helps to guide the unfolding process of personality integration. David Buss's revisioning of the factor-analytic trait approach marked a return to Darwin in order to draw on contemporary insights from evolutionary biology. In its efforts to efficiently and effectively adjust to environmental niches, the adaptive ego (to use Freud's language) became evolutionarily disposed to employ the strategies of surgency, agreeableness, conscientiousness, emotional stability, and openness. The personality's adaptive dimensions were loosened from the grip of self-deception and illusion, and personality theorizing itself became more integrational with the introduction of epigenetics. However, ontogeny is not destiny, and neither is phylogeny. Human begins are born with a predisposition to develop certain kinds of traits over others, but human personality is mutable, plastic, and subject to repeated transformations over the course of the lifespan. It is, moreover, much more complex.

Engaging cognitive social learning perspectives, personality came to be viewed in an even more self-regulating light, teasing out the subtleties intrinsic to the power of human adaptation in contributing to personal integration. This was due to the cognitive social learning theorists' insights concerning the role of the human intellect in structuring self–world–other interactions. Cognitive social learning approaches noted how the active, interpreting intellect is informed by the past to deal with the contingencies of the here and now, and to plan for a possible future. Individual cognitive processes (e.g., predictive proclivities, locus of control, attention, representation, memory, self-reaction, self-efficacy, cognitive-affective "units," etc.) were observed to have ongoing reciprocal causational relations to the cognitive processes of others and the world at large. Further, goal formation and the establishment of individual values emerged as themes.

George Kelly's approach to personality brought this kind of thinking into an expanded horizon of thought, operating in certain ways outside the strictures of the logico-analytic thinking that dominates cognitive social learning theory. Kelly offered a theoretical framework for approaching the adaptive functioning of the personality that showcases the way in which people construe and conceptualize reality, generating evolving, dynamical construction systems with varying degrees of awareness. Significantly, such a theory allows one to critically assess both personality and personality theories themselves! Kelly's approach, more in tune with the distinctly human aspect of personality, called attention to the finite, real-life dynamics inherent in any system of constructs in dealing with the overflowing complexity of one's culturally informed, linguistically codified engagement with oneself, other people, and the world at large. A forerunner of dynamic systems thinking, Kelly opened the door to understanding intellectual functioning in a non-linear, holistic–dialectical manner, working with pairs like self–other, uniqueness–commonality, freedom–determinism, and permeability–impermeability. One of the more important dynamic tensions in his work concerned the tension between stability and change. Constructs are continually "tried on for size" in the manner of a freeform quasi-experiment, and so it is that the person is always more or less in the process of learning and creating. Learning and creating together lie at the core of personality integration and personal becoming (see DeRobertis, 2017). Yet, there is only so much change that the personality can handle at a given time. People need a modicum of constancy and stability in their construction systems, which confronts the larger existential issue of how human beings deal with their finitude, the radical contingency of their lives, and the ever-present threat of non-being or death (a theme that would reappear in the theories of Erik Erikson and Carl Jung, and, most prominently, in the theories of Erich Fromm and Rollo May). Kelly thus offered a more holistic, synoptic approach to personality integration, and in the process added a decidedly existential dimension to it. The confrontation with finitude means the challenge of personal becoming is how to achieve relative integration in a manner that is permeable and open enough to allow for ongoing reorganization and growth.

Complementing Kelly's theoretical foci, Erik Erikson's psychosocial ego theory contributed an impressive breadth of socially structured emotional dynamisms to the agentic aspects of human personality. Whereas Freud provided an undercurrent of tumultuous emotionality and conflict to personality theorizing, Erikson provided a means to journey in a contrasting direction, exploring socio-emotional forces of integration without ignoring or denying the existence of normal conflict within the structure of personality. Recall that Erikson built upon Freud's theory; he never sought to replace it. The psychosexual is enveloped within the psychosocial, making for a theoretical scheme that integrates biology and culture. Crucially, Erikson's theory also (like Kelly's) contained elements that left the standard foci of adaptive ego functioning, pointing the way to a still more comprehensive integrative approach to personality: macro-theorizing. Without disavowing

Freud's depths or the tragic aspects of human development, Erikson showed how functional interpersonal relationships can give rise to various strengths or virtues indicative of the truly personal in personality. An existential shift in focus toward these strengths and their paradoxical nature as the organizational centerpiece of the theory grants one access to the realm of optimal becoming (see Knowles, 1986).

Together, the theories of Kelly and Erikson acted as footholds to transition toward the theories of William Stern and Gordon Allport, both of whom introduced the reader to concepts such as person and proprium (i.e., selfhood or the multifaceted self-system). Stern and Allport each, in their own ways, exposed the core of human personality by highlighting its warm, owned, and multidimensional unifying aspects. Stern outlined various hierarchically interrelated constituents of the person, and Allport extended this exposition by detailing the diverse aspects of both the proprium and the personality as a whole. Personality was shown to be a self-organizing, world-relating, goal-directed *unitas multiplex*. Here, the Gestalt of human personality was decisively established, as was the macro-integrational orientation toward personality. The schematic understanding introduced by these two thinkers provided a significantly enlarged clearing within which the more restrictive foci of previous chapters could begin to be synthesized. The chapters to follow assisted in this process.

Alfred Adler brought the warm, owned, multidimensional, goal-directed integrative tendencies of human personality more squarely within the realm of interpersonal relations. In order to do so, Adler emphasized the fact that personality integration is the result of cooperative creative effort and mutual meaning making. In particular, Adler emphasized the fact that healthy personality development is best facilitated in an environment conducive to social interest. The creative self came to the foreground, and it was observed that it is only really nurtured when it is assisted in developing, maintaining, and fostering community feeling. Significantly, one is more human and more oneself when forging a lifestyle wherein one is freed from egotism and freed for genuine social encounter.

Karen Horney and Carl Rogers extended this line of thought by detailing the familial conditions most conducive to the actualization of the relational self that resides at the core of personality integration. Horney and Rogers brought the significant issue of the relative genuineness of the self to prominence, thus implicating the relative genuineness of the personality's integrative character as well. Rogers and Horney both observed that self-development must proceed unimpeded by conditions of worth that compromise the personal insight, wholeheartedness, and psycho-emotional integrity of the personality. Psychological health was seen as a function of the relative match or mismatch between the total organismic experiences of the person and the self-ideals that guide their personality development.

With the theories of Abraham Maslow and Viktor Frankl, the transcendent self came into focus. In spite of their terminological differences, both Maslow and Frankl highlighted the inherently meaning-oriented, value-laden interpenetration of person and world. They extended the boundaries within which personality theory engages notions of health and fulfillment with their respective approaches to motivational diversity and stratified growth potential. They studied states of consciousness that reside in the boundary area between psychology and spirituality, opening into the arena of the transpersonal. They each dedicated focused attention to the profound connectivity of human personality with all of creation and beyond. But, in pursuing these aims, they maintained the need for a macro-integrative outlook that builds upon and incorporates more elementary, less synoptic levels of functioning and analysis. Maslow advanced a hierarchical-integrative model that utilized his often-misunderstood needs hierarchy, while Frankl developed a multidimensional ontology consisting of endogenic, psychogenic, sociogenic, and noögenic factors. The Gestalt of human personality emerged as a bio-psycho-social-spiritual Gestalt.

Carl Jung's personality theory marked the beginning of a series of discussions having a dedicated focus on the contextual–relational dynamics inherent in personality formation. His contributions related to evolution, but outside of the reductionistic strictures imposed by the contrasting explanatory styles of Freud and Buss. In Jung's work, one finds the personality nested within a composite bio-psycho-social-spiritual ancestry. The components of this ancestry were found to be embedded within human cultures, particularly in their symbolic forms of expression (a theme that would reemerge in the theories of Erich Fromm and Rollo May). Jung saw the personality as involved in ongoing processes of differentiation/individuation and as structured in accord with the transcendent function of the archetypal Self. Where the Self outranks the ego as the integrative center of the personality, the personality is able to fully develop and harmonize its many opposing psychological tendencies (i.e., archetypes, character orientations, characteristic functions, and life experiences in general).

Jung's emphasis on culture then lead to an acknowledgment of the inherently multicultural nature of differentiation/individuation and personal integration. Individual identity was taken up as a dialogue with myriad potential cultural identities occurring on different levels of awareness. As an illustration of the power of culture, the concepts of individualism and collectivism were reviewed. In addition, the importance of geographic location by way of natural ecology was discussed. This was not a reversion to any form of reductionism or micro-integrative theorizing. The self (recall the return of self-construal) was embraced as a nested subsystem, an ecosystem operating within a socially and symbolically mediated field. The need for a systematic body of multicultural literature on personality was noted, particularly one that can work hand in hand with a transpersonal ecopsychology. Erich Fromm's notion of the self-transcending, biophilic personality was introduced as a guiding concept for the ecologically nested personality in its ongoing quest for integration and fulfillment.

Erich Fromm contributed to the expansion and contextualization of personality dynamics by illuminating the sociopolitical and economic context of personality integration and personal becoming. Fromm saw that the uniquely human striving to attain a unified character orientation is co-constituted in dialogue with the values embedded within one's sociopolitical and economic milieu. Fromm warned that in today's day and age, rampant consumerism has made it more difficult than ever to make strides in coming to terms with the existential dichotomies that typify the human condition and to successfully work toward forms of personality integration that are conducive to biophilia. Fromm's theory stands as a testament to the contemporary relevance of individual discernment when it comes to enculturation. Specifically, Fromm stressed the need to think, feel, and act in ways that are at variance with the forces of mass culture when these forces prove to be deleterious to human becoming. Here, personality formation involves the emergence of an authentic self, standing in loving defiance of the anonymity fostered by corporatized culture. Like Adler before him, Fromm looked to education for prophylaxis against the dehumanization of contemporary society. Adding a Jungian twist, Fromm ventured that a cultural therapeutic might be accomplished by way of a renewed appreciation for symbolic forms of communication, which was taken up by Rollo May.

Rollo May's theory provided a fitting means for understanding the integration of the personality at its highest levels of analysis by way of his emphasis on narrative. May pointed out that the striving to find and fulfill a destiny is a vitalizing, integrative force like no other. May shared Fromm's sentiments concerning the need for authentic, biophilic selfhood, noting that the anonymity that appears to be engulfing humanity is further rooted in rigid, depersonalizing life narratives. May's insights have yet to achieve full recognition within the ranks of personality psychology, but there are signs of awakening. McAdams and Pals (2006), for instance, noted, "The complex interplay between culture and human individuality may be most evident at the level of narrative identity" (211). From within May's own tradition of existential psychology, Edward L. Murray (1986) has convincingly argued that optimal personality integration is dependent upon robust myths, life narratives rich in literal, metaphorical, and symbolic meaning that can act as a guide for navigating life's broad array of challenges. Like Erich Fromm, Murray held that personal fulfillment in the ongoing quest for personality integration depends on the experiential realization of genuine poetic living, facilitated by the strong presence of both imaginative and rational thinking. The cooperative dynamic tension of reason and imagination optimizes the creative, paradox-negotiating power of the personality and, in the process, supports the differential–integrative process of personality formation and personal becoming. As humanistic psychologists have been arguing for decades, personality theorizing itself is optimized by the strong presence of imaginative and rational thinking as well.

Coda

This text has been a journey from the impotent nothingness of materialist reductionism to the synergistic expanses of mystical consciousness, ending with a series of situational–relational refinements that illuminated the multicultural and very human nature of personality development. The bio-psycho-social-spiritual Gestalt of human personality came to land on terra firma in a place where the personality stands in confrontation with the very pregnant, existential nothingness that calls to one's conscience. What is that call, dare one listen? It issues forth whenever one is in danger of squandering time. The message is: "You do not have to be here, but you are, and this life is temporary, so make the absolute best of the limited time that you have." Again, May (1953) states:

> I think it was C. G. Jung who said, accurately enough, that a person is afraid of growing old to the extent that he [sic] is not

really living now. Hence it follows that the best way to meet the anxiety about growing old is to make sure one at the moment is fully alive. (p. 222)

Viktor Frankl (2006) reminds us that the call is laced with a question, the origins of which lie both inside and outside the self:

> What was really needed was a fundamental change in our attitude toward life. We had to learn ourselves and, furthermore, we had to teach the despairing . . . that *it did not really matter what we expected from life, but rather what life expected from us.* We needed to stop asking about the meaning of life, and instead to think of ourselves as those who were being questioned by life—daily and hourly. Our answer must consist, not in talk and meditation, but in right action and in right conduct. Life ultimately means taking the responsibility to find the right answer to its problems and to fulfill the tasks which it constantly sets for each individual. (pp. 76–77)

To properly hear the call of one's own conscience, one must paradoxically dereflect one's consciousness outward, not in a posture of blind conformity or obedience, but in genuine investment and authentic responsibility. Where consciousness meets conscience, the self is indubitably confronted with its inherently paradoxical nature (Fromm, 1966).

Between the self as deluded illusion and the Self as archetypal conduit to the limitless vistas of transpersonal psychology lies the paradoxical self, which Kirk J. Schneider describes as a fluid center (as we saw in Chapter 10, the same description was offered by Carl Rogers). Schneider, arguably Rollo May's chief contemporary spokesman (e.g., see Schneider, 1990, 1999, 2004, 2011, 2013, 2015), notes as follows:

> The fluid center . . . is a condition of being rented by paradox. The chief paradox . . . is that between our smallness, nothingness before creation, and our greatness, vastness before creation. These poles, these rivaling positions, are the crux of both our enormous hope, richness, and marvel as human beings, as well as our pitiable folly, corruption, and debasement. (Schneider, 1999, pp. 115–116)

Elsewhere, he goes on:

> The human psyche is a constrictive/expansive continuum only degrees of which are conscious. Denial or avoidance of these polarities associates with extreme or polarized counterreactions (e.g., "disorders," violence), whereas the encounter with, integration of, or coexistence with the polarities associates with more vital and dynamic living—a form of living that I've since termed the "fluid center" (Schneider, 2004, 2013). The fluid center is structured inclusiveness, pliability and constraint, and humility and boldness as context and circumstance demand. (It is no accident that the fluid center is akin to Kierkegaard's . . . "self as synthesis.") (Schneider, 2015, p. 3)

Crucially, the fluidity of the paradoxical self depends on its capability for "empathy, identification with otherness, discovery" (Schneider, 1999, p. 122). It is "a vision of self and culture . . . that can go hand in hand" (p. 126).

The fluid center is a fitting concept for reflecting on the long and winding road we have travelled in the pages above. The personality has transitioned from the very constrictive, cumulative result of environmental contingencies, to the very expansive transpersonal self, to contingent existence achieving relative integration in a characteristically human, yet unique, and inherently paradoxical striving to fulfill a destiny. Embracing the fluid center, we can say that in every case, it has always been "us," all profiles of a multidimensional life that generates varying blends of objectivity and subjectivity. Kidder (1987) refers to this as Husserl's paradox, so named after a theme within the philosophy of Edmund Husserl (1970):

> On the one hand, subjectivity does not fabricate truth but seeks it, and thus it is dependent upon reality; on the other hand, objectivity is nothing without the meaning-intentions of subjectivity. But thinking in terms of this double-dependency, one refuses to settle upon a final articulation of what is absolutely prior to what. (Kidder, 1987, p. 240)

Sometimes biosocial pawn, sometimes would-be god, through it all we are each inevitably faced with the question of what we will make of our ineffable existence. Whether we seek to address the question in good faith or perpetually avoid it is, of course, quite another question.

The ever-present threat of death harbors the potential to keep one honest. And, in keeping with the themes of this text, it is fitting to conclude with the observation that even death itself takes on a conspicuously paradoxical character as human sociality is realized in the lifelong differential–integrative process of personal becoming. In the explicitly humanistic portions of this text, human sociality has been described in many ways: as irreducible relationality, as community feeling, as self-transcendent devotion, and as linguistically/symbolically, rationally, and imaginatively mediated interpersonal engagement. These qualities make it possible for one to imperfectly yet empathically put oneself in the place of another. With the realization of this possibility, the fear of death loses any lingering pretense of egoism. In further keeping with the themes of this text, allow me to revert to the way I began, as an experiencing person speaking in first-person voice.

For most of my life, my fear of death has been my own. Of course, I feared for the death of others, but the fear of my death was *mine*. But that changed when I met my wife. Suddenly, the fear of my death had somewhat less to do with me missing what I hold dear. It became just as much to do with my fear of what would happen to her if I were gone. And on the day that we learned that we were having a little girl, this experiential shift progressed even further. Today, I fear my death, of course. But the fear of my death is typically and mostly the fear of how it will impact the lives of my wife and daughter. The fear of "my" death is, for me now, primarily a concern for those whose welfare I put before my own in *agape*. Peperzak (1993), reflecting on the phenomenological philosophy of Emmanuel Levinas (1969), once commented:

> To lose one's life for the other(s) *is* to be meaningful in living for a time after one's own life. If death—and suffering—were a purely individual event, it would be meaningless; its having a place within the horizon of the metaphysical (i.e., intersubjective) relation saves it from absurdity. (p. 189)

I am inclined to agree.

References

Abraham, K. (1965). *Selected papers of Karl Abraham*. Hogarth Press and Institute of Psychoanalysis.

Adler, A. (1935). Introduction. *International Journal of Individual Psychology, 1*, 5–8.

Adler, A. (1958). *What life should mean to you*. Capricorn Books.

Adler, A. (1979). *Superiority and social interest*. Norton.

Adler, A. (1992). *Understanding human nature* (C. Brett, Trans.). Oneworld Publications.

Adler, A. (1998). *Social interest: Adler's key to the meaning of life*. Oneworld Publications.

Adler, A. (2012). Individual psychological education. In J. Carlson and M. P. Maniacci (Eds.) *Alfred Adler revisited* (pp. 129–138). Routledge.

Allport, G. W. (1937). The personalistic psychology of William Stern. *Journal of Personality, 5*(3), 231–246. https://doi.org/10.1111/j.1467-6494.1937.tb02222.x

Allport, G. W. (1955). *Becoming: Basic considerations for a psychology of personality*. Yale.

Allport, G. W. (1961). *Pattern and growth in personality*. Holt, Rinehart and Winston.

Allport, G. W. (1968). *The person in psychology: Selected essays*. Beacon Press.

Allport G. W. & Odbert, H. S. (1936). Trait-names: A psycho-lexical study. *Psychological Monographs, 47*, 1–171. https://doi.org/10.1037/h0093360

Alter A. (2013). *Drunk tank pink and other unexpected forces that shape how we think, feel, and behave*. Penguin.

Ansbacher, H. L. (1971). Alfred Adler and humanistic psychology. *Journal of Humanistic Psychology, 11*, 53–63. https://doi.org/10.1177/002216787101100106

Asante, M. (1980). *Afrocentricity: Theory of social change*. Amulefi Publishing Company.

Ashton, M. C., Lee, K., Perugini, M., Szarota, P., de Vries, R. E., Di Blas, L., Boies, K., & De Raad, B. (2004). A six-factor structure of personality-descriptive adjectives: Solutions from psycholexical studies in seven languages. *Journal of Personality and Social Psychology, 86*(2), 356–366. https://doi.org/10.1037/0022-3514.86.2.356

Bandura, A. (1977). *Social learning theory*. Prentice-Hall.

Bandura, A. (1989). Human agency in social cognitive theory. *American Psychologist, 44*, 1175–1184. https://doi.org/10.1037/0003-066X.44.9.1175

Bandura, A. (2008). Reconstrual of "free will" from the agentic perspective of social cognitive theory. In J. Baer, J. C. Kaufman, & R. F. Baumeister (Eds.),

Are we free? Psychology and free will (pp. 86–127). Oxford University Press.

Barker, R. (1968). *Ecological psychology: Concepts and methods for studying the environment of human behavior.* Stanford University Press.

Bauer, J. J., Schwab, J. R., & McAdams, D. P. (2011). Self-actualizing: Where ego development finally feels good? *The Humanistic Psychologist, 39*(2), 121–136. https://doi.org/10.1080/08873267.2011.564978

Baumgartner, A. I., & Tavris, C. (1983). How would your life be different if you'd been born a boy? *Redbook, 160*, 92–95.

Beck, A. T. (1979). *Cognitive therapy and the emotional disorders.* Penguin.

Behrends, R. S. (1986). The integrated personality: Maximal utilization of information. *Journal of Humanistic Psychology, 26*(1), 27–59. https://doi.org/10.1177/0022167886261003

Benedict, R. (1934). *Patterns of culture.* Houghton Mifflin.

Bergson, H. (1998). *Creative evolution.* Dover Publications, Inc.

Bijnen E. J., & Poortinga, Y. H. (1988). The questionable value of cross-cultural comparisons with the Eysenck personality questionnaire. *Journal of Cross-Cultural Psychology, 19*(2), 193–202. https://doi.org/10.1177/0022022188192005

Binswanger, L. (1967). *Being-in-the-world: Selected papers of Ludwig Binswanger.* Harper Torchbooks.

Bland, A. M. (2019). The personal hero technique: A therapeutic strategy that promotes self-transformation and interdependence. *Journal of Humanistic Psychology, 59*(4), 634–657. https://doi.org/10.1177/0022167818763207

Bland, A.M., & DeRobertis, E.M. (2017). Humanistic Perspective. In V. Zeigler-Hill, & T. Shackelford (Eds.), *Encyclopedia of Personality and Individual Differences.* Springer. https://doi.org/10.1007/978-3-319-28099-8_1484-2

Bland, A. M., & DeRobertis, E. M. (2020). Maslow's unacknowledged contributions to developmental psychology. *Journal of Humanistic Psychology, 60*(6), 934–958. https://doi.org/10.1177/0022167817739732

Bland, A. M., & Swords, B. A. (In press). Eupsychian versus authoritarian leadership: Existential-humanistic underpinnings and empirical support. *Journal of Humanistic Psychology.*

Block, J. (2000). Millennial Contrarianism: The five-factor approach to personality description 5 years later. *Journal of Research in Personality, 35*, 98–107. https://doi.org/10.1006/jrpe.2000.2293

Bohart, A. C., Held, B. S., Mendelowitz, E., & Schneider, K. J. (Eds.) (2013). *Humanity's dark side: Evil, destructive experience, and psychotherapy.* American Psychological Association.

Boss, M. (1982). Psychoanalysis and daseinsanalysis. DaCapo Press.

Breuer, J., & Freud, S. (1955). Studies on hysteria. In J. Strachey (Ed. & Trans.), *The standard edition of the complete psychological works of Sigmund Freud* (Vol. 2). The Hogarth Press.

Bronfenbrenner, U. (1981). *The ecology of human development: Experiments by nature and design.* Harvard University Press.

Bühler, C. (1971). Basic theoretical concepts of humanistic psychology. *American Psychologist, 26*(4), 378–386. https://doi.org/10.1037/h0032049

Buss, D. M. (1991). Evolutionary personality psychology. *Annual Review of Psychology, 42*, 459–491. https://doi.org/10.1146/annurev.ps.42.020191. 002331

Buss, D. M. (1995). Evolutionary psychology: A new paradigm for psychological science. *Psychological Inquiry, 6*, 1–49. https://doi.org/10.1207/s15327965pli0601_1

Buss, D. M. (2001). Human nature and culture: An evolutionary psychological perspective. *Journal of Personality, 69*, 955–978. https://doi.org/10.1111/1467-6494.696171

Buss, D. M. (2004). *Evolutionary psychology: The new science of the mind.* Allyn & Bacon.

Buss, D. M. (2008). Human nature and individual differences: Evolution of human personality. In O. P. John, R. W. Robins, & L. A. Pervin (Eds.), *Personality: Theory and research* (pp. 29-60). Guilford Press.

Buss, D. M. & Craik, K. H. (1981). The act frequency analysis of interpersonal dispositions: Aloofness, gregariousness, dominance and submissiveness. *Journal of Personality, 49*, 175–192. https://doi.org/10.1111/j.1467-6494.1981.tb00736.x

Buss, D. M. & Craik, K. H. (1985). Why *not* measure that trait? Alternative criteria for identifying important dispositions. *Journal of Personality and Social Psychology, 48*(4), 934–946. https://doi.org/10.1037/0022-3514.48.4.934

Buss, D. M., & Craik, K. H. (1983). The act frequency approach to personality. *Psychological Review, 90*(2), 105–126. https://doi.org/10.1037/0033-295X.90.2.105

Calhoun, J. B. (1962). Population density and social pathology. *Scientific American 306*, 139–148. https://www.gwern.net/docs/sociology/1962-calhoun.pdf

Cattell, R. B. (2007). *The scientific analysis of personality.* Aldine Transaction.

Chiao, J. Y., Harada, T., Komeda, H., Li, Z., Mano, Y., Saito, D., Parrish, T. B., Sadato, N., & Iidaka, T. (2009). Neural basis of individualistic and collectivistic views of self. *Human Brain Mapping, 30*, 2813–2820. https://doi.org/10.1002/hbm.20707

Cook-Greuter, S. (2000). Mature ego development: A gateway to ego transcendence? *Journal of Adult Development, 7*(4), 227–240. https://doi.org/10.1023/A:1009511411421

Coonan, D. J. (2016). *Hierarchies of brain and being: Abraham Maslow and the origins of the hierarchy of needs in German brain science* [Undergraduate honors thesis]. The University of Texas Digital Archive. https://repositories.lib.utexas.edu/handle/2152/36662

Costa, P. T., Jr., & McCrae, R. R. (2011). The five-factor model, five-factor theory, and interpersonal psychology. In L. M. Horowitz & S. Strack (Eds.), *Handbook of interpersonal psychology: Theory, research, assessment, and therapeutic interventions* (pp. 91–104). John Wiley & Sons, Inc.

Cushman, P. (2012). Defenseless in the face of the status quo: Psychology without a critical humanities. *The Humanistic Psychologist, 40*(3), 262–269. https://doi.org/10.1080/08873267.2012.696411

Dabrowski, K. (1967). *Personality shaping through positive disintegration.* Little, Brown and Co.

Davis, J. (1998). The transpersonal dimensions of ecopsychology: Nature, nonduality, and spiritual practice. *The Humanistic Psychologist, 26,* 60–100. https://doi.org/10.1080/08873267.1998.9976967

DeCarvalho, R. J. (1990). Who coined the term "humanistic psychology"? *The Humanistic Psychologist, 18*(3), 350–351. https://doi.org/10.1080/08873267.1990.9976902

Deci, E. L., & Ryan, R. M. (2000). The "what" and the "why" of goal pursuits: Human needs and the self-determination of behavior. *Psychological Inquiry, 11*(4), 227–268. ttps://doi.org/10.1207/S15327965PLI1104_01

de Graaf, J., Wann, D., & Naylor, T. H. (2005). *Affluenza: The all-consuming epidemic.* Berrett-Koehler Publishers.

Deichmann, U. (2016). Epigenetics: The origins and evolution of a fashionable topic. *Developmental Biology, 416,* 249–254. https://doi.org/10.1016/j.ydbio.2016.06.005

De Long, A. J. (1981). Phenomenological space-time: Towards an experiential relativity. *Science 213,* 681–683. https://doi.org/10.1126/science.7256273

DeRobertis, E. M. (2008). *Humanizing child developmental theory: A holistic approach.* iUniverse.

DeRobertis, E. M. (2012). *The whole child: Selected papers on existential-humanistic child psychology.* CreateSpace.

DeRobertis, E. M. (2015). Philosophical-anthropological considerations for an existential-humanistic ecopsychology, *The Humanistic Psychologist, 43*(4), 323–337. https://doi.org/10.1080/08873267.2014.961637

DeRobertis, E. M. (2017). *The phenomenology of learning and becoming: Enthusiasm, creativity, and self-development.* Palgrave.

DeRobertis, E. M. (2020). The humanistic revolution in psychology: Its inaugural vision. *Journal of Humanistic Psychology, 61*(1), 8–32. https://doi.org/10.1177/0022167820956785

DeRobertis, E. M. (2021). Piaget and Husserl: Comparisons, contrasts, and challenges for future research. *The Humanistic Psychologist.* Advance online publication. https://doi.org/10.1037/hum0000183

DeRobertis, E. M., & Bland, A. M. (2020). From personal threat to cross-cultural learning: An eidetic investigation. *Journal of Phenomenological Psychology, 51*(1), 1–15. https://doi.org/10.1163/15691624-12341368

DeYoung, C. G., Hirsh, J. B., Shane, M. S., Papademetris, X., Rajeevan, N., & Gray, J. R. (2012). Testing predictions from personality neuroscience: Brain structure and the big five. *Psychological Science*, 21, 820–828. https://doi.org/10.1177/0956797610370159

Dillon, M. (1983). The implications of Merleau-Ponty's thought for the practice of psychotherapy. *Journal of Phenomenological Psychology, 14*(1), 21–41. https://doi.org/10.1163/156916283X00036

Dinwiddie, F.W. (1975). Humanistic behaviorism. *Child Psychiatry and Human Development, 5*, 254–259. https://doi.org/10.1007/BF01433419

Dollard, J., & Miller, N. E. (1950). *Personality and psychotherapy: An analysis in terms of learning, thinking and culture.* McGraw-Hill.

Eisendrath, C. R. (1971). *The unifying moment: The psychological philosophy of William James and Alfred North Whitehead.* Harvard University Press.

Ellis, A. (2006). *How to stubbornly refuse to make yourself miserable about anything—yes, anything!* Citadel.

Epstein, M. (1995). *Thoughts without a thinker: Psychotherapy from a Buddhist perspective.* Basic Books.

Epting, F. R., & Paris, M. E. (2006). A constructive understanding of the person: George Kelly and humanistic psychology. *The Humanistic Psychologist, 34*(1), 21–37.

Erikson, E. H. (1961). The roots of virtue. In J. Huxley (Ed.), *The humanist frame* (147–165). Harper and Brothers.

Erikson, E. H. (1963). *Childhood and society.* W. W. Norton.

Erikson, E. H. (1968). *Identity: Youth and crisis.* W. W. Norton.

Erikson, E. H., & Erikson, J. M. (1997). *The life cycle completed.* W. W. Norton.

Eysenck, H. J. (1991). Dimensions of personality: 16, 5, or 3?--Criteria for a taxonomic paradigm. *Personality and Individual Differences, 12*, 773–790. https://doi.org/10.1016/0191-8869(91)90144-Z

Eysenck, H. J., & Eysenck, S. B. G. (2006). *The biological basis of personality.* Aldine Transaction

Feral, C. (1998). The connectedness model and optimal development: Is ecopsychology the answer to emotional well-being? *The Humanistic Psychologist, 26*, 243–274. https://doi.org/10.1080/08873267.1998.9976975

Ferenczi, S. (2013). *Further contributions to the theory and technique of psychoanalysis.* Read Books Ltd.

Ferster, C. B., & Skinner, B. F. (1957). *Schedules of reinforcement.* Appleton-Century-Crofts.

Fischer, K. W. (2009). Mind, brain, and education: Building a scientific groundwork for learning and teaching. *Mind, Brain, and Education, 3*, 3–16. https://doi.org/10.1111/j.1751-228X.2008.01048.x

Franco, Z. E., Allison, S. T., Kinsella, E. L., Kohen, A., Langdon, M., & Zimbardo, P. G. (2016). Heroism research: A review of theories, methods, challenges, and trends. *Journal of Humanistic Psychology, 58*(4), 382–396. https://doi.org/10.1177/0022167816681232

Franco, Z. E., Efthimiou, O., & Zimbardo, P. G. (2016). Heroism and eudaimonia: Sublime actualization through the embodiment of virtue. In J. Vittersø (Ed.), *Handbook of eudaimonic well-being, international handbooks of quality-of-life* (pp. 337–348). Springer International Publishing.

Frankl, V. E. (1967). *Psychotherapy and existentialism: Selected papers on logotherapy.* Simon and Schuster/Touchstone.

Frankl, V. E. (1969). *The will to meaning: Foundations and applications of logotherapy.* Nal.

Frankl, V. E. (1978). *The unheard cry for meaning.* Washington Square Press.

Frankl, V.E. (1986). *The doctor and the soul.* Vintage.

Frankl, V. E. (2006). *Man's search for meaning.* Beacon Press.

Freud, A. (1936). *The ego and the mechanisms of defense.* Hogarth.

Freud, S. (1949). *An outline of psycho-analysis.* Norton.

Freud, S. (1950). Project for a scientific psychology. In J. Strachey (Ed. & Trans.), *The standard edition of the complete psychological works of Sigmund Freud* (Vol. 1). The Hogarth Press.

Freud, S. (1960). *Three essays on the theory of sexuality.* Basic Books.

Freud, S. (1961). *Beyond the pleasure principle.* Norton.

Freud, S. (1965a). *New introductory lectures on psychoanalysis.* Norton.

Freud, S. (1965b). *The psychopathology of everyday life.* Norton.

Fromm, E. (1941). *Escape from freedom.* Rinehart.

Fromm, E. (1947). *Man for himself: An inquiry into the psychology of ethics.* Holt, Rinehart and Winston.

Fromm, E. (1951). *The forgotten language: An introduction to the understanding of dreams, fairy tales and myths.* Rinehart.

Fromm, E. (1955). *The sane society.* Holt, Rinehart and Winston.

Fromm, E. (1956). *The art of loving.* Harper & Row.

Fromm, E. (1966). *You shall be as gods.* Holt, Rinehart and Winston

Fromm, E. (1973). *The anatomy of human destructiveness.* Henry Holt & Company.

Fromm, E. (1986). *For the love of life.* The Free Press.

Garcia, J., Kimeldorf, D.J., & Koelling, R.A. (1955). Conditioned aversion to saccharin resulting from exposure to gamma radiation. *Science, 122* (3160), 157–158. https://doi.org/10.1126/science.122.3160.157

Gibson, E. J. (1969). *Principles of perceptual learning and development.* Prentice Hall.

Gibson, J. J. (1986). *The ecological approach to visual perception.* Lawrence Erlbaum.

Gigerenzer, G. (1993). The superego, the ego, and the id in statistical reasoning. In G. Keren & C. Lewis (Eds.), *A handbook for data analysis in the behavioral science: Methodological Issues* (pp. 311–339). Lawrence Erlbaum Associates.

Giorgi, A. (1992). Whither humanistic psychology? *The Humanistic Psychologist, 20*(2–3), 422–438. https://doi.org/10.1080/08873267.1992.9986807

Giorgi, A. (2009). *The descriptive phenomenological method in psychology: A modified Husserlian approach.* Duquesne University Press.

Goldstein, K. (1995). *The organism.* Zone Books.

Gray, J.A. (1981). A critique of Eysenck's theory of personality. In H.J. Eysenck (Ed.) *A model for personality* (pp. 246–276). Springer.

Gruel, N. (2015). The plateau experience: An exploration of its origins, characteristics, and potential. *The Journal of Transpersonal Psychology, 47*(1), 44–63. http://www.atpweb.org/jtparchive/trps-47-15-01-44.pdf

Hall, C. S., & Lindzey, G. (1978). *Theories of personality.* Wiley.

Hall, E. T. (1977). *Beyond culture.* Anchor.

Hall, E. T. (1990a). *The hidden dimension.* Anchor.

Hall, E. T. (1990b). *The silent language.* Anchor.

Hall, M. H. (1968, July). The psychology of universality: A conversation with the president of the American Psychological Association, Abraham H. Maslow. *Psychology Today,* 35–37, 54–57. https://www.psychologytoday.com/us/articles/199201/abraham-maslow

Hartmann, H. (1939). *Ego psychology and the problem of adaptation.* International Universities Press.

Heidegger, M. (1962). *Being and time.* Harper Collins.

Heisler, V. (1973). The transpersonal in Jungian theory and therapy. *Journal of Religion and Health, 12*(4), 337–341. https://doi.org/10.1007/BF01532422

Hergenhahn, B. R., & Olson, M. H. (2007). An introduction to theories of personality (7th ed.). Pearson.

Herring, E. (2018). 'Great is Darwin and Bergson his poet': Julian Huxley's other evolutionary synthesis. *Annals of Science, 75*(1), 40–54. https://doi.org/10.1080/00033790.2017.1407442

Hillman, J. (1993). *Archetypal psychology: A brief account.* Spring Publications.

Hoffman, L. (2008). An existential framework for Buddhism, world religions, and psychotherapy: Culture and diversity considerations. In F. Kaklauskas, S. Nimmanheminda, L. Hoffman, & M. Jack (Eds.), *Brilliant sanity: Buddhist approaches to psychotherapy* (pp. 19–38). University of the Rockies Press.

Hoffman, L., Stewart, S., Warren, D., and Meek, L. (2009). Toward a sustainable myth of self: An existential response to the postmodern condition. *Journal of Humanistic Psychology, 49,* 135–173. https://doi.org/10.1177/0022167808324880

Hofstede, G. (1997). *Cultures and organizations, software of the mind: Intercultural cooperation and its importance for survival.* McGraw-Hill.

Holland, R. L., Sayers, J. A., Keatinge, W. R., Davis, H. M., & Peswani, R. (1985). Effects of raised body temperature on reasoning, memory, and mood. *Journal of Applied Physiology, 59,* 1823–1827. https://doi.org/10.1152/jappl.1985.59.6.1823

Horney, K. (1937). *The neurotic personality of our time.* W. W. Norton.

Horney, K. (1939). *New ways in psychoanalysis.* W. W. Norton.

Horney, K. (1945). *Our inner conflicts: A constructive theory of neurosis.* W. W. Norton.

Horney, K. (1950). *Neurosis and human growth: The struggle toward self-realization.* W. W. Norton.

Horney, K. (1967). *Feminine psychology.* W. W. Norton.

Hunter, G. (2019). The self: Can behaviorism inform the study of the self? *Journal of Psychiatry Depression & Anxiety, 5*: 021. https://doi.org/10.24966/PDA-0150/100021

Husserl, E. (1970). *The crisis of European sciences and transcendental phenomenology.* Northwestern University Press.

Husserl, E. (1977). *Phenomenological psychology.* Martinus Nijhoff.

Husserl, E. (1999). *Cartesian meditations.* Kluwer.

Husserl, E. (2001). *Analyses concerning passive and active synthesis: Lectures on transcendental logic.* Kluwer.

Jung, C. G. (1961). *Memories, dreams, reflections* (A. Jaffé, Ed.). Random House.

Jung, C. G. (1964). *Man and his symbols.* Doubleday.

Jung, C. G. (1969). *The archetypes and the collective unconscious.* Princeton University Press.

Jung, C. G. (1980). *Psychology and alchemy.* Princeton University Press.

Jung, C. G. (1999). *Two Essays on analytical psychology.* Routledge.

Kanner, A. D. (1998). Mount Rushmore syndrome: When narcissism rules the earth. *The Humanistic Psychologist, 26,* 101–122. https://doi.org/10.1080/08873267.1998.9976968

Kaufman, S. B. (2020). *Transcend: The new science of self-actualization.* Tarcher Perigee.

Kelly, G. A. (1980). A psychology of the optimal man. In A. W. Landfield, & L. M. Leitner (Eds.), *Personal construct psychology: Psychotherapy and personality* (pp.18–35). Wiley.

Kelly, G. A. (1963). *A theory of personality: The psychology of personal constructs.* Norton.

Kelly, G. A. (1965). The threat of aggression. *Journal of Humanistic Psychology, 5*(2), 195–201. https://doi.org/10.1177/002216786500500208

Kersting, K. (2004, June). Driving teen egos—and buying—through 'branding.' *Monitor on Psychology, 35,* 60–61. https://www.apa.org/monitor/jun04/driving

Kidder, P. (1987). Husserl's paradox. *Research in Phenomenology, 17,* 227–242. https://www.jstor.org/stable/24654861

Kierkegaard, S. (1954). Fear and trembling and the sickness unto death. Princeton University Press.

Kierkegaard, S. (1962). *The present age.* Harper Torchbooks.

Knowles, R. T. (1986). *Human development and human possibility: Erikson in the light of Heidegger.* University Press of America.

Koydemir, S., Şimşek, Ö. F., & Demir, M. (2014). Pathways from personality to happiness: Sense of uniqueness as a mediator. *Journal of Humanistic Psychology, 54*(3), 314-335. https://doi.org/10.1177/0022167813501226

Kuhn, T. (1996). *The structure of scientific revolutions.* University of Chicago Press.

Kvale, S., & Grennes, C. E. (1975). Skinner and Sartre: Towards a radical phenomenology of behavior? In A. Giorgi, C. Fischer, & E. Murray (Eds.), *Duquesne studies in phenomenological psychology,* Vol. II (pp. 38–59). Duquesne University Press.

Laher, S. (2013). Understanding the five-factor model and five-factor theory through a South African cultural lens. *South African Journal of Psychology, 43*(2), 208–221. https://doi.org/10.1177/0081246313483522

Lamiell, J. T. (2013). Statisticism in personality psychologists' use of trait constructs: What is it? How was it contracted? Is there a cure? *New Ideas in Psychology, 31*(1), 65–71.

Levinas, E. (1969). *Totality and infinity: An essay on exteriority.* Duquesne University Press.

Lewin, K. (1935). *Dynamic theory of personality: Selected papers.* McGraw-Hill.

Lewin, K. (1951). *Field theory is social science: Selected theoretical papers.* Harper & Row.

Louv, R. (2008). *Last child in the woods: Saving our children from nature-deficit disorder.* Algonquin.

Loye, D. (2010). *Darwin's lost theory.* Benjamin Franklin Press.

Luijpen, W. A., & Koren, H. J. (1969). *A first introduction to existential phenomenology.* Duquesne University Press.

Markus, H. R., Crane, M. Bernstein, S., & Siladi, M. (1982). Self-schemas and gender. *Journal of Personality and Social Psychology, 42*(1), 38–50. https://doi.org/10.1037/0022-3514.46.6.1222

Markus, H. R., & Kitayama, S. (1991). Culture and the self: Implications for cognition, emotion, and motivation. *Psychological Review, 98,* 224–253. https://doi.org/10.1037/0033-295X.98.2.224

Marsh, T., & Boag, S. (2013). Evolutionary and differential psychology: Conceptual conflicts and the path to integration. *Frontiers in Psychology, 4,* Article 10.3389. https://doi.org/10.3389/fpsyg.2013.00655

Martinez-Conde, S., Alexander, R. G., Blum, D., Britton, N., Lipska, B. K., Quirk, G. J., Swiss, J. I., Willems, R. M., & Macknik, S. L. (2019). The storytelling brain: How neuroscience stories help bridge the gap between research and society. *The Journal of Neuroscience, 39*(42), 8285–8290. https://doi.org/10.1523/JNEUROSCI.1180-19.2019

Maslow, A. (1961). Health as transcendence of environment. *Journal of Humanistic Psychology, 1*(1), 1–7. https://doi.org/10.1177/002216786100100102

Maslow, A. H. (1970). *Motivation and personality*. Longman.

Maslow, A. H. (1993). *The farther reaches of human nature*. Penguin/Arkana.

Maslow, A. H. (1999). *Toward a psychology of being*. John Wiley & Sons.

Maslow, A. H., & Mintz, N. L. (1956). Effects of esthetic surroundings: Initial effects of three esthetic conditions upon perceiving energy and well-being in faces. *The Journal of Psychology: Interdisciplinary and Applied, 41*, 247–254. https://doi.org/10.1080/00223980.1956.9713000

Maslow, A. H., & Mittelmann, B. (1951). *Principles of abnormal psychology: The dynamics of psychic illness* (2nd ed.). Cotler.

Massey, R. F. (1986). Erik Erikson: Neo-Adlerian. *Individual Psychology: Journal of Adlerian Theory, Research & Practice, 42*(1), 65–91.

Matsumoto, D., & Juang, L. (2013). *Culture and personality*. Wadsworth.

May, R. (1953). *Man's search for himself*. W. W. Norton.

May, R. (1958). Contributions to existential psychotherapy. In R. May, E. Angel, & H. Ellenberger (Eds.), *Existence: A new dimension in psychology and psychiatry* (pp. 37–91). Basic Books.

May, R. (1969). *Love and will*. W. W. Norton.

May, R. (1979). *Psychology and the human dilemma*. W. W. Norton.

May, R. (1981). *Freedom and destiny*. W. W. Norton.

May, R. (1991). *The cry for myth*. W. W. Norton.

May, R., Angel, E., & Ellenberger H. (1958). *Existence: A new dimension in psychiatry and psychology*. Basic Books.

McAdams, D. P., & Pals, J. L. (2006). A new big five: Fundamental principles for an integrative science of personality. *American Psychologist, 61*, 204–217. https://doi.org/10.1037/0003-066X.61.3.204

McCall, R. J. (1983). *Phenomenological psychology*. The University of Wisconsin Press.

McCrae, R. R., & Costa, P. T., Jr. (1996). Toward a new generation of personality theories: Theoretical contexts for the five-factor model. In J. S. Wiggins (Ed.), *The five-factor model of personality: Theoretical perspectives* (pp. 51–58). Guilford Press.

McCrae, R. R., & Costa, P. T., Jr. (1999). A five-factor theory of personality. In L. Pervin & O. John (Eds.), *Handbook of personality: Theory and research* (pp. 139–153). Guilford Press.

McCrae, R. R., & Costa, P. T., Jr. (2003). *Personality in adulthood* (2nd ed.): *A five-factor theory perspective*. Guilford.

McCrae, R. R., & Costa, P. T., Jr. (2008). The five-factor theory of personality. In O. P. John, R. W. Robins, & L. A. Pervin (Eds.), *Handbook of personality: Theory and research* (3rd ed., pp. 159–181). Guilford.

Midgley, M. (2005). *The essential Mary Midgley*. Routledge.

Mischel, W. (1971). *Introduction to personality*. Holt, Rinehart and Winston.

Mischel, W. (1973). Toward a cognitive social learning reconceptualization of personality. *Psychological Review, 80*(4), 252–283. https://doi.org/10.1037/h0035002

Mischel, W. (2004). Toward an integrative science of the person. *Annual Review of Psychology, 55*, 1–22. https://doi.org/10.1146/annurev.psych.55.042902.130709

Mischel, W., Ayduk, O., Berman, M. G., Casey, B. J., Gotlib, I. H., Jonides, J., Kross, E., Teslovich, T., Wilson, N. L., Zayas, V., & Shoda, Y. (2011). 'Willpower' over the life span: Decomposing self-regulation. *Social Cognitive and Affective Neuroscience, 6*(2), 252–256. https://doi.org/10.1093/scan/nsq081

Mischel, W., & Shoda, Y. (1995). A cognitive-affective system theory of personality: Reconceptualizing situations, dispositions, dynamics, and invariance in personality structure. *Psychological Review, 102*(2), 246–268. https://doi.org/10.1037/0033-295X.102.2.246

Mitchell, S. A., & Black, M. J. (1995). *Freud and beyond: A history of modern psychoanalytic thought.* Basic Books.

Moore, K. (1944). The effect of controlled temperature changes on the behavior of the white rat. *Journal of Experimental Psychology, 34*, 70–79. https://doi.org/10.1037/h0058187

Morawski, J. G. (1988). *The rise of experimentation in American psychology.* Yale.

Murray, E. L. (1986). *Imaginative thinking and human existence.* Duquesne University Press.

Nettle, D. (2006). The evolution of personality variation in humans and other animals. *American Psychologist, 61*(6), 622–631. https://doi.org/10.1037/0003-066X.61.6.622

Nicholson, I. (1997). Humanistic psychology and intellectual identity: The "open" system of Gordon Allport. *Journal of Humanistic Psychology, 37*(3) 61–79. https://doi.org/10.1177/00221678970373005

Nisbett, R. (2003). *The geography of thought: How Asians and Westerners think differently...and why.* The Free Press.

Nuttin, J. (1962). *Psychoanalysis and personality: A dynamic theory of normal personality.* Mentor-Omega.

O'Hara, M. (2016). Natalie Rogers: Artist, healer, activist—1927–2015. *Journal of Humanistic Psychology, 56*(5), 561–566. https://doi.org/10.1177/0022167816639420

Oishi, S. & Graham, J. (2010). Social ecology: Lost and found in psychological science. *Perspectives on Psychological Science, 5*, 356–377. https://doi.org/10.1177/1745691610374588

Oyserman, D., Coon, H. M., & Kemmelmeier, M. (2002). Rethinking individualism and collectivism: Evaluation of theoretical assumptions and meta-analyses. *Psychological Bulletin, 128*, 3–72. https://doi.org/10.1037/0033-2909.128.1.3

Panksepp, J., & Panksepp, J. B. (2000). The seven sins of evolutionary psychology. *Evolution and Cognition, 6*(2), 108–131. http://www.flyfishingdevon.co.uk/salmon/year3/psy364criticisms-evolutionary-psychology/panksepp_seven_sins.pdf

Paunonen, S. V., & Jackson, D. N. (2000). What is beyond the big five? Plenty! *Journal of Personality, 68,* 821–835. https://doi.org/10.1111/1467-6494.00117

Pavlov, I. P. (1927). *Conditioned reflexes.* Oxford University Press.

Peperzak, A. (1993). *To the other: An introduction to the philosophy of Emmanuel Levinas.* Purdue University Press.

Perluss, B. (2012). Following the raven: The paradoxical path toward a depth ecopsychology. *Ecopsychology, 4*(3), 181–186. https://doi.org/10.1089/eco.2012.0045

Pfaffenberger, A. H. (2005). Optimal adult development: An inquiry into the dynamics of growth. *Journal of Humanistic Psychology, 45*(3), 279–301. https://doi.org/10.1177/0022167804274359

Pfaffenberger, A. (2007). Different conceptualizations of optimum development. *Journal of Humanistic Psychology, 47,* 501–523. https://doi.org/10.1177/0022167806296858

Phillips, R. W. (1997). Educational facility and the academic achievement and attendance of upper elementary school students. Unpublished doctoral dissertation, University of Georgia, Athens.

Piaget, J., & Garcia, R. (1989). *Psychogenesis and the history of science.* Columbia University Press.

Piaget, J., & Inhelder, B. (1969). *The psychology of the child.* Basic Books.

Piekkola, B. (2011). Traits across cultures: A neo-Allportian perspective. *Journal of Theoretical and Philosophical Psychology, 31*(1), 2–24. https://doi.org/10.1037/a0022478

Plomin, R., DeFries, J. C., & McClearn, G. E. (1990). *Behavioral genetics: A primer* (2nd ed.). Freeman.

Pluess, M., Belsky, J., Baldwin, M. W., & Shelley, E. T. (2010). 5-HTTLPR moderates effects of current life events on neuroticism: Differential susceptibility to environmental influences. *Progress in Neuropsychopharmacoly and Biological Psychiatry, 34*(6), 1070–1074. https://doi.org/10.1016/j.pnpbp.2010.05.028

Popper, K. R. (1959). *The logic of scientific discovery.* Hutchinson.

Radtke, K. M., Ruf, M., Gunter, H. M., Dohrmann, K., Schauer, M., Meyer A., & Elbert, T. (2011). Transgenerational impact of intimate partner violence on methylation in the promoter of the glucocorticoid receptor. *Translational Psychiatry, 1*(7), 1–6. https://doi.org/10.1038/tp.2011.21

Ricoeur, P. (1970). *Freud & philosophy: An essay on interpretation.* Yale.

Ricoeur, P. (1992). *Oneself as another.* University of Chicago Press.

Ritvo, L. B. (1990). *Darwin's influence on Freud: A tale of two sciences.* Yale University Press.

Robbins, B. D. (2015). The heart of humanistic psychology: Human dignity disclosed through a hermeneutic of love. *Journal of Humanistic Psychology, 53*(6), 1–15. https://doi.org/10.1177/0022167815591408

Rodgers, J. L. (2010). The epistemology of mathematical and statistical modeling: A quiet methodological revolution. *American Psychologist, 65*(1), 1–12. https://doi.org/10.1037/a0018326

Roesler, C. (2012). Are archetypes transmitted more by culture than biology? Questions arising from conceptualizations of the archetype. *Journal of Analytical Psychology, 57(2)*, 223–246. https://doi.org/10.1111/j.1468-5922.2011.01963.x

Rogers, C. R. (1951). *Client-centered therapy: Its current practice, implications and theory*. Houghton Mifflin.

Rogers, C. R. (1959). A theory of therapy, personality, and interpersonal relationships, as developed in the client-centered framework. In S. Koch (Ed.), *Psychology: A study of a science (*Vol. 3) (184–256). McGraw Hill.

Rogers, C. R. (1961). *On becoming a person: A therapist's view of psychotherapy*. Houghton Mifflin.

Rogers, C. R. (1969). *Freedom to learn*. Charles E. Merrill Publishing Company.

Rogers, C. R. (1980). *A way of being*. Houghton Mifflin.

Rogers, N. (1993). *The creative connection: Expressive arts as healing*. Science and Behavior Books.

Rogers, N., Tudor, K., Embleton Tudor, L., & Keemar, K. (2012). Person-centered expressive arts therapy: A theoretical encounter, *Person-Centered & Experiential Psychotherapies, 11*(1), 31–47. https://doi.org/10.1080/14779757.2012.656407

Romanyshyn, R. D. (1989). *Technology as symptom and dream*. Routledge.

Roszak, T. (1995). *Where the wasteland ends*. Celestial Arts.

Rotter, J. B. (1966). Generalized expectancies for internal versus external control of reinforcement. *Psychological Monographs, 80*(1), 1–28. https://doi.org/10.1037/h0092976

Rotter, J. B. (1982). *The development and applications of social learning theory: Selected papers*. Praeger.

Rotter, J. B., & Hochreich, D. J. (1975). *Personality*. Scott, Foresman.

Ryan, R. M., & Deci, E. L. (2004). Overview of self-determination theory: An organismic dialectical perspective. In E. L. Deci & R. M. Ryan (Eds.), *Handbook of self-determination research* (pp. 3–33). University of Rochester Press.

Salmon, C. A., & Daley, M. (1998). Birth order and familial sentiment: Middleborns are different. *Evolution and Human Behavior, 19*, 299–312. https://doi.org/10.1016/S1090-5138(98)00022-1

Sampson, E. E. (1988). The debate on individualism: Indigenous psychologies and their role in personal and social functioning. *American Psychologist, 43*, 15–22. https://doi.org/10.1037/0003-066X.43.1.15

Saudino, K. J., & Micalizzi, L. (2015). Emerging trends in behavioral genetic studies of child temperament. *Child Development Perspectives, 9*(3), 144–148. https://doi.org/10.1111/cdep.12123

Schneider, K. J. (1990). *The paradoxical self: Toward an understanding of our contradictory nature.* Insight Books.

Schneider, K. J. (1993). *Horror and the holy: Wisdom-teachings of the monster tale.* Open Court Publishing Company.

Schneider, K. J. (1999). The fluid center: A third millennium challenge to culture, *The Humanistic Psychologist, 27,* 114–130. https://doi.org/10.1080/08873267.1999.9986901

Schneider, K. J. (2004). *Rediscovery of awe: Splendor, mystery, and the fluid center of life.* Paragon House.

Schneider, K. J. (2011). Humanistic psychology's chief task: To reset psychology on its rightful existential–humanistic base. *Journal of Humanistic Psychology, 51*(4), 436–438. https://doi.org/10.1177/0022167811412190

Schneider, K. J. (2013). *The polarized mind: Why it's killing us and what we can do about it.* University Professors Press.

Schneider, K. J. (2015). My journey with Kierkegaard: From the paradoxical self to the polarized mind. *Journal of Humanistic Psychology, 55,* 1–8. https://doi.org/10.1177/0022167814537889

Schor, J. B. (2004). *Born to buy: The commercialized child and the new consumer culture.* Scribner.

Shaw, F. J. (1961). The problem of acting and the problem of becoming. *Journal of Humanistic Psychology, 1*(1), 64–69. https://doi.org/10.1177/002216786100100107

Shaw, C., & Proctor, G. (2005). Women at the margins: A critique of the diagnosis of borderline personality disorder. *Feminism & Psychology, 15*(4), 483–490. https://doi.org/10.1177/0959-353505057620

Siegel, D. J. (2001). Toward an interpersonal neurobiology of the developing mind: Attachment relationships, "mindsight," and neural integration. *Infant Mental Health Journal, 22,* 6–94. https://doi.org/10.1002/1097-0355(200101/04)22:1<67::AID-IMHJ3>3.0.CO;2-G

Sipiora, M. P. (1991). Alienation, the self, and television: Psychological life in mass culture. *The Humanistic Psychologist, 19*(2), 158–169. https://doi.org/10.1080/08873267.1991.9986759

Skinner, B. F. (1953). *Science and human behavior.* Free Press.

Skinner, B. F. (1969). *Contingencies of reinforcement: A theoretical analysis.* Appleton-Century-Crofts.

Skinner, B. F. (1971). *Beyond freedom and dignity.* Hackett Publishing Company, Inc.

Slife, B. (2000). The practice of theoretical psychology. *Journal of Theoretical and Philosophical Psychology, 20,* 97–115. https://doi.org/10.1037/h0091300

Smith, M. B. (1982). Psychology and humanism. *Journal of Humanistic Psychology, 22*(2), 44–55. https://doi.org/10.1177/0022167882222003

Smith, D. L. (2004). Implicit philosophies and therapeutic theories: How theoretical constructs conceal phenomena. *The Humanistic Psychologist, 32*(2), 198–218. https://doi.org/10.1080/08873267.2004.9961751

Smits, D. J. M., & Boeck, P. D. (2006). From BIS/BAS to the Big Five. *European Journal of Personality, 20*, 255–270. https://doi.org/10.1002/per.583

Smuts, J. (1926). *Holism and evolution.* Macmillan.

Snygg, D. (1959). Preface. In A. E. Kuenzli (Ed.), *The phenomenological problem* (pp. vii–x). Harper & Brothers.

Stern, W. (1924). *Psychology of early childhood.* Henry Holt and Company.

Stern, W. (2010). Psychology and personalism (James T. Lamiell, Trans.). *New Ideas in Psychology, 28*, 110-134. https://doi.org/10.1016/j.newideapsych.2009.02.005

Sternberg, R. J., Grigorenko, E. L., & Kalmar, D. A. (2001). The role of theory in unified psychology. *Journal of Theoretical and Philosophical Psychology, 21*, 99–117. https://doi.org/10.1037/h0091200

Stortelder, F. (2014). Varieties of male-sexual-identity development in clinical practice: A neuropsychoanalytic model. *Frontiers in Psychology, 5*, Article 10.3389. https://doi.org/10.3389/fpsyg.2014.01512

Strasser, S. (1977). *Phenomenology of feeling.* Duquesne University Press.

Straus, E. (1963). *The primary world of the senses: A vindication of sensory experience.* The Free Press of Glencoe.

Sulloway, F. J. (1996). *Born to rebel: Birth order, family dynamics, and creative lives.* Pantheon/Vintage.

Sweeney, T. J. (1998). *Adlerian counseling: A practitioner's approach.* Accelerated Development.

Szurmak, J., & Thuna, M. (2013). Tell me a story: The use of narrative as tool for instruction. In D. M. Mueller (Ed.), *Imagine, innovate, inspire: The proceedings of the ACRL 2013 conference.* Retrieved from http://www.ala.org/acrl/sites/ala.org.acrl/files/content/conferences/confsandpreconfs/2013/papers/SzurmakThuna_TellMe.pdf

Taber, K. S. (2020). Constructive alternativism: George Kelly's personal construct theory. In B. Akpan & T. Kennedy (Eds.), *Science education in theory and practice: An introductory guide to learning theory* (pp. 373–388). Springer.

Taylor, A., & Gousie, G. (1988). The ecology of learning environments for children. *CEFPI Journal, 26*, 23–28.

Taylor, E. (2000). "What is man, psychologist, that thou art so unmindful of him?"" Henry A. Murray on the historical relation between classical personality theory and humanistic psychology. *Journal of Humanistic Psychology, 40(3)*, 29–42. https://doi.org/10.1177/0022167800403003

Teo, T. (2003). Wilhelm Dilthey (1833–1911) and Eduard Spranger (1882–1963) on the developing person. *The Humanistic Psychologist, 31*(1), 74–94. https://doi.org/10.1080/08873267.2003.9986920

Tesch, R. (1990). *Qualitative research: Analysis types and software tools.* Routledge Falmer.

Thelen, E. (1996). The improvising infant: Learning about learning to move. In M. R. Merrens & G. G. Brannigan (Eds.), *The developmental psychologists: Research adventures across the life span* (pp. 21–35). McGraw-Hill.

Thomas, A., & Chess, S. (1977). *Temperament and development.* Brunner/Mazel.

Thorndike, E. L. (1932). *The fundamentals of learning.* Teachers College.

Tillich, P. (1980). *The courage to be.* Yale University Press.

Tooby, J., & Cosmides, L. (1990). On the universality of human nature and the uniqueness of the individual: The role of genetics and adaptation. *Journal of Personality, 58,* 17–68. https://doi.org/10.1111/j.1467-6494.1990.tb00907.x

Tornstam, L. (1996). Gerotranscendence: A theory about maturing into old age. *Journal of Aging and Identity, 1,* 37–50.

Tornstam, L. (2005). *Gerotranscendence: A developmental theory of positive aging.* Springer.

Triandis, H. C. (1995). *Individualism and collectivism.* Westview Press.

Tully, J. B. (1976). Personal construct theory and psychological changes related to social work training. *British Journal of Social Work, 6*(4), 481–499. https://doi.org/10.1093/oxfordjournals.bjsw.a056764

Twitmyer, E. B. (1902). *A study of the knee jerk.* Winston.

Twitmyer, E. B. (1905). Knee jerks without simulation of the patellar tendon. *Psychological Bulletin, 2,* 43.

Vaihinger, H. (1924). *The philosophy of 'as if': A system of the theoretical, practical and religious fictions of mankind.* Routledge and Kegan Paul.

Valsala, P., & Menon, P. (2019). Psychospiritual basis of altruism: A review. *Journal of Humanistic Psychology.* Advance online publication. https://doi.org/10.1177/0022167819830517

Valsiner, J. (2005). *Heinz Werner and developmental science.* Kluwer.

van den Berg, J. H. (1972). *A different existence: Principles of phenomenological psychopathology.* Duquesne University Press.

van Kaam, A. (1961). Humanistic psychology and culture. *Journal of Humanistic Psychology, 1*(1), 94–100. https://doi.org/10.1177/002216786100100110

van Kaam, A. (1966). *Existential foundations of psychology.* Duquesne University Press.

Varela, F., Thompson, E., & Rosch, E. (1991). *The embodied mind.* MIT Press.

von Bertalanffy, L. (1968). *Organismic psychology and systems theory.* Clark University Press.

von Eckartsberg, R. (1979). The eco-psychology of personal culture building: An existential-hermeneutic approach. In A. Giorgi, R. Knowles, & D. L. Smith (Eds.), *Duquesne studies in phenomenological psychology* (Vol. III; 227–244). Duquesne University Press.

von Uexküll, J. (2010). *A foray into the worlds of animals and humans.* University of Minnesota Press.

Vygotsky, L. S. (1986). *Thought and language*. MIT Press.

Vygotsky, L. S. (2004). Imagination and creativity in childhood. *Journal of Russian & East European Psychology, 42*(1), 7–79. https://doi.org/10.1080/10610405.2004.11059210

Walker, B. M., & Winter, D. A. (2007). The elaboration of personal construct theory. *Annual Review of Psychology, 58*, 453–477. https://doi.org/10.1146/annurev.psych.58.110405.085535

Waller, N. G., & Zavala, J. (1993). Evaluating the big five. *Psychological Inquiry, 4*, 131–134. https://doi.org/10.1207/s15327965pli0402_13

Walsh, R. (2015). What is wisdom? Cross-cultural and cross-disciplinary syntheses. *Review of General Psychology, 19*, 278–293. https://doi.org/10.1037/gpr0000045

Watson, J. B. (1994). Psychology as the behaviorist views it. *Psychological Review, 101*(2), 248–253. https://doi.org/10.1037/0033-295X.101.2.248

Watson, J. B., & Rayner, R. (1920). Conditioned emotional reactions. *Journal of Experimental Psychology, 3*, 1–14. https://doi.org/10.1037/h0069608

Webster, G. D., Urland, G. R., & Correll, J. (2012). Can uniform color aggression? Quasi-experimental evidence from professional ice hockey. *Social Psychological and Personality Science, 3*, 274–281. https://doi.org/10.1177/1948550611418535

Winnicott, D. W. (1960). Ego distortion in terms of the true and false self. In D. W. Winnicott & M. M. R. Khan (Eds.), *The maturational processes and the facilitating environment: Studies in the theory of emotional development* (pp. 140–152). The Hogarth Press.

Winston, C. N. (2016). An existential-humanistic-positive theory of human motivation. *The Humanistic Psychologist, 44*(2), 142–163. https://doi.org/10.1037/hum0000028

Winston, C. N. (2018). To be *and* not to be: A paradoxical narrative of self-actualization. *The Humanistic Psychologist, 46*(2), 159–174. https://doi.org/10.1037/hum0000082

Winston, C. N., Maher, H., & Easvaradoss, V. (2017). Needs and values: An exploration. *The Humanistic Psychologist, 45*(3), 295–311. https://doi.org/10.1037/hum0000054

Woodworth, R. S., & Schlosberg, H. (1954). *Experimental psychology*. Henry Holt.

Index

About the Author

Eugene Mario DeRobertis is a Professor of Psychology at Brookdale College in New Jersey and a Lecturer at Rutgers University-Newark. He received his PhD in psychology from Duquesne University. He has been teaching at the college level since 1996. Prior to committing himself to teaching full-time, Professor DeRobertis worked as a developmentally oriented psychotherapist, an academic counselor, and an addictions counselor. He has published multiple peer-reviewed works in the areas of phenomenological psychology, existential-humanistic psychology, psychological theory, and child psychology. His publications include *Humanizing Child Developmental Theory: A Holistic Approach* (2008), *The Whole Child: Selected Papers on Existential-Humanistic Child Psychology* (2012), *Existential-Phenomenological Psychology: A Brief Introduction* (2012), and *The Phenomenology of Learning and Becoming: Enthusiasm, Creativity, and Self-Development* (2017). He is currently the Review Editor for the *Journal of Phenomenological Psychology*.

CPSIA information can be obtained
at www.ICGtesting.com
Printed in the USA
BVHW040218170821
614603BV00014B/638

9 781939 686749